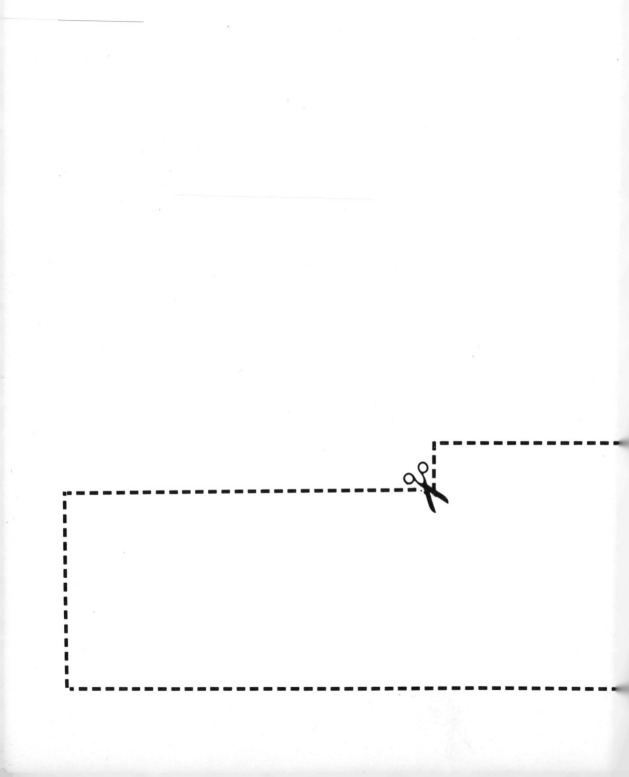

BASICS OF PHONOLOGICAL ANALYSIS

BASICS OF PHONOLOGICAL ANALYSIS
A Programmed Learning Text

Linda M. L. Khan
Callier Center for Communication Disorders
University of Texas at Dallas

 COLLEGE-HILL PRESS, San Diego, California

College-Hill Press, Inc.
4284 41st Street
San Diego, California 92105

© 1985 by College-Hill Press, Inc.

Library of Congress Cataloging in Publication Data

Khan, Linda M. L., 1948–
Basics of phonological analysis.

Bibliography: p.
1. Grammar, Comparative and general—Phonology—
Programmed instruction.   I. Title.
P217.3.K49   1985   414′.07′7   84-29269
ISBN 0-88744-109-2

Printed in the United States of America

To Amer and Ziad, for placing both normal and disordered phonology on my doorstep. And to all children, for attacking phonological development with such energy and determination.

LMLK

Contents

Foreword

The improvement of inadequate articulation was one of the earliest tasks undertaken by speech pathologists. Throughout the years, more professional time in terms of percentage of caseload has been devoted to disorders of articulation by school therapists, in particular, than to any other type of speech problem. The accepted approach to remediation became fairly routine over the years. The basic assumption into the 1960s was that acquisition of the oral medium of language involved learning to produce speech sounds or phonemes, and that remediation required the identification and teaching of those that were missing or incorrectly produced.

In the late 1960s and early 1970s, however, speech pathologists began to observe the practical application of theories by then rather widely accepted among scholars in linguistics, which held that children learn to speak by decoding and mastering the sound system (phonology) of language. That is, the child focuses on sound contrasts, classes, or patterns that enable him or her to expand phonemic and sound sequence repertoire. The impact of this concept upon the analysis and remediation of phonological (systematic) disorders has been considerable, particularly in the case of the severely or profoundly unintelligible child.

A theory that has seemed especially meaningful to many speech pathologists for explaining how children deal with skills which they have not yet acquired is David Stampe's natural process theory. Briefly, Stampe proposes that the child reduces target utterances through an array of inherent simplification processes to a form that reflects his or her current production and perception constraints. These processes, such as fronting of velars, cluster reduction, and liquid gliding, have become the basis for most of the phonological analysis procedures currently reported and for several newer remediation approaches.

Acquiring the terminology and an understanding of the common phonological processes has thus become important to speech-language pathologists in training and to those who completed their formal education before courses in phonology were an accepted part of the curriculum. This volume addresses that need. It concerns knowledge that can easily be mastered with a minimum of tutorial assistance. It will be learned at rates that vary widely among individuals depending on their background. The material is therefore well suited to the programmed learning method. The author has taken advantage of the opportunity to minimize an instructor's somewhat routine teaching tasks and allow the student to move as slowly or rapidly as required for absorbing the material. Both students and practicing professionals may find this volume a useful introduction to a more complete understanding of the applications of phonological theory.

Elaine Paden

Preface

This is a programmed learning text for teaching yourself the basic components of phonological analysis. It is intended for those who wish to become more proficient in using phonological patterns to analyze disordered speech production. The book is recommended for use as a supplementary text for courses in normal and disordered articulation or phonology and language acquisition and disorders. The user progresses at a comfortable pace, and advanced users are free to skim sections that may be familiar to them. The sample productions used to illustrate phonological analysis procedures were collected from the speech samples of children with phonological disorders over a three year period. Although the text was written with the disordered child in mind, the procedures are equally applicable for analyzing the speech production patterns of adults with disorders. Partial samples from children with unintelligible speech have been included for the purpose of illustrating patterns of phonological process usage. Extensive practice in the phonological analysis of complete samples is available in a companion volume, entitled *Applications of Phonological Analysis*.

 The content of this self-instructional text has been sequentially arranged from basic to more complex material. The format is consistent throughout. The user reads a sentence or short paragraph and supplies answers as required. This involves filling in a blank within a sentence, providing the requested phonemes and phonetic symbols, or identifying the sound changes and phonological processes involved in specific productions. A user card has been included. As the user reads each entry, the correct answer will be covered by this card. When the user advances the card, the answer to the previous item will be exposed along with the next item to be completed. Throughout the text, there are sample children's productions to be analyzed by the user. Upon completion of the text, the reader should be prepared to (1) identify sound changes; (2) recognize major phonological processes; and (3) assign phonological processes to sound changes.

 The appendices are intended to serve as references for improved analysis of altered productions. Appendix I consists of phonetic symbols and diacritical markings that would be used to transcribe speech production using either broad or narrow transcription. Appendix II includes a table of equivalent names for specific phonological processes from several phonological assessment procedures. Appendix III contains one complete speech sample to be scored, and a key is provided. Appendix IV covers syllabication issues.

Readers desiring additional practice in transcription should refer to the workbook with cassette tapes by Shriberg and Kent (1982) or the programmed textbook by Paden (1971). It is beyond the scope of this book to provide exercises in transcription. However, a chapter that explains the system used in this textbook has been included.

A number of people, either knowingly or unknowingly, have contributed to the conception and completion of this text. I am especially grateful to my students for suggesting the need for an organized, step-by-step procedural guide to phonological analysis. This book was written for them. Nancy Lewis, Lori LeGrow, Jan Lougeay, and Sondra Lockard reviewed and critiqued earlier versions of the manuscript. Jeri Logemann reviewed the manuscript for content and format. Her suggestions were constructive and are reflected in the manuscript's final version. Several editors at College-Hill Press deserve credit for tireless proofreading and accurate editing: Anna Congdon, Marie McAuliffe, John Chaimov, and Garry Burton. Their attention to detail assisted in identifying possible inaccuracies in the text. It was reassuring to know that several pairs of knowledgeable eyes were reviewing the extensive phonetic notations. I am also grateful for the technical assistance of Marge Bichsel, Jan Blair, Trish Lindemann, Lisa Middleton, Judy Simpson-Mika, and Lisa Williams, who helped with the word processing, and formatting.

I owe special thanks to those phonologists whose knowledge and enthusiasm for phonology and love of children have contributed to this work both through personal communications and through their own published works. These include Mary Louise Edwards, Barbara Hodson, Elaine Paden, Barbaranne Benjamin, Carla Dunn, David Ingram, and Larry Shriberg.

All work on this manuscript was completed in addition to supervising student clinicians, teaching, and raising a family. Therefore, I am particularly grateful for Peji Khan's support and encouragement, which have been offered generously at critical times.

Introduction

PHONOLOGY is the study of the sound systems and sound patterns of spoken language. Some of these patterns are natural and predictable and examples are found *cross-linguistically*.

The term "natural" is used to describe these *sound patterns*, or *phonological processes*, which have been found to occur _____.

cross-linguistically

phonological process

_____ is another term for sound pattern.

According to Stampe (1969), who first described these *natural* patterns, or processes, there are certain innate tendencies to simplify speech production. For example, word-final voiced consonants tend to be devoiced, as in /bɛd/ → [bɛt], read as "bed BECOMES bet." Because this process is found universally, developmentally, and because English-speaking adults tend to partially devoice final consonants, the process is said by Stampe to be a _____ process, which is innate.

natural

The concept of searching for patterns within a speech sample is not new. Templin and Darley (1960) developed a system for recognizing patterns of errors from performance on their articulation test. Fisher and Logemann (1971) have arranged their scoring protocol into a grid, which is organized in such a way that the clinician can recognize immediately those error patterns which share specific distinctive features. The type of error analysis presented here includes elements of both of these analyses, but presents an additional set of patterns. These patterns are called _____.

phonological processes

In this text, we are primarily concerned with the sound patterns, or processes, that are used by young normal children who are acquiring spoken language, and by children who have disordered speech production. In contrast to those which Stampe described, disordered speech sound patterns include processes which are not necessarily _____.

natural processes

By examination of the speech sample, patterns of sound production may become apparent. Examine the following sample for evidence of a phonological pattern, or process:

	Adult Form	*Child's Form*
CAT	/kæt/	→ [kæ]
HOUSE	/haʊs/	→ [haʊ]
BED	/bɛd/	→ [bɛ]
MAN	/mæn/	→ [mæ]

All four words are altered in the same way: the word-final consonant has been deleted. POSTVOCALIC is a term that refers to the _____ consonant.

word-final

The pattern which is evident from the four sample words given above is that all word-final consonants have been _____.

deleted

As we examine the speech samples of young children, we find that many different _____ are present, altering the adult forms of words into manageable productions for the child.

sound patterns, OR phonological processes

These phonological processes constitute the focus of this text. Their application results in some degree of change from the target adult word, or *underlying* form, in the language. The adult form of a word is the _____.

underlying form

There are both underlying forms and surface forms. "Surface form" is the term used to identify the speaker's actual _____.

production, response

We will view the speaker's production as an alteration of the underlying form or, basically, as the *surface form* of the underlying representation. For the child who changes CAT /kæt/ to [tæt], an altered _____ form has resulted in the surface form, [tæt].

underlying

There are several theories regarding the exact nature of the child's underlying form. The child may have the underlying adult target in mind but for some reason may alter the adult representation in production of the speech sounds, or the child may have a unique underlying representation that is not the adult form. For example, when a child alters BLUE /blu/ to [bu], the underlying representation may be /bu/ rather than /blu/. The assumption made here is that the child has an adult _____ to correspond with the actual altered production.

representation, OR underlying form

Thus, we will use Stampe's view, which states that the underlying form, or representation, is the _____ form of the word, available to the child for alteration.

adult

One must be able to recognize sound changes in order to determine which phonological processes were used by the speaker to alter the production. The next section introduces various types of *sound changes* produced by the speaker. Each _____ accounts for one difference between the adult form of the word and the speaker's actual production.

sound change

Once all _____ within a word have been determined, the phonological processes that contributed to each sound change are identified.

sound changes

SUMMARY
Introduction

1. A phonological process is a sound pattern that has been observed in the speech of an individual.
2. The underlying form of a word is generally considered to be the same as the adult form of the word.
3. The surface form of a word is the speaker's actual production, which may or may not be identical to the adult form of the word.
4. Each sound change accounts for one difference between the speaker's actual production and the adult form of the word.

1
RECOGNIZING SOUND CHANGES

A sound change is a way of noting the alteration of a target consonant, cluster, or syllable. The change may result in a deletion, a substitution, a distortion, or a phoneme sequence alteration. Any deviation from the adult form represents at least one _____.

sound change

In order to determine which phonological processes have been used to alter the underlying representation, one must first identify the *sound changes*. Each difference between the child's form and its underlying representation (the adult form) is called a _____.

sound change

Prior to assignment of phonological processes, each _____ must be identified.

sound change

If the underlying representation is CAT /kæt/ and the child's form is [kæk], then the sound change is represented as /t/ → [k], "/t/ becomes [k]." If the adult form is PEAK /pik/ and the child's form is [bik], then the sound change is represented as /p/ → [___].

[b]

If the adult form HOUSE /haʊs/ becomes [haʊf], then the sound change is /___/ → [f].

/s/

If CARROT /kɛrət/ → [kɛwət], the sound change is /r/ → [___].

[w]

If STOVE /stov/ → [stof], the sound change is /___/ → [___].

/v/ → [f]

1

ø

/g/ → [ø]

/b/ → [ø]

/t/ → [ø]

/k/ → [ø]

/f/ → [ø]

/b/ → [ø]

[t]

[gw]

If STOVE /stov/ → [sto], then the sound change is recorded as /v/ → [ø], which is the symbol for a deletion. This null sign is used to the right of the arrow whenever a deletion has been made. The symbol for a deletion is _____.

If BAG /bæg/ → [bæ], the sound change is recorded as /___/ → [___].

If BAG /bæg/ → [æg], the sound change is recorded as /___/ → [___].

Identify the *sound changes* for the following words, which include deletions of phonemes.

	Adult Form	Child's Form	Sound Change
HAT	/hæt/	→ [hæ]	/___/ → [_]
TALK	/tɔk/	→ [tɔ]	/___/ → [_]
FINGER	/fɪŋgɚ/	→ [ɪŋgɚ]	/___/ → [_]
BOY	/bɔɪ/	→ [ɔɪ]	/___/ → [_]

Sound changes also involve clusters. A common sound change involves the deletion of one member of the cluster. For example, if BLUE /blu/ → [bu], the sound change would be written as /bl/ → [b]. Note that the entire cluster is included in the sound change notation. Similarly, if TREE /tri/ → [ti], the sound change would be noted as /tr/ → [___].

Clusters are included in their *complete adult form* to the left of the sound change arrow. Clusters are considered to be a whole unit. If GRASS /græs/ → [gwæs], then the sound change is NOT written as /r/ → [w]; instead, the entire cluster is included and the sound change is written as /gr/ → [___].

Another common sound change that applies to clusters is the replacement of one consonant by another within the cluster. The child produces the correct number

of consonants in the cluster, but produces an altered
form. For example, TREE /tri/ might become [twi]. In
this case, the sound change is represented by /tr/ → [tw].
Similarly, if BLUE /blu/ → [bwu], the sound change is
written as /____/ → [____].

/bl/ → [bw]

To summarize, the phoneme(s) or syllable(s) to the
left of the arrow are those included in the target, or *adult*,
form of the word. The phoneme(s) or syllable(s) to the
right of the arrow represent the child's form of
production. Recall that the sound changes are listed in
order from _____ to _____: the adult form
→ the child's actual production.

left, right

Identify the sound changes in the following examples:

	Adult Form	Child's Form	Sound Change	
BACK	/bæk/	→ [bæt]	/___/ → [___]	/k/ → [t]
CAR	/kar/	→ [kaʊ]	/___/ → [___]	/r/ → [ʊ]
SUN	/sʌn/	→ [tʌn]	/___/ → [___]	/s/ → [t]
ZIPPER	/zɪpɚ/	→ [zɪpɛ]	/___/ → [___]	/ɚ/ → [ɛ]
HAT	/hæt/	→ [hæʔ]	/___/ → [___]	/t/ → [ʔ]
MOUSE	/maʊs/	→ [maʊts]	/___/ → [___]	/s/ → [ts]
BASKET	/bæskɪt/	→ [bæksɪt]	/___/ → [___]	/sk/ → [ks]
CLOWN	/klaʊn/	→ [kaʊn]	/___/ → [___]	/kl/ → [k]
SMALL	/smɔl/	→ [smɔ]	/___/ → [___]	/l/ → [ø]
NEST	/nɛst/	→ [nɛs]	/___/ → [___]	/st/ → [s]
SMOKE	/smok/	→ [fok]	/___/ → [___]	/sm/ → [f]

Sound changes can involve entire syllables. If
BANANA /bənænə/ → [nænə], the sound change would
be noted as /bə/ → [____].

[ø]

/dʒə/ → [ø]

Similarly, if GIRAFFE /dʒəræf/ → [ræf], the sound change would be /____/ → [____].

Identify the sound changes between the following multisyllabic words and their productions.

	Adult Form		Child's Form	Sound Change
WAGON	/wægən/	→ [wæ]		/____/ → [____]
TELEPHONE	/tɛləfon/	→ [tɛfon]		/____/ → [____]
AIRPLANE	/ɛɪrplen/	→ [plen]		/____/ → [____]
CHICKEN	/tʃɪkɪn/	→ [tʃɪk]		/____/ → [____]
PRETTY	/prɪtɪ/	→ [prɪ]		/____/ → [____]
VACATION	/vekeʃən/	→ [keʃən]		/____/ → [____]

/gən/ → [ø]

/lə/ → [ø]

/ɛɪr/ → [ø]

/ɪn/ → [ø]

/tɪ/ → [ø]

/ve/ → [ø]

Each response involved only one sound change. However, more than one sound change may be present when the child's production is compared with the adult form. For example, when TELEPHONE /tɛləfon/ becomes [fɛləbon], there are *two* sound changes: /t/ → [____] and /f/ → [____].

[f], [b]

Multiple sound changes are listed as several single sound changes. When two or more sound changes are present, we say that _____ sound changes have occurred.

multiple

Whenever we list each multiple sound change, we go from _____ to _____ through the word.

left, right

When HOUSE /haʊs/ → [aʊf], the sound changes include (from left to right) /h/ → [____] and /s/ → [____].

[ø], [f]

When CARROT /kɛrət/ → [tɛwət], the sound changes include /____/ → [____] and /____/ → [____].

/k/ → [t],
/r/ → [w]

Identify the multiple sound changes in the following examples. Each child's form has resulted from the application of two sound changes.

	Adult Form	Child's Form	Sound Changes	
SNAKE	/snek/	→ [net]	/___/ → [___] /___/ → [___]	/sn/ → [n] /k/ → [t]
CAR	/kar/	→ [taɔ]	/___/ → [___] /___/ → [___]	/k/ → [t] /r/ → [ɔ]
BAD	/bæd/	→ [dæ]	/___/ → [___] /___/ → [___]	/b/ → [d] /d/ → [ø]
SHOVEL	/ʃʌvəl/	→ [dʌbəl]	/___/ → [___] /___/ → [___]	/ʃ/ → [d] /v/ → [b]
BRUSH	/brʌʃ/	→ [bʌtʃ]	/___/ → [___] /___/ → [___]	/br/ → [b] /ʃ/ → [tʃ]
KNIFE	/naɪf/	→ [maɪp]	/___/ → [___] /___/ → [___]	/n/ → [m] /f/ → [p]
ZIPPER	/zɪpɚ/	→ [dɪpɔ]	/___/ → [___] /___/ → [___]	/z/ → [d] /ɚ/ → [ɔ]
BASKET	/bæskɪt/	→ [bæʔɪk]	/___/ → [___] /___/ → [___]	/sk/ → [ʔ] /t/ → [k]

The following productions contain one or more sound changes. List the single and multiple sound changes. List them in order from left to right. Remember to list clusters as whole clusters to the left of the arrow, as in /tr/ → [t], rather than /r/ → [ø].

	Adult Form	Child's Form	Sound Change	
LEG	/lɛg/	→ [jɛk]	/___/ → [___] /___/ → [___]	/l/ → [j] /g/ → [k]

/r/ → [w]	RABBIT	/ræbɪt/	→ [wædɪ]	/___/ → [___]
/b/ → [d]				/___/ → [___]
/t/ → [ø]				/___/ → [___]
/sn/ → [sən]	SNAKE	/snek/	→ [səneʔ]	/___/ → [___]
/k/ → [ʔ]				/___/ → [___]
/p/ → [g]	PIG	/pɪg/	→ [gɪp]	/___/ → [___]
/g/ → [p]				/___/ → [___]
/s/ → [st]	SUN	/sʌn/	→ [stʌn]	/___/ → [___]
/z/ → [d]	ZIPPER	/zɪpɚ/	→ [dɪʔə]	/___/ → [___]
/p/ → [ʔ]				/___/ → [___]
/ɚ/ → [ə]				/___/ → [___]
/sk/ → [s]	BASKET	/bæskɪt/	→ [bæsɪʔ]	/___/ → [___]
/t/ → [ʔ]				/___/ → [___]
/sm/ → [f]	SMALL	/smɔl/	→ [fɔ]	/___/ → [___]
/l/ → [ø]				/___/ → [___]
/t/ → [s]	TELEPHONE	/tɛləfon/	→ [sɛdəso]	/___/ → [___]
/l/ → [d]				/___/ → [___]
/f/ → [s]				/___/ → [___]
/n/ → [ø]				/___/ → [___]

sound change
Recall that there may be more than one _____ observed between the adult form and the child's response.

sound changes
Before assigning phonological processes, all _____ must be identified.

process, OR phonological process
Each sound change is then analyzed for the applicable phonological processes. A _____ is a rule, or fairly consistent pattern of altered speech production.

phonological processes
In a word that has three sound changes, there may be as many as six _____ that account for those sound changes.

In the next chapter, some notes on transcription are presented with examples. This is followed by a section on each of 22 phonological processes and when they apply.

SUMMARY
Recognizing Sound Changes

1. A sound change is a way of noting the alteration of a target consonant, cluster, or syllable. The change may result in a deletion, a substitution, a distortion, or a phoneme sequence alteration.
2. Any deviation from the adult form represents at least one sound change.
3. The null sign (ø) is used as the symbol for a deletion.
4. The entire cluster is included in the sound change notation when any part of it has become altered in the surface form.
5. Sound changes are written so that the adult form is placed to the left of the arrow and the speaker's actual production is placed to the right of the arrow.
6. Any production may contain multiple sound changes.

2
NOTES ON TRANSCRIPTION

Transcription is a difficult skill to master. For this reason, several programs have been developed to provide practice for the speech-language clinician. Some of these are accompanied by audio tapes (Shriberg and Kent, 1982; Compton and Hutton, 1978; Edwards, in preparation). Some provide practice in transcribing the target adult forms of words and phrases (Paden, 1971). These programs provide excellent means for improving transcription skills. It is beyond the scope of this text to train the user in transcription. However, the consonant phonemes of English, the vowels, and useful diacritical markings are introduced here and defined with examples.

In general, the *phonemic* form of the target word has been used in this text. The _____ form includes the general consonants and vowels without regard to variations resulting from dialects or fast speech forms.

phonemic

This is also referred to as *broad* transcription. The phonemes without their variants are used to represent the adult form of a word or the child's response. When the phonemic form is used, it is referred to as _____ transcription.

broad

For example, when broad transcription is used, CAT is transcribed as /kæt/. A type of "generic" /k/ is used without indicating whether it is released or unreleased, anterior or posterior, and so on. The form /kæt/ is an example of _____ transcription.

broad

Each phoneme has a number of acceptable variations, called *allophones*. Since they are acceptable allophones, they can be grouped together and represented by the use of the generic _____.

phoneme

Another example of phonemic, or broad, transcription would be SOAP /sop/, where the expected anticipatory lip rounding on the /s/ is not specified. The transcription /sop/ is an example of _____ transcription.

phonemic,
OR broad

The symbols used in this text are primarily those used for phonemic transcription, with some exceptions. In this section, each symbol will be introduced with examples. The symbols introduced are those used in this text. Additional symbols can be found in Appendix I.

The consonants of English are familiar to most clinicians. They will be reviewed briefly here. The stop consonants consist of /p/, /b/, /t/, /d/, /k/, /g/. Transcribe the word-initial consonants for the following words. The first one has been done for you.

Words Containing a Stop	*Transcription*
PEANUT	/p/
BED	/___/
TELEPHONE	/___/
DOG	/___/
KITTEN	/___/
GOAT	/___/

/b/

/t/

/d/

/k/

/g/

Transcribe the word-final consonants for the following words:

Words Containing a Stop	*Transcription*
CUP	/___/
BATHTUB	/___/
BOAT	/___/

/p/

/b/

/t/

MAD	/___/	/d/
BOOK	/___/	/k/
DOG	/___/	/g/

Transcribe the word-medial stop consonants for the following words:

Words Containing a Stop	*Transcription*	
HAPPY	/___/	/p/
MAYBE	/___/	/b/
KITTEN	/___/	/t/
RADISH	/___/	/d/
OKAY	/___/	/k/
TIGER	/___/	/g/

Give the six stop consonants of English: /___/, /___/, /___/, /___/, /___/, /___/

/p/, /b/, /t/, /d/, /k/, /g/

Of these, three are voiceless and three are voiced. List the voiceless stop consonants: /___/, /___/, /___/

/p/, /t/, /k/

List the voiced stop consonants: /___/, /___/, /___/

/b/, /d/, /g/

There are two bilabial stop consonants. List them: /___/, /___/

/p/, /b/

There are two alveolar stop consonants. List them: /___/, /___/

/t/, /d/

There are two velar stop consonants. List them: /___/, /___/

/k/, /g/

Give the phoneme that fits each of the following descriptions:

/p/   voiceless bilabial stop: /_p_/

/g/   voiced velar stop: /_g_/

/d/   voiced alveolar stop: /_d_/

/k/   voiceless velar stop: /_K_/

/t/   voiceless alveolar stop: /_t_/

/b/   voiced bilabial stop: /_b_/

The transcription for each of these stop consonants matches its orthographic form. That is, the symbols appear just as they do in lower-case print.

However, some words containing *medial* /t/ are not transcribed using a /t/. This is because the tongue tip flaps back slightly and there is a slight addition of voicing. In words like WATER and BUTTER the/t/ is produced as an alveolar "flap." The symbol for this is /ɾ/.

Transcribe the word-medial consonant in the following words containing alveolar flaps:

Word Containing a Flap	Transcription
/ɾ/ WATER	/____/
/ɾ/ MOTOR	/____/
/ɾ/ TURTLE	/____/
/ɾ/ MATTER	/____/
/ɾ/ BITTER	/____/

orthographic, OR lower-case print   Medial /t/ is the one stop consonant that may not be transcribed in its _____ form.

In the word KITTEN, used above as an example of word-medial /t/, this does not typically occur because of coarticulatory constraints (context). The symbol for an alveolar flap is /____/.

/ɾ/

There are nine (9) fricatives in the English language. A fricative is a phoneme that is produced with a continuous airstream through the oral cavity or glottis. The nine fricatives are /f/, /v/, /θ/, /ð/, /s/, /z/, /ʃ/, /ʒ/, /h/. Transcribe the word-initial fricatives in the following words:

	Transcription	
FATHER	/____/	/f/
VACATION	/____/	/v/
THUMB	/____/	/θ/
THIS	/____/	/ð/
SUPPER	/____/	/s/
ZEBRA	/____/	/z/
SHOE	/____/	/ʃ/
HAPPY	/____/	/h/

The phoneme /ʒ/ was not included. There are no English words that contain word-initial /ʒ/. Transcribe the word-final fricatives in the following words:

	Transcription	
LEAF	/____/	/f/
HAVE	/____/	/v/
BATH	/____/	/θ/
SMOOTH	/____/	/ð/

/s/	BUS	/___/
/z/	TOYS	/___/
/ʃ/	WASH	/___/
/ʒ/	ROUGE	/___/

The phoneme /h/ was not included. There are no English words that contain word-final /h/. Transcribe the word-medial fricatives in the following words:

Transcription

/f/ (PH)	TELEPHONE	/___/
/v/	OVER	/___/
/θ/	NOTHING	/___/
/ð/	FATHER	/___/
/s/ (C)	RACING	/___/
/z/	BULLDOZER	/___/
/ʃ/ (C)	SPECIAL	/___/
/ʒ/	TREASURE	/___/

/f/, /v/, /θ/, /ð/, /s/, /z/, /ʃ/, /ʒ/, /h/

Give the nine fricatives of English: /___/, /___/, /___/, /___/, /___/, /___/, /___/, /___/, /___/

/f/, /θ/, /s/, /ʃ/, /h/

Of those five are voiceless and four are voiced. List the voiceless fricatives: /___/, /___/, /___/, /___/, /___/

/v/, /ð/, /z/, /ʒ/

List the four voiced fricatives: /___/, /___/, /___/, /___/

There are two labiodental fricatives. List them: /____/, /____/

/f/, /v/

There are two linguadental fricatives. List them: /____/, /____/

/θ/, /ð/

There are two alveolar fricatives. List them: /____/, /____/

/s/, /z/

There is one glottal fricative, which is /____/

/h/

There are two palatal fricatives. List them: /____/, /____/

/ʃ/, /ʒ/

Stridency is the aperiodic noise that accompanies the production of a fricative or affricate. When you pronounce each individual fricative, you can tell that /θ/, /ð/, and /h/ are not _____ because they are "quieter."

strident

Of the nine fricatives, six are strident and three are not. The three that are not strident are /θ/, /ð/, and /h/. Those which are strident are /____/, /____/, /____/, /____/, /____/, /____/

/f/, /v/, /s/, /z/, /ʃ/, /ʒ/

Give the phoneme that fits each of the following descriptions:

voiceless labiodental fricative: /__f__/

/f/

voiced alveolar fricative: /__z__/

/z/

voiced palatal fricative: /__ʒ__/

/ʒ/

voiceless linguadental fricative: /__θ__/

/θ/

voiceless alveolar fricative: /__s__/

/s/

voiced labiodental fricative: /__v__/

/v/

voiceless glottal fricative: /__h__/

/h/

voiceless palatal fricative: /__ʃ__/

/ʃ/

/ð/ | voiced linguadental fricative: /____/

/θ/ | non-strident voiceless fricative: /____/

/ð/ | non-strident voiced fricative: /____/

/f/, /v/, /s/, /z/, /ʃ/, /ʒ/ | List the strident fricatives: /____/, /____/, /____/, /____/, /____/, /____/

/p/, /b/, /f/, /v/ | List the stops and fricatives that are labial (they include bilabial and labiodental): /____/, /____/, /____/, /____/

/θ/, /ð/; there are no linguadental stops in Standard English. | List the stops and fricatives that are linguadental: /____/, /____/

/t/, /d/, /s/, /z/ | List the stops and fricatives that are alveolar: /____/, /____/, /____/, /____/

/ʃ/, /ʒ/; there are no palatal stops in Standard English. | List the stops and fricatives that are palatal: /____/, /____/

/k/, /g/; there are no velar fricatives in Standard English. | List the stops and fricatives that are velar: /____/, /____/

A class of sounds that shares both stop and fricative characteristics is called the affricates. There are two affricates in Standard English. They are /tʃ/ and /dʒ/. The stop components are represented by /t/ and /d/. The fricative components are represented by /ʃ/ and /ʒ/. The affricates are considered to be palatal, or sometimes are referred to as palatal-alveolar. Transcribe the word-initial fricatives in the following words:

Transcription

/tʃ/ | CHAIR | /____/

/dʒ/ | GIANT | /____/

The voiceless affricate is /____/.

/tʃ/

The voiced affricate is /____/.

/dʒ/

When a child alters a fricative, an affricate is sometimes what the fricative becomes. That is, when the target word is SEE /si/, the child may produce [tʃi]. When this occurs, the alveolar /s/ becomes the palatal /____/.

/tʃ/

However, sometimes the production remains alveolar. In this case, the child may produce [tsi]. The /s/ has become an alveolar affricate. The alveolar _____ are /ts/ and /dz/.

affricates

Transcribe the word-final affricates in the following words:

	Transcription
CATCH	/____/
BRIDGE	/____/

/tʃ/

/dʒ/

Transcribe the word-medial affricates in the following words:

	Transcription
MATCHES	/____/
BADGER	/____/

/tʃ/

/dʒ/

There are three nasal consonants in English. They are /m/, /n/, and /ŋ/. /ŋ/ occurs only in word-medial and word-final position within Standard English words. Transcribe the word-initial nasal consonants in the following words:

	Transcription
MAN	/____/
NOSE	/____/

/m/

/n/

Transcribe the word-final nasal consonants in the following words:

		Transcription
/m/	HAM	/___/
/n/	GUN	/___/
/ŋ/	RING	/___/

Transcribe the word-medial nasal consonants in the following words:

		Transcription
/n/	PENNY	/___/
/m/	HAMMER	/___/
/ŋ/	SINGER	/___/

/m/   There is one bilabial nasal. It is /___/.

/n/   The alveolar nasal is /___/.

/ŋ/   The velar nasal is /___/.

/p/, /b/, /f/, /v/, /m/; no affricates

List the labial stops, fricatives, affricates, and nasals: /___/, /___/, /___/, /___/, /___/

/θ/, /ð/; no stops, affricates, or nasals

List the linguadental stops, fricatives, affricates, and nasals: /___/, /___/

/t/, /d/, /s/, /z/, /ts/, /dz/, /n/

List the alveolar stops, fricatives, affricates, and nasals: /___/, /___/, /___/, /___/, /___/, /___/, /___/

/ʃ/, /ʒ/ /tʃ/, /dʒ/; no stops or nasals

List the palatal stops, fricatives, affricates, and nasals: /___/, /___/, /___/, /___/

List the velar stops, fricatives, affricates, and nasals: /____/, /____/, /____/

/k/, /g/, /ŋ/

There are two glides in the English language: /w/ and /j/. /j/ is pronounced "YUH" as in YELLOW /jɛlo/. Transcribe the word-initial consonants in the following words:

	Transcription	
WATER	/____/	/w/
YESTERDAY	/____/	/j/

Transcribe the word-medial glides in the following words:

	Transcription	
HALLOWEEN	/____/	/w/
CRAYON	/____/	/j/

The palatal glide is /____/.

/j/

The liquids in English are basically /l/ and /r/. Transcribe the word-initial liquids in the following words:

	Transcription	
LEMON	/____/	/l/
RABBIT	/____/	/r/

Transcribe the word-final liquids in the following words:

	Transcription	
BALL	/____/	/l/
CAR	/____/	/r/

Transcribe the word-medial liquids in the following words:

		Transcription
/l/	ELEPHANT	/___/
/r/	CARROT	/___/

In addition to consonantal /l/ and /r/, there are syllabic /l̩/ and /r̩/. The dot beneath the consonants indicates that they are syllabic. That is, they represent an entire syllable. Examples of these syllabics are SISTER /sistr̩/ and CHANNEL /tʃænl̩/. Both /l̩/ and /r̩/ can also be transcribed with a schwa to represent the syllable. For example, SISTER /sistɚ/ and CHANNEL /tʃænəl/. Transcribe the syllabic liquids in the following words:

		Transcription
/r̩/ OR /ɚ/	CALENDAR	/___/
/l̩/ OR /əl/	TABLE	/___/

When /ɚ/ is used in a primary syllable, as in the word HER /hɝ/, it is transcribed as /ɝ/. The only difference is one of stress. You can hear the difference between HER /hɝ/ and MOTHER /mʌðɚ/. Transcribe the stressed /ɝ/ in each of the following words:

		Transcription
/ɝ/	PERSON	/___/
/ɝ/	SHIRT	/___/
/ɝ/	TURKEY	/___/

There are allophonic variations in /r/ and /ɚ/, which are related to the context in which the /r/ is produced. These variations have been included in Appendix I.

In addition to /h/, there is another glottal phoneme, the glottal stop. It is represented by the symbol /ʔ/. This phoneme is not common in Standard English, although it is in some dialects. For example, the word BOTTLE may be pronounced /baʔl̩/ in some areas of the northeastern

United States. Glottal stops may also replace consonants in children's productions. For example, TEACHER /titʃɚ/ → [tiʔɚ]. The two glottal phonemes presented here are /___/ and /___/.

/h/, /ʔ/

The vowels of English are somewhat more difficult to transcribe than the consonants. There are regional differences, which make transcription confusing, at best. The vowels used in this text match as closely as possible those presented in Kenyon and Knott (1953). In general, regional dipthongization of vowels (non-phonemic diphthongs) was avoided. For example, the word GO was transcribed as /go/ instead of the diphthongized /goʊ/. The user is urged to be aware of this and to transcribe as closely as possible to LOCAL dialect. If the local production of the /o/ in GO is, in fact, a diphthong, then the user should transcribe it as one. In comparing the responses with the answers provided, an [oʊ] for an [o] would then be correct.

The vowel in WHEEL is represented by /i/. Transcribe the vowel in the following words:

	Transcription	
CHEAP	/___/	/i/
LEAF	/___/	/i/

This is sometimes referred to as a "long E." The "long E" sound is transcribed as the /___/ phoneme.

/i/

The vowel in HILL is represented by /ɪ/. Transcribe the vowel in each of the following words:

	Transcription	
SICK	/___/	/ɪ/
FISH	/___/	/ɪ/

This is sometimes referred to as a "short I." The "short I" sound is transcribed as the /___/ phoneme.

/ɪ/

The vowel in PLANE is represented by /e/. Transcribe the vowel in each of the following words:

	Transcription
DATE	/___/
LAKE	/___/

/e/

/e/

This is sometimes referred to as "long A." The "long A" sound is transcribed as the /___/ phoneme.

/e/

When this vowel is lengthened regionally, it may become /eɪ/. This is an acceptable transcription for the /e/, which is used in this text. In fact, when the vowel occurs at the end of the word, as in PLAY, it may be diphthongized to /pleɪ/. The symbol used for this vowel is /___/ in this text.

/e/

The vowel in BED is represented by /ɛ/. Transcribe the vowel in each of the following words:

	Transcription
DESK	/___/
SAID	/___/

/ɛ/

/ɛ/

This is sometimes referred to as "short E." The "short E" sound is transcribed as the /___/ phoneme.

/ɛ/

The vowel in SAD is transcribed as /æ/. Transcribe the vowel in each of the following words:

	Transcription
BACK	/___/
HAND	/___/

/æ/

/æ/

This is sometimes referred to as "short A." The "short A" sound is transcribed as the /___/ phoneme.

/æ/

In parts of Texas and the South, the /æ/ is diphthongized to /æjə/, as in BAD /bæd/ → [bæjəd]. If this sound is characteristic of local dialect, you may wish to transcribe the longer /æ/ as [___].

[æjə]

The vowel in HOT is transcribed as /a/. Transcribe the vowel in each of the following words:

	Transcription	
BOX	/___/	/a/
WASH	/___/	/a/

This is sometimes referred to as "short O." The "short O" sound is transcribed as the /___/ phoneme.   /a/

The vowel in TALK is transcribed as /ɔ/. Transcribe the vowel in each of the following words:

	Transcription	
SMALL	/___/	/ɔ/
LONG	/___/	/ɔ/

The /ɔ/ is often used by children to replace a syllabic /ɚ/. When FATHER /faðɚ/ becomes [faðɔ], the /ɚ/ has become an /___/.   /ɔ/

The vowel in STOVE is transcribed as /o/. Transcribe the vowel in each of the following words:

	Transcription	
BOAT	/___/	/o/
GO	/___/	/o/

This is sometimes referred to as "long O." The "long O" sound is transcribed as the /___/ phoneme.   /o/

In some regions, and in some phonetic contexts, the /o/ is elongated and pronounced /___/, a non-phonemic diphthong.   /oʊ/

The vowel in PUT is transcribed as /ʊ/. Transcribe the vowel in each of the following words:

	Transcription	
BOOK	/___/	/ʊ/·
PUSH	/___/	/ʊ/

The vowel in BLUE is transcribed as /u/. Transcribe the vowel in each of the following words:

		Transcription
/u/	FRUIT	/___/
/u/	DO	/___/

This is sometimes referred to as "long U." The "long U" sound is transcribed as the /___/ phoneme.

/u/

The vowel in CUP is transcribed as /ʌ/. Transcribe the vowel in each of the following words:

		Transcription
/ʌ/	RUN	/___/
/ʌ/	TRUCK	/___/

This is sometimes referred to as "short U." The "short U" sound is transcribed as the /___/ phoneme.

/ʌ/

A phoneme that is very similar, except that it is not stressed (/ʌ/ is stressed), is the *schwa*. The symbol for a schwa is /ə/. The first vowel in AFRAID is a schwa: /əfred/. Transcribe the schwa vowels in the following words:

		Transcription
/ə/	*A*GO	/___/
/ə/	DRAG*O*N	/___/

When it is used in a word like CARR*O*T, it is sometimes transcribed as /ə/. This often depends upon the individual speaker or the regional dialect. The /___/ is basically an "UH" that does not occur within a stressed syllable.

/ə/

There are several diphthongs in Standard English. The diphthong in KNIFE is transcribed as /aɪ/. Transcribe the vowel in each of the following words:

Transcription

FIGHT /____/   /aɪ/

ICE /____/   /aɪ/

This is sometimes referred to as "long I." The "long I" sound is transcribed as /____/.   /aɪ/

Another diphthong is the vowel in SHOUT. This is represented by the diphthong /aʊ/. Transcribe the vowel in each of the following words:

Transcription

COUCH /____/   /aʊ/

HOUSE /____/   /aʊ/

The vowel in BOY is also a diphthong and is transcribed as /ɔɪ/. Transcribe the vowel in each of the following words:

Transcription

TOY /____/   /ɔɪ/

NOISE /____/   /ɔɪ/

There are several diacritical markings that are useful during transcription. They have been included in Appendix I. In general, diacritics are used to specify non-redundant characteristics of articulatory production. For example, /k/ may be released, as in CUP /kʌp/. The /k/ is typically released prevocalically and therefore need not be represented by [kᴸ]. The small "ᴸ" to the upper right of the consonant indicates that it has been released. When specific characteristics of a phoneme are represented by diacritical markings such as "ᴸ", the transcription is said to be *narrow* rather than _____.   broad

In contrast, the /k/ in the word SCOTT /skˀat/ is unreleased because of coarticulatory constraints. The /k/ would be represented by [kˀ]. The small "ˀ" to the upper right of the consonant indicates that it is unreleased.

| narrow | When diacritical markings are used to represent as closely as possible the exact articulatory characteristics of a production, the transcription is called _____ transcription. |

When phonemic, or broad, transcription is used, these variations in /k/ production are ignored. Since /k/ is inherently unreleased in /sk/-clusters, it is redundant to specify this. However, if the /k/ is *released* in the context of an /sk/-cluster, it may be important to note this. The production would then be transcribed as [skᴸat], which is no longer broad transcription. When diacritical marks are used to specify characteristics of phoneme production, the

narrow | transcription is called _____.

Several diacritical markings are included in Appendix I. When attempting narrow transcription, refer to these

diacritical markings | _____.

Thus far, the user has been introduced to some of the basic terminology of phonology, sound changes, and transcription. In the next section, patterns of errors will be described. The next chapter contains a general introduction to phonological processes, which is followed by a section on each of 22 phonological processes. Each process is defined, examples are provided, and exercises in analysis are included.

SUMMARY
Notes on Transcription
1. The phonemic, or broad, transcription of a word includes general consonants and vowels without noting specific allophonic differences.
2. The phonetic, or narrow, transcription of a word specifies allophonic differences in the speaker's production.
3. Diacritical markings are used to represent allophonic variations.
4. Local dialect must be considered acceptable when speech production is analyzed.

3
ASSIGNING PHONOLOGICAL PROCESSES TO SOUND CHANGES

After identification of all the sound changes in a word, the next step involves assigning a phonological process (or processes) to each identified _____.

sound change

One of the major phonological processes described in the literature can be assigned to most identified _____. Other sound changes may be IDIOSYNCRATIC, or otherwise novel, and will require a unique descriptive label.

sound changes

For each sound change, an attempt should be made to identify the phonological _____ that produced the sound change.

process(es)

A single sound change may result from the application of more than one _____.

phonological process

For example, the word THING /θɪŋ/, if produced as [dɪŋ], represents the single _____, /θ/ → [d].

sound change

That single sound change, however, has resulted from the application of two _____.

phonological processes

In this case, /θ/ → [d] results from the application of STOPPING and PREVOCALIC VOICING. STOPPING of the /θ/ results in [t]. The /t/ is then voiced, producing a [d]. The single sound change has resulted from the application of _____ phonological processes.

two

Following is a list of the phonological processes that will be covered in this text. It is not intended to be an exhaustive list. Additional processes are described in Edwards and Shriberg (1983), Ingram (1981), and Hodson (1980).

There are also processes that are unique to individual children. Some of them are discussed under "Idiosyncratic Processes." Examples will be given as each process is defined. Opportunities to analyze productions for phonological processes are provided throughout.

Twenty-two phonological processes (listed here) are included in this text. Of these, the first 13 are presented in approximately developmental order. They are processes that are frequently produced by normally developing young children. Processes 14 through 21 are generally not characteristic of young normal development, although they are used occasionally by some children who do not have articulation/phonological disorders. A 22nd category, "Idiosyncratic Processes," includes examples of processes that may be novel or unique to an individual child.

PROCESSES CHARACTERISTIC OF NORMAL SPEECH DEVELOPMENT

	Phonological Process	Abbreviation	Examples
1.	DELETION OF FINAL CONSONANT—page 32	DFC	HAT /hæt/ → [hæ] CUP /kʌp/ → [kʌ]
2.	PREVOCALIC VOICING —page 38	PVV	TALK /tɔk/ → [dɔk] CUP /kʌp/ → [gʌp]
3.	SYLLABLE REDUCTION —page 49	SR	WAGON /wægən/ → [wæ] CRACKER /krækɚ/ → [kræ]
4.	VELAR FRONTING —page 61	VF	CUP /kʌp/ → [tʌp] DUCK /dʌk/ → [dʌt]

5.	STOPPING OF FRICATIVES AND AFFRICATES —page 71	ST	SUN /sʌn/ → [tʌn] CHAIR /tʃɛr/ → [tɛr]
6.	CLUSTER REDUCTION —page 86	CR	TREE /tri/ → [ti] NEST /nɛst/ → [nɛs]
7.	STRIDENCY DELETION —page 104	STR	SUN /sʌn/ → [θʌn] CHAIR /tʃɛr/ → [tɛr]
8.	CONSONANT HARMONY —page 115	CH	DUCK /dʌk/ → [gʌk] or [dʌt] FISH /fɪʃ/ → [ʃɪʃ]
9.	POSTVOCALIC DEVOICING—page 127	PVD	BAG /bæg/ → [bæk] CAGE /kedʒ/ → [ketʃ]
10.	VOCALIZATION—page 139	VOC	MOTHER /mʌðɚ/ → [mʌðʊ] TABLE /tebl̩/ → [tebo]
11.	PALATAL FRONTING —page 155	PF	SHOE /ʃu/ → [su] CHAIR /tʃɛr/ → [tsɛr]
12.	GLIDING OF LIQUIDS —page 163	GL	LEAF /lif/ → [wif] READ /rid/ → [jid]
13.	DEAFFRICATION—page 172	DEAFF	CHAIR /tʃɛr/ → [ʃɛr] JAM /dʒæm/ → [zæm]

PROCESSES NOT CHARACTERISTIC OF
NORMAL SPEECH DEVELOPMENT

	Phonological Process	**Abbreviation**	**Examples**
14.	DELETION OF INITIAL CONSONANT —page 182	DIC	HAT /hæt/ → [æt] TREE /tri/ → [i]

15. GLOTTAL REPLACEMENT
    —page 188 GR WAGON /wægən/ → [wæʔən]
                   CAT /kæt/ → [kæʔ]

16. BACKING—page 198 BK FISH /fɪʃ/ → [gɪʃ]
                           KNIFE /naɪf/ → [naɪk]

17. EPENTHESIS—page 207 EPEN BLUE /blu/ → [bəlu]
                                SPOON /spun/ → [səpun]

18. METATHESIS —page 210 METATH FISH /fɪʃ/ → [ʃɪf]
                                   BASKET /bæskɪt/ → [bæksɪt]

19. COALESCENCE —page 217 COAL SWING /swɪŋ/ → [fɪŋ]
                                  RADISH /rædɪʃ/ → [ræʃ]

20. PALATALIZATION
    —page 220 PAL SEE /si/ → [ʃi]
                    TOYS /tɔɪz/ → [tɔɪʒ]

21. DENASALIZATION
    —page 223 DENAS MAD /mæd/ → [bæd]
                      TEN /tɛn/ → [tɛd]

22. IDIOSYNCRATIC
    PROCESSES —page 226

Processes Characteristic
of Normal Speech Development

SECTION 1. DELETION OF FINAL CONSONANT

DELETION OF FINAL CONSONANT

DELETION OF FINAL CONSONANT is a process that results in the deletion of the word-final consonant from an attempted word. BOAT /bot/ → [bo] is an example of _____.

DFC

The abbreviation for DELETION OF FINAL CONSONANT is _____. A list of processes and abbreviations appears below and on all succeeding left-hand pages.

/g/

Another example of DFC would be DOG /dɔg/ → [dɔ], where the sound change is represented by /___/ → [ø].

DFC, or DELETION OF FINAL CONSONANT

Since the deletion occurs word-finally (at the end of the word) we recognize the process as _____.

DFC

The child may change WALK /wɔk/ → [wɔ] and HOUSE /haʊs/ → [haʊ]. Similarly, WASH /waʃ/ may change to [wa] with the application of the process _____.

List the productions that would result from the application of DFC to the following attempted words:

		Adult Form	*Child's Form*
[haʊ]	HOUSE	/haʊs/	→ [_____]
[dɔ]	DOG	/dɔg/	→ [_____]

Deletion of Final Consonant	DFC	Consonant Harmony	CH	Backing to Velars	BK
Prevocalic Voicing	PVV	Postvocalic Devoicing	PVD	Epenthesis	EPEN
Syllable Reduction	SR	Vocalization	VOC	Metathesis	METATH
Velar Fronting	VF	Palatal Fronting	PF	Coalescence	COAL
Stopping of Fricatives and Affricates	ST	Gliding of Liquids	GL	Palatalization	PAL
Cluster Reduction	CR	Deaffrication	DEAFF	Denasalization	DENAS
Stridency Deletion	STR	Deletion of Initial Consonant	DIC	Idiosyncratic Processes	
		Glottal Replacement	GR		

CUP   /kʌp/   → [_____]   [kʌ]

MOON   /mun/   → [_____]   [mu]

DFC is also applied to words that end with clusters.
Thus, CARD /kard/ → [ka] when DFC is applied. The
result is a production that lacks a _____   postvocalic, OR
consonant.   word-final

That is, the production ends with a vowel when the
underlying or adult form contains one or more word-final
_____.   consonants

Apply the process of DFC to the following words
containing clusters:

	Adult Form		*Child's Form*	
FAST	/fæst/	→	[_____]	[fæ]
LAMP	/læmp/	→	[_____]	[læ]
MILK	/mɪlk/	→	[_____]	[mɪ]
TENT	/tɛnt/	→	[_____]	[tɛ]

Whether an attempted word ends with a singleton or
a cluster, if the child's production lacks the postvocalic
consonant(s), then the process of _____ has been   DFC
applied.

The sound change still includes the entire cluster to
the _____ of the arrow.   left

/p/ PIG	/n/ NO	/ʃ/ SHE	/w/ WAGON	/ɛ/ BED	/ʌ/ GUN
/b/ BED	/ŋ/ STING	/ʒ/ ROUGE	/ʍ/ WHEEL	/æ/ CAT	/ə/ ABOUT
/t/ TOY	/f/ FOX	/h/ HAVE	/ɚ/ FINGER	/a/ GOT	/aɪ/ KITE
/d/ DUCK	/θ/ THINK	/tʃ/ CHICKEN	/ɝ/ CHURCH	/ɔ/ TALK	/ɔɪ/ TOY
/k/ KEEP	/ð/ THIS	/dʒ/ JUMPING	/i/ SEE	/o/ GOAT	/aʊ/ OUT
/g/ GOAT	/s/ SEE	/l/ LAKE	/ɪ/ PIG	/ʊ/ BOOK	
/m/ ME	/z/ ZOO	/j/ YOU	/eɪ, e/ MAKE	/u/ GLUE	

For each of the following attempted words, determine the sound change and predictable production that result from applying the process of DELETION OF FINAL CONSONANT:

	Adult Form	Child's Form	Sound Change
SOUP	/sup/	→ [_____]	/___/ → [___]
LEG	/lɛg/	→ [_____]	/___/ → [___]
CLAP	/klæp/	→ [_____]	/___/ → [___]
DRINK	/drɪŋk/	→ [_____]	/___/ → [___]
FROG	/frɔg/	→ [_____]	/___/ → [___]
NEST	/nɛst/	→ [_____]	/___/ → [___]

Left margin answers:

[su]
/p/ → [ø]

[lɛ]
/g/ → [ø]

[klæ]
/p/ → [ø]

[drɪ]
/ŋk/ → [ø]

[frɔ]
/g/ → [ø]

[nɛ]
/st/ → [ø]

DFC

When the attempted word contains no word-final consonant (as in SHOE /ʃu/ or MY /maɪ/) then there is no opportunity for the process of _____ to be applied.

When a cluster is reduced to a singleton, it is not considered to be deleted. For example, when GHOST /gost/ → [gos], only the cluster has been reduced, with one member of the cluster retained. The process of

Deletion of Final Consonant	DFC	Consonant Harmony	CH	Backing to Velars	BK
Prevocalic Voicing	PVV	Postvocalic Devoicing	PVD	Epenthesis	EPEN
Syllable Reduction	SR	Vocalization	VOC	Metathesis	METATH
Velar Fronting	VF	Palatal Fronting	PF	Coalescence	COAL
Stopping of Fricatives and Affricates	ST	Gliding of Liquids	GL	Palatalization	PAL
		Deaffrication	DEAFF	Denasalization	DENAS
Cluster Reduction	CR	Deletion of Initial Consonant	DIC	Idiosyncratic Processes	
Stridency Deletion	STR	Glottal Replacement	GR		

_____ has NOT been applied because a word-final consonant is present in the child's production (CVC).

| | DFC |

Indicate whether each of the following attempted words provides an opportunity for DFC to be applied:

	Adult Form	
LAMP	/læmp/	YES, /mp/
BLUE	/blu/	NO
WINDOW	/wɪndo/	NO
SLEEPING	/slipɪŋ/	YES, /ŋ/
DUCK	/dʌk/	YES, /k/
HOUSE	/haʊs/	YES, /s/
SAY	/seɪ/	NO

Of the seven attempted words listed above, a total of _____ provided the opportunity for DFC to be applied.

| | four |

Note that the orthographic spellings (as in DOUGH) may contain word-final consonants while their phonemic forms, or pronunciations, do not (as in /do/). Deciding whether there is an opportunity to apply a certain process must be made using the _____ transcription for the word.

| | phonemic |

/p/ PIG	/n/ NO	/ʃ/ SHE	/w/ WAGON	/ɛ/ BED	/ʌ/ GUN
/b/ BED	/ŋ/ STING	/ʒ/ ROUGE	/ʍ/ WHEEL	/æ/ CAT	/ə/ ABOUT
/t/ TOY	/f/ FOX	/h/ HAVE	/ɚ/ FINGER	/a/ GOT	/aɪ/ KITE
/d/ DUCK	/θ/ THINK	/tʃ/ CHICKEN	/ɝ/ CHURCH	/ɔ/ TALK	/ɔɪ/ TOY
/k/ KEEP	/ð/ THIS	/dʒ/ JUMPING	/i/ SEE	/o/ GOAT	/aʊ/ OUT
/g/ GOAT	/s/ SEE	/l/ LAKE	/ɪ/ PIG	/ʊ/ BOOK	
/m/ ME	/z/ ZOO	/j/ YOU	/eɪ, e/ MAKE	/u/ GLUE	

identifiable context	Any phonological process may be applied in every identifiable context. When this happens, the process is applied *uniformly* or *consistently*. Any phonological process may also be applied *selectively* or *optionally*. When a process is applied selectively, it is not applied in every _____.
four	DFC may be applied *uniformly* or *selectively*. In the list of words above, there are four opportunities for DFC to be applied. If it had been applied to all _____, then it would have been applied uniformly.
selectively	If it had been applied to some but not all contexts, then the process of DFC would have been _____ applied.
selective	DFC may have been applied to all consonants that share a certain distinctive feature, such as stridency. When a process applies to certain, but not all, consonants potentially affected, it is called a _____ process, or an optional process.
	It is important to look for these specific patterns within a process category. For example, DFC may be *optionally* applied to postvocalic *stops* only. Indicate whether each of the following attempted words would have DFC applied if this OPTIONAL rule is used:
	Adult Form
YES, /t/ is a stop.	CAT /kæt/

Deletion of Final Consonant	DFC	Consonant Harmony	CH	Backing to Velars	BK
Prevocalic Voicing	PVV	Postvocalic Devoicing	PVD	Epenthesis	EPEN
Syllable Reduction	SR	Vocalization	VOC	Metathesis	METATH
Velar Fronting	VF	Palatal Fronting	PF	Coalescence	COAL
Stopping of Fricatives and Affricates	ST	Gliding of Liquids	GL	Palatalization	PAL
Cluster Reduction	CR	Deaffrication	DEAFF	Denasalization	DENAS
Stridency Deletion	STR	Deletion of Initial Consonant	DIC	Idiosyncratic Processes	
		Glottal Replacement	GR		

BUS	/bʌs/	NO, /s/ is not a stop
FROG	/frɔg/	YES, /g/ is a stop
CUP	/kʌp/	YES, /p/ is a stop

There are three words with word-final *stop* consonants. These three provide the opportunity for this optional process to be applied. When there are specific conditions that must be met before a process can be applied, the process is termed an _____ process.

optional, OR selective

SUMMARY
Deletion of Final Consonant

1. DFC is a process that results in the deletion of a singleton or cluster from word-final position.
2. When a cluster has been reduced to a singleton, it is not considered to have been deleted.
3. Orthographic spellings may contain word-final consonants while their phonemic forms do not.

/p/ *PIG*	/n/ *NO*	/ʃ/ *SHE*	/w/ *WAGON*	/ɛ/ *BED*	/ʌ/ *GUN*
/b/ *BED*	/ŋ/ *STING*	/ʒ/ *ROUGE*	/ʍ/ *WHEEL*	/æ/ *CAT*	/ə/ *ABOUT*
/t/ *TOY*	/f/ *FOX*	/h/ *HAVE*	/ɚ/ *FINGER*	/a/ *GOT*	/aɪ/ *KITE*
/d/ *DUCK*	/θ/ *THINK*	/tʃ/ *CHICKEN*	/ɝ/ *CHURCH*	/ɔ/ *TALK*	/ɔɪ/ *TOY*
/k/ *KEEP*	/ð/ *THIS*	/dʒ/ *JUMPING*	/i/ *SEE*	/o/ *GOAT*	/aʊ/ *OUT*
/g/ *GOAT*	/s/ *SEE*	/l/ *LAKE*	/ɪ/ *PIG*	/ʊ/ *BOOK*	
/m/ *ME*	/z/ *ZOO*	/j/ *YOU*	/eɪ, e/ *MAKE*	/u/ *GLUE*	

SECTION 2. PREVOCALIC VOICING

PREVOCALIC
VOICING,
or PVV

PREVOCALIC VOICING (PVV) is the inappropriate voicing of a word-initial voiceless consonant. It applies only to prevocalic voiceless consonants. The change from CUP /kʌp/ → [gʌp] is an example of _____ where the consonant /k/ has changed from voiceless to voiced.

[b]

Another example of PVV would be PAJAMAS /pədʒæməz/ → [bədʒæməz], where the /p/ → [___].

PVV

Since the process involves an alteration in voicing word-initially (from voiceless to voiced), we recognize the process as _____.

PVV

_____ is used by very young children. Its use may produce homonyms.

homonyms

Homonyms are words that are produced identically but have different meanings. That is, the child's actual production represents two separate words. One example might be [du] when used to indicate both DO and TWO. When one surface form is used to represent two underlying forms, the underlying forms are called _____.

PVV

Another example might be when SUE and ZOO are both produced [zu]. The word-initial /s/ becomes [z] when _____ is applied.

homonyms

With the application of PVV to SUE, the words SUE and ZOO become _____.

Deletion of Final		Consonant Harmony	CH	Backing to Velars	BK
Consonant	DFC	Postvocalic Devoicing	PVD	Epenthesis	EPEN
Prevocalic Voicing	PVV	Vocalization	VOC	Metathesis	METATH
Syllable Reduction	SR	Palatal Fronting	PF	Coalescence	COAL
Velar Fronting	VF	Gliding of Liquids	GL	Palatalization	PAL
Stopping of Fricatives		Deaffrication	DEAFF	Denasalization	DENAS
and Affricates	ST	Deletion of Initial		Idiosyncratic	
Cluster Reduction	CR	Consonant	DIC	Processes	
Stridency Deletion	STR	Glottal Replacement	GR		

When two words have different meanings but share an identical surface form, they are called _____.

homonyms

When many words share an identical surface form, that is, a child's speech contains frequent _____, that speech tends to be unintelligible.

homonyms

When there are considerably more underlying representations than surface forms, the listener has difficulty following the conversation. The child is unintelligible because of the number of _____ present.

homonyms

In the most recent example given, if an adult asks, "Where did you go today?" and the child answers "[zu]", the response is ambiguous because [zu] has become a homonym for both _____ and _____ through the application of PREVOCALIC VOICING.

zoo, Sue

Eventually, the adult will uncover the correct information.

Adult: "Zoo? What animals did you see?"

Child: "No, [zu] house."

Adult: "The zoo house?"

Child: "No, [zu] house. Play with [zu]."

In this example, ZOO and SUE are _____.

homonyms

Give the other member of the homonym pair that would result if the child applied the process of PVV to the

---

/p/ *PIG*	/n/ *NO*	/ʃ/ *SHE*	/w/ *WAGON*	/ɛ/ *BED*	/ʌ/ *GUN*	
/b/ *BED*	/ŋ/ *STING*	/ʒ/ *ROUGE*	/ʍ/ *WHEEL*	/æ/ *CAT*	/ə/ *ABOUT*	
/t/ *TOY*	/f/ *FOX*	/h/ *HAVE*	/ɚ/ *FINGER*	/a/ *GOT*	/aɪ/ *KITE*	
/d/ *DUCK*	/θ/ *THINK*	/tʃ/ *CHICKEN*	/ɝ/ *CHURCH*	/ɔ/ *TALK*	/ɔɪ/ *TOY*	
/k/ *KEEP*	/ð/ *THIS*	/dʒ/ *JUMPING*	/i/ *SEE*	/o/ *GOAT*	/aʊ/ *OUT*	
/g/ *GOAT*	/s/ *SEE*	/l/ *LAKE*	/ɪ/ *PIG*	/ʊ/ *BOOK*		
/m/ *ME*	/z/ *ZOO*	/j/ *YOU*	/eɪ, e/ *MAKE*	/u/ *GLUE*		

following words. The surface form that the child uses for both homonyms in each pair is listed below. The first example has been completed.

	Adult Form		Child's Form	
SUE	/su/	→	[zu]	__ZOO__
TO	/tu/	→	[du]	_____
PIE	/paɪ/	→	[baɪ]	_____
CAP	/kæp/	→	[gæp]	_____
CHEAP	/tʃip/	→	[dʒip]	_____

DO

BYE

GAP

JEEP

In the examples just given, [zu], [du], [baɪ], [gæp], and [dʒip] are used by the child to represent the following _____: SUE/ZOO, TO/DO, PIE/BYE, CAP/GAP, and CHEAP/JEEP.

homonyms

The more homonyms there are in the child's speech, the greater the listener's confusion. It is not unusual to find many _____ in the speech of unintelligible children.

homonyms

Children's homonyms are often the result of the application of several phonological processes. For example, the word TOAST /tost/ may undergo PVV (/t/ → [d]) along with DFC (/st/ → [ø]) to result in DOUGH → [do]. In this case the homonyms are _____ and _____.

TOAST, DOUGH

Deletion of Final Consonant	DFC	Consonant Harmony	CH	Backing to Velars	BK
Prevocalic Voicing	PVV	Postvocalic Devoicing	PVD	Epenthesis	EPEN
Syllable Reduction	SR	Vocalization	VOC	Metathesis	METATH
Velar Fronting	VF	Palatal Fronting	PF	Coalescence	COAL
Stopping of Fricatives and Affricates	ST	Gliding of Liquids	GL	Palatalization	PAL
Cluster Reduction	CR	Deaffrication	DEAFF	Denasalization	DENAS
Stridency Deletion	STR	Deletion of Initial Consonant	DIC	Idiosyncratic Processes	
		Glottal Replacement	GR		

As more phonological processes are introduced, there will be additional opportunities to recognize homonyms that result from the application of more than one process.

List the productions that would result from applying PVV to the following adult forms.

	Adult Form		Child's Form	
PIG	/pɪg/	→ [_____]		[bɪg]
CAR	/kar/	→ [_____]		[gar]
FIVE	/faɪv/	→ [_____]		[vaɪv]
SHOE	/ʃu/	→ [_____]		[ʒu]
CHIN	/tʃɪn/	→ [_____]		[dʒɪn]

For each of the following target words, determine the sound change and child's form that result from applying the process of PVV:

	Adult Form	Child's Form	Sound Change		
CAR	/kar/	→ [_____]	/___/ → [___]	[gar]	/k/ → [g]
PENCIL	/pɛnsl̩/	→ [_____]	/___/ → [___]	[bɛnsl̩]	/p/ → [b]
FINGER	/fɪŋgɚ/	→ [_____]	/___/ → [___]	[vɪŋgɚ]	/f/ → [v]
SHOE	/ʃu/	→ [_____]	/___/ → [___]	[ʒu] /ʃ/ → [ʒ]

/p/ PIG	/n/ NO	/ʃ/ SHE	/w/ WAGON	/ɛ/ BED	/ʌ/ GUN	
/b/ BED	/ŋ/ STING	/ʒ/ ROUGE	/ʍ/ WHEEL	/æ/ CAT	/ə/ ABOUT	
/t/ TOY	/f/ FOX	/h/ HAVE	/ɚ/ FINGER	/a/ GOT	/aɪ/ KITE	
/d/ DUCK	/θ/ THINK	/tʃ/ CHICKEN	/ɝ/ CHURCH	/ɔ/ TALK	/ɔɪ/ TOY	
/k/ KEEP	/ð/ THIS	/dʒ/ JUMPING	/i/ SEE	/o/ GOAT	/aʊ/ OUT	
/g/ GOAT	/s/ SEE	/l/ LAKE	/ɪ/ PIG	/ʊ/ BOOK		
/m/ ME	/z/ ZOO	/j/ YOU	/eɪ, e/ MAKE	/u/ GLUE		

[ðʌm] /θ/ → [ð]	THUMB /θʌm/ → [_____] /___/ → [___]

PVV will apply only if the prevocalic, or word-initial, consonant is voiceless. Indicate whether each of the following words provides an opportunity for PVV to be applied:

		Adult Form	*YES/NO*
YES, /p/ is voiceless.	PIE	/paɪ/	_____
NO, /m/ is voiced.	MATCHES	/mætʃɪz/	_____
YES, /k/ is voiceless.	COOK	/kʊk/	_____
YES, /ʃ/ is voiceless.	SHOWER	/ʃaʊɚ/	_____
NO, /b/ is voiced.	BUTTON	/bʌtn/	_____
NO, /g/ is voiced.	GOAT	/got/	_____
YES, /θ/ is voiceless.	THINK	/θɪŋk/	_____

four | Of the seven words just listed, _____ provide the opportunity for PVV to be applied.

optional | Of those seven, if a child applies PVV to the fricatives only, the process would be _____, because it was applied selectively.

PVV | PVV can also be applied to words that begin with clusters. For example, TREE /tri/ → [dri] with the application of _____.

Deletion of Final Consonant	DFC	Consonant Harmony	CH	Backing to Velars	BK
Prevocalic Voicing	PVV	Postvocalic Devoicing	PVD	Epenthesis	EPEN
Syllable Reduction	SR	Vocalization	VOC	Metathesis	METATH
Velar Fronting	VF	Palatal Fronting	PF	Coalescence	COAL
Stopping of Fricatives and Affricates	ST	Gliding of Liquids	GL	Palatalization	PAL
Cluster Reduction	CR	Deaffrication	DEAFF	Denasalization	DENAS
Stridency Deletion	STR	Deletion of Initial Consonant	DIC	Idiosyncratic Processes	
		Glottal Replacement	GR		

Similarly, CLASS /klæs/ → [_____] when
PVV is applied.

[glæs]

The underlying forms CLASS and GLASS are both
realized by one surface form, [_____], making
them homonyms.

[glæs]

Apply the process of PVV to the following attempted
words, which begin with clusters. Indicate the child's form
that would result.

	Adult Form		*Child's Form*
TRAP	/træp/	→ [_____]	[dræp]
CLOWN	/klaʊn/	→ [_____]	[glaʊn]
SWING	/swɪŋ/	→ [_____]	[zwɪŋ]
FROG	/frɔg/	→ [_____]	[vrɔg]
SHRINK	/ʃrɪŋk/	→ [_____]	[ʒrɪŋk]
PRINCE	/prɪnts/	→ [_____]	[brɪnts]
CRY	/kraɪ/	→ [_____]	[graɪ]
QUICK	/kwɪk/	→ [_____]	[gwɪk]

In each case, the word-initial voiceless consonant
became voiced as a result of the application of
_____.

PVV

./p/ *PIG* /n/ *NO* /ʃ/ *SHE* /w/ *WAGON* /ɛ/ *BED* /ʌ/ *GUN*
/b/ *BED* /ŋ/ *STING* /ʒ/ *ROUGE* /ʍ/ *WHEEL* /æ/ *CAT* /ə/ *ABOUT*
/t/ *TOY* /f/ *FOX* /h/ *HAVE* /ɚ/ *FINGER* /a/ *GOT* /aɪ/ *KITE*
/d/ *DUCK* /θ/ *THINK* /tʃ/ *CHICKEN* /ɝ/ *CHURCH* /ɔ/ *TALK* /ɔɪ/ *TOY*
/k/ *KEEP* /ð/ *THIS* /dʒ/ *JUMPING* /i/ *SEE* /o/ *GOAT* /aʊ/ *OUT*
/g/ *GOAT* /s/ *SEE* /l/ *LAKE* /ɪ/ *PIG* /ʊ/ *BOOK*
/m/ *ME* /z/ *ZOO* /j/ *YOU* /eɪ, e/ *MAKE* /u/ *GLUE*

	And, in each case, the second consonant of the cluster remained intact. However, it is not unusual for both members of a consonant cluster to be altered by the child. That is, the child may apply PVV to the word-initial consonant and may apply another _____ to
process	the second consonant.
	For example, when _____ is applied to words
PVV	like FLAG and PLAY, the result is [vlæg] and [bleɪ]
	However, it is more common to hear a child use [vwæg] and [bweɪ] for these two words. The /l/ members of the clusters have become [____] by the application of
[w]	GLIDING OF LIQUIDS (see Section 12).
	Thus, the child's forms for those two words have resulted from the alteration of both members of the consonant clusters. The important thing to note is that since the word-initial voiceless consonants were voiced in the child's production, the process of _____ was
PVV	applied.
	Clusters may be simplified in many ways because there are inherently more consonants available for alteration. Additional information on clusters appears in Section 6.
	The detection of PREVOCALIC VOICING is a perceptual judgement by the listener. There is a range of amount of voicing that is acceptable to the listener. Once the speaker crosses over this perceptual boundary, the listener detects an error. Some voicing errors are more detectable than others. That is, they lie outside the
boundary	perceptual _____.

Deletion of Final Consonant	DFC	Consonant Harmony	CH	Backing to Velars	BK
Prevocalic Voicing	PVV	Postvocalic Devoicing	PVD	Epenthesis	EPEN
Syllable Reduction	SR	Vocalization	VOC	Metathesis	METATH
Velar Fronting	VF	Palatal Fronting	PF	Coalescence	COAL
Stopping of Fricatives and Affricates	ST	Gliding of Liquids	GL	Palatalization	PAL
		Deaffrication	DEAFF	Denasalization	DENAS
Cluster Reduction	CR	Deletion of Initial Consonant	DIC	Idiosyncratic Processes	
Stridency Deletion	STR	Glottal Replacement	GR		

There is a diacritical symbol to represent the addition of voicing to a voiceless consonant when the listener detects some voicing, but not complete _____, on the consonant.

voicing

The symbol for noting the addition of voicing (*partial voicing*) to a voiceless consonant is a small "v" placed just below the consonant. For example, if the word TIE /taɪ/ is produced with partial voicing on the /t/, it would be noted in this way: [ṭaɪ]. A [d] is not used because the additional voicing is not complete, but rather _____.

partial

In general, partial voicing of word-initial consonants does not interfere with intelligibility as much as complete _____, which results in homonyms.

voicing

If the word-initial consonant is partially voiced, then it may still be possible that a contrast exists between the voiced cognate and the partially voiced "voiceless" cognate. For example, if TIE /taɪ/ → [ṭaɪ] and DIE /daɪ/ → [daɪ], it might enable the listener to perceive a difference between the two. The words TIE and DIE would therefore not be _____.

homonyms

However, if the /t/ had been completely voiced, the words TIE and DIE would have been homonyms because both would have been pronounced as [_____].

[daɪ]

Whether partial voicing is influential enough to interfere with intelligibility is dependent upon the degree of _____ that is added by the child.

voicing

/p/ *PIG*	/n/ *NO*	/ʃ/ *SHE*	/w/ *WAGON*	/ɛ/ *BED*	/ʌ/ *GUN*	
/b/ *BED*	/ŋ/ *STING*	/ʒ/ *ROUGE*	/ʍ/ *WHEEL*	/æ/ *CAT*	/ə/ *ABOUT*	
/t/ *TOY*	/f/ *FOX*	/h/ *HAVE*	/ɚ/ *FINGER*	/a/ *GOT*	/aɪ/ *KITE*	
/d/ *DUCK*	/θ/ *THINK*	/tʃ/ *CHICKEN*	/ɝ/ *CHURCH*	/ɔ/ *TALK*	/ɔɪ/ *TOY*	
/k/ *KEEP*	/ð/ *THIS*	/dʒ/ *JUMPING*	/i/ *SEE*	/o/ *GOAT*	/aʊ/ *OUT*	
/g/ *GOAT*	/s/ *SEE*	/l/ *LAKE*	/ɪ/ *PIG*	/ʊ/ *BOOK*		
/m/ *ME*	/z/ *ZOO*	/j/ *YOU*	/eɪ, e/ *MAKE*	/u/ *GLUE*		

A particular child uses the processes of PVV and DFC consistently. Recall that DFC is the deletion of postvocalic (or word-final) consonants. Both of these processes are applied to the following words. How would these words be produced by the child?

		Adult Form		Child's Form
[bɪ]	PIG	/pɪg/	→	[_____]
[ga]	CAR	/kar/	→	[_____]
[zu]	SOUP	/sup/	→	[_____]
[glæ]	CLASS	/klæs/	→	[_____]
[glæ]	CLAP	/klæp/	→	[_____]
[glæ]	CLAM	/klæm/	→	[_____]
[glæ]	GLASS	/glæs/	→	[_____]
[glæ]	GLAD	/glæd/	→	[_____]

The last five words are all produced by the child as [glæ]. Since there is one surface form for five words, these words are _____ for this child.

homonyms

When there are several underlying forms which are represented by one surface form (in this case, [glæ]), there is greater listener confusion. Children with _____ speech tend to have more underlying forms per surface form in their speech output than do their intelligible peers.

unintelligible

Deletion of Final Consonant	DFC	Consonant Harmony	CH	Backing to Velars	BK
Prevocalic Voicing	PVV	Postvocalic Devoicing	PVD	Epenthesis	EPEN
Syllable Reduction	SR	Vocalization	VOC	Metathesis	METATH
Velar Fronting	VF	Palatal Fronting	PF	Coalescence	COAL
Stopping of Fricatives and Affricates	ST	Gliding of Liquids	GL	Palatalization	PAL
Cluster Reduction	CR	Deaffrication	DEAFF	Denasalization	DENAS
Stridency Deletion	STR	Deletion of Initial Consonant	DIC	Idiosyncratic Processes	
		Glottal Replacement	GR		

There are eight words in the list just given. Of these, _____ provided opportunities for PVV to be applied.

six

That is, there were six adult forms that began with word-initial _____ consonants and were therefore available for the application of PVV.

voiceless

Of the eight words, _____ provided opportunities for DFC to be applied.

eight

That is, there were eight adult forms that ended with word-final _____ and were therefore available for the application of DFC.

consonants

In this last example, both PVV and DFC are considered to be obligatory rules, or processes, because they are applied in every possible context (uniformly). Thus, both PVV and DFC were applied to _____% of possible contexts.

100

Examine the following target forms and children's productions. Determine which processes of those we have discussed so far (PVV, DFC) were applied to each of them.

	Adult Form	*Child's Form*	*Processes*	
LEAF	/lif/	→ [li]	_____	DFC
PIE	/paɪ/	→ [baɪ]	_____	PVV
CAP	/kæp/	→ [gæ]	_____	PVV, DFC

/p/ *PIG*	/n/ *NO*	/ʃ/ *SHE*	/w/ *WAGON*	/ɛ/ *BED*	/ʌ/ *GUN*
/b/ *BED*	/ŋ/ *STING*	/ʒ/ *ROUGE*	/ʍ/ *WHEEL*	/æ/ *CAT*	/ə/ *ABOUT*
/t/ *TOY*	/f/ *FOX*	/h/ *HAVE*	/ɚ/ *FINGER*	/a/ *GOT*	/aɪ/ *KITE*
/d/ *DUCK*	/θ/ *THINK*	/tʃ/ *CHICKEN*	/ɝ/ *CHURCH*	/ɔ/ *TALK*	/ɔɪ/ *TOY*
/k/ *KEEP*	/ð/ *THIS*	/dʒ/ *JUMPING*	/i/ *SEE*	/o/ *GOAT*	/aʊ/ *OUT*
/g/ *GOAT*	/s/ *SEE*	/l/ *LAKE*	/ɪ/ *PIG*	/ʊ/ *BOOK*	
/m/ *ME*	/z/ *ZOO*	/j/ *YOU*	/eɪ, e/ *MAKE*	/u/ *GLUE*	

DFC	CHEAP	/tʃip/	→ [tʃi]	_____
PVV	PIG	/pɪg/	→ [bɪg]	_____
PVV, DFC	FISH	/fɪʃ/	→ [vɪ]	_____
PVV	CARROT	/kɛrət/	→ [gɛrət]	_____

Of the seven words, PVV was applied to _____ of them; and DFC was applied to _____ of them.

five, four

Both PVV and DFC were applied to _____ of the seven words.

two

SUMMARY
Prevocalic Voicing

1. PVV is the inappropriate voicing of a word-initial voiceless consonant.
2. When two words have different meanings but share an identical surface form, they are called homonyms.
3. The more homonyms that a speaker uses, the less intelligible the speech.
4. PVV may be applied to clusters.
5. Complete or partial voicing of the word-initial consonant may occur.
6. The per cent of occurence for a process may be calculated using this formula:

$$\frac{Number\ of\ Occurrences}{Number\ of\ Possible\ Occurrences}$$

Deletion of Final Consonant	DFC	Consonant Harmony	CH	Backing to Velars	BK
Prevocalic Voicing	PVV	Postvocalic Devoicing	PVD	Epenthesis	EPEN
Syllable Reduction	SR	Vocalization	VOC	Metathesis	METATH
Velar Fronting	VF	Palatal Fronting	PF	Coalescence	COAL
Stopping of Fricatives and Affricates	ST	Gliding of Liquids	GL	Palatalization	PAL
Cluster Reduction	CR	Deaffrication	DEAFF	Denasalization	DENAS
Stridency Deletion	STR	Deletion of Initial Consonant	DIC	Idiosyncratic Processes	
		Glottal Replacement	GR		

SECTION 3. SYLLABLE REDUCTION

SYLLABLE REDUCTION (SR) is a process that results in a production with fewer syllables than the attempted word. BANANA /bənænə/ → [nænə] is an example of _____.

SYLLABLE
REDUCTION,
or SR

The abbreviation for SYLLABLE REDUCTION is _____.

SR

Give the phonological processes for the following abbreviations:

DFC   _____

DELETION OF
FINAL
CONSONANT

PVV   _____

PREVOCALIC
VOICING

SR   _____

SYLLABLE
REDUCTION

Another example of SR would be TELEPHONE /tɛləfon/ → [tɛfon], where the syllable /lə/ has been deleted. This reduces the number of syllables in the word from _____ to _____.

three, two

When a syllable has been deleted, this can be expressed as the REDUCTION of the number of _____ within a word.

syllables

Any word that contains two or more syllables provides the opportunity for _____ to be applied.

SR

/p/ *PIG*	/n/ *NO*	/ʃ/ *SHE*	/w/ *WAGON*	/ɛ/ *BED*	/ʌ/ *GUN*	
/b/ *BED*	/ŋ/ *STING*	/ʒ/ *ROUGE*	/ʍ/ *WHEEL*	/æ/ *CAT*	/ə/ *ABOUT*	
/t/ *TOY*	/f/ *FOX*	/h/ *HAVE*	/ɚ/ *FINGER*	/a/ *GOT*	/aɪ/ *KITE*	
/d/ *DUCK*	/θ/ *THINK*	/tʃ/ *CHICKEN*	/ɝ/ *CHURCH*	/ɔ/ *TALK*	/ɔɪ/ *TOY*	
/k/ *KEEP*	/ð/ *THIS*	/dʒ/ *JUMPING*	/i/ *SEE*	/o/ *GOAT*	/aʊ/ *OUT*	
/g/ *GOAT*	/s/ *SEE*	/l/ *LAKE*	/ɪ/ *PIG*	/ʊ/ *BOOK*		
/m/ *ME*	/z/ *ZOO*	/j/ *YOU*	/eɪ, e/ *MAKE*	/u/ *GLUE*		

[ø]

The sound change (or "syllable change") is noted in the same way that any deletion is noted. The syllable (or consonant) becomes deleted, and the symbol for this deletion is [____].

[ø]

In the example of TELEPHONE, the sound change would be noted as /lə/ → [____].

Write the sound change for the following attempted words and their altered forms:

	Adult Form		Child's Form	Sound Change
/dʒə/ → [ø]	GIRAFFE	/dʒəræf/ →	[ræf]	/___/ → [___]
/lə/ → [ø]	TELEPHONE	/tɛləfon/ →	[tɛfon]	/___/ → [___]
/pə/ → [ø]	PAJAMAS	/pədʒæməz/→	[dʒæməz]	/___/ → [___]
/bə/ → [ø]	BANANA	/bənænə/ →	[nænə]	/___/ → [___]
/lə/ → [ø]	ELEPHANT	/ɛləfənt/ →	[ɛfənt]	/___/ → [___]

A word can be reduced by one or more syllables. That is, TELEPHONE /tɛləfon/ can become [tɛfon] (as in our example); or it may become [tɛ]. In this case, *two* syllables have been deleted. They are /_____/ and

/lə/, /fon/

/_____/. The three-syllable word has been reduced to one syllable.

To determine whether SYLLABLE REDUCTION has been applied to an adult target word, compare the target word with the child's production. If the child's production includes fewer syllables than the adult target word, then

SR

_____ has been applied.

Deletion of Final Consonant	DFC	Consonant Harmony	CH	Backing to Velars	BK
Prevocalic Voicing	PVV	Postvocalic Devoicing	PVD	Epenthesis	EPEN
Syllable Reduction	SR	Vocalization	VOC	Metathesis	METATH
Velar Fronting	VF	Palatal Fronting	PF	Coalescence	COAL
Stopping of Fricatives and Affricates	ST	Gliding of Liquids	GL	Palatalization	PAL
Cluster Reduction	CR	Deaffrication	DEAFF	Denasalization	DENAS
Stridency Deletion	STR	Deletion of Initial Consonant	DIC	Idiosyncratic Processes	
		Glottal Replacement	GR		

The process of SYLLABLE REDUCTION *can/cannot* be applied to words containing only one syllable.

cannot

The attempted word must contain a minimum of _____ syllables to provide an opportunity for SR to be applied.

two

For example, TELEPHONE, BANANA, PUMPKIN all provide the opportunity for reduction in number of syllables; while HOUSE, CUP, FROG do not. When a sample contains both monosyllabic and multisyllabic attempted (target) words, the opportunity for SR to be applied is NOT provided by the _____ words.

monosyllabic

Multisyllabic words contain both stressed and unstressed syllables. The accented syllable is another name for the _____ syllable.

stressed

Stressed syllables carry more acoustic energy and are therefore more readily retained during word production. When young children reduce attempted words to fewer syllables than the target form, they generally retain the _____ syllable(s) and delete the _____ syllables.

stressed, unstressed

Underline the most stressed syllable in each of the following words:

GIRAFFE   /dʒəræf/

/dʒə<u>ræf</u>/

TELEPHONE /tɛləfon/

/<u>tɛ</u>ləfon/

PAJAMAS   /pədʒæməz/

/pə<u>dʒæ</u>məz/

/p/ *PIG*	/n/ *NO*	/ʃ/ *SHE*	/w/ *WAGON*	/ɛ/ *BED*	/ʌ/ *GUN*
/b/ *BED*	/ŋ/ *STING*	/ʒ/ *ROUGE*	/ʍ/ *WHEEL*	/æ/ *CAT*	/ə/ *ABOUT*
/t/ *TOY*	/f/ *FOX*	/h/ *HAVE*	/ɚ/ *FINGER*	/a/ *GOT*	/aɪ/ *KITE*
/d/ *DUCK*	/θ/ *THINK*	/tʃ/ *CHICKEN*	/ɝ/ *CHURCH*	/ɔ/ *TALK*	/ɔɪ/ *TOY*
/k/ *KEEP*	/ð/ *THIS*	/dʒ/ *JUMPING*	/i/ *SEE*	/o/ *GOAT*	/aʊ/ *OUT*
/g/ *GOAT*	/s/ *SEE*	/l/ *LAKE*	/ɪ/ *PIG*	/ʊ/ *BOOK*	
/m/ *ME*	/z/ *ZOO*	/j/ *YOU*	/eɪ, e/ *MAKE*	/u/ *GLUE*	

/m<u>æ</u>tʃɪz/	MATCHES /mætʃɪz/
/bə<u>næ</u>nə/	BANANA /bənænə/
/<u>ɛ</u>ləfənt/	ELEPHANT /ɛləfənt/
/əm<u>brɛ</u>lə/	UMBRELLA /əmbrɛlə/

stress

In each of these examples, it would be predictable that the child would delete the unstressed syllable(s) and retain the syllable with the most _____ .

stressed

Although this is generally the case, sometimes children retain one of the unstressed syllables and delete the _____ syllable(s).

SR

As long as at least one syllable has been deleted from the attempted word, the process of _____ has been applied.

[wæ]

When a word contains two syllables, it is easier to predict which of the syllables will be deleted. For example, if WAGON /wægən/ undergoes SYLLABLE REDUCTION, the production is most likely to become [_____], because this is the stressed syllable.

stressed

Several of the words just given contain more than two syllables. If the child reduces these words by one syllable, it is again likely that the most _____ syllable will be retained.

It is also likely that the other syllable that is retained will have secondary stress. For example, in the word TELEPHONE, if the child reduces by one syllable, [tɛlə]

Deletion of Final Consonant	DFC	Consonant Harmony	CH	Backing to Velars	BK	
Prevocalic Voicing	PVV	Postvocalic Devoicing	PVD	Epenthesis	EPEN	
Syllable Reduction	SR	Vocalization	VOC	Metathesis	METATH	
Velar Fronting	VF	Palatal Fronting	PF	Coalescence	COAL	
Stopping of Fricatives and Affricates	ST	Gliding of Liquids	GL	Palatalization	PAL	
Cluster Reduction	CR	Deaffrication	DEAFF	Denasalization	DENAS	
Stridency Deletion	STR	Deletion of Initial Consonant	DIC	Idiosyncratic Processes		
		Glottal Replacement	GR			

is not likely to be produced. /tɛ/ contains the primary stress and /fon/ contains the secondary stress. So the most likely production for TELEPHONE when it is reduced by one syllable is [_____].

[tɛfon]

The following list contains those words just listed that contain more than two syllables. Underline the syllable that receives primary stress and circle the syllable that receives secondary stress:

TELEPHONE /tɛləfon/

/tɛ̲ləfon/

PAJAMAS /pədʒæməz/

/pəd̲ʒæ(məz)/

BANANA /bənænə/

/bənæ̲nə/

ELEPHANT /ɛləfənt/

/ɛ̲lə(fənt)/

UMBRELLA /əmbrɛlə/

/əmbrɛ̲lə/

If the child retains two of the three syllables, and if they are the syllables receiving the most stress, then the five words would be produced as follows:

	Adult Form		Child's Form
TELEPHONE	/tɛləfon/	→ [_____]	[tɛfon]
PAJAMAS	/pədʒæməz/	→ [_____]	[dʒæməz]
BANANA	/bənænə/	→ [_____]	[nænə]
ELEPHANT	/ɛləfənt/	→ [_____]	[ɛfənt]

/p/ PIG	/n/ NO	/ʃ/ SHE	/w/ WAGON	/ɛ/ BED	/ʌ/ GUN
/b/ BED	/ŋ/ STING	/ʒ/ ROUGE	/ʍ/ WHEEL	/æ/ CAT	/ə/ ABOUT
/t/ TOY	/f/ FOX	/h/ HAVE	/ɚ/ FINGER	/a/ GOT	/aɪ/ KITE
/d/ DUCK	/θ/ THINK	/tʃ/ CHICKEN	/ɝ/ CHURCH	/ɔ/ TALK	/ɔɪ/ TOY
/k/ KEEP	/ð/ THIS	/dʒ/ JUMPING	/i/ SEE	/o/ GOAT	/aʊ/ OUT
/g/ GOAT	/s/ SEE	/l/ LAKE	/ɪ/ PIG	/ʊ/ BOOK	
/m/ ME	/z/ ZOO	/j/ YOU	/eɪ, e/ MAKE	/u/ GLUE	

[brɛlə] | UMBRELLA /əmbrɛlə/ → [_____]

We recognize these productions as common simplifications used by young children. In each case, the number of syllables was reduced by deleting the

unstressed

_____ syllable.

Knowing that a child generally retains the stressed syllable(s) and deletes the unstressed syllable(s), apply the process of SR to the following attempted words and assume that only one syllable (the least stressed) is deleted.

		Adult *Form*		*Child's* *Form*
[ræf]	GIRAFFE	/dʒəræf/	→	[_____]
[tɛfon]	TELEPHONE	/tɛləfon/	→	[_____]
[dʒæməz]	PAJAMAS	/pədʒæməz/	→	[_____]
[næna]	BANANA	/bənænə/	→	[_____]
[ɛfənt]	ELEPHANT	/ɛləfənt/	→	[_____]
[slip]	SLEEPING	/slipɪŋ/	→	[_____]
[wæ]	WAGON	/wægən/	→	[_____]

The established syllable boundaries within the native language are not necessarily recognized by the child. For example, MATCHES /mætʃɪz/ may be divided into two syllables: as /mæ-tʃɪz/, or as /mætʃ-ɪz/. In either example, the child has reduced the attempted word to one

Deletion of Final		Consonant Harmony	CH	Backing to Velars	BK
Consonant	DFC	Postvocalic Devoicing	PVD	Epenthesis	EPEN
Prevocalic Voicing	PVV	Vocalization	VOC	Metathesis	METATH
Syllable Reduction	SR	Palatal Fronting	PF	Coalescence	COAL
Velar Fronting	VF	Gliding of Liquids	GL	Palatalization	PAL
Stopping of Fricatives		Deaffrication	DEAFF	Denasalization	DENAS
and Affricates	ST	Deletion of Initial		Idiosyncratic	
Cluster Reduction	CR	Consonant	DIC	Processes	
Stridency Deletion	STR	Glottal Replacement	GR		

syllable: [mæ] or [mætʃ]. The two possible syllable boundaries for MATCHES are between _____ and _____; _____ and _____.

/æ/, /tʃ/; /tʃ/, /ɪ/

    The two possible syllable boundaries for WAGON /wægən/ are between _____ and _____; _____ and _____. (See Appendix IV.)

/æ/, /g/; /g/, /ə/

    Two children, each reducing /wægən/ by deleting one syllable, may produce different surface forms. Predictably, these forms would be [_____] and [_____], because the children's syllable boundaries differed.

[wæ], [wæg]

    Give two predictable productions for each of the following attempted words based on different syllable boundaries:

	Adult Form	Child's Forms	
MATCHES	/mætʃɪz/	[_____], [_____]	[mæ], [mætʃ]
GIRAFFE	/dʒəræf/	[_____], [_____]	[ræf], [æf]
SLEEPING	/slipɪŋ/	[_____], [_____]	[slip], [sli]
ZIPPER	/zɪpɚ/	[_____], [_____]	[zɪ], [zɪp]
FINGER	/fɪŋgɚ/	[_____], [_____]	[fɪ], [fɪŋ]

    In each of the reduced forms listed here, SR has been applied. Since children's perception of syllable boundaries may not match the adult system, we expect some children to divide a word in one place and some in another. Wherever the child divides the word, if the production has

./p/ *PIG*	/n/ *NO*	/ʃ/ *SHE*	/w/ *WAGON*	/ɛ/ *BED*	/ʌ/ *GUN*
/b/ *BED*	/ŋ/ *STING*	/ʒ/ *ROUGE*	/ʍ/ *WHEEL*	/æ/ *CAT*	/ə/ *ABOUT*
/t/ *TOY*	/f/ *FOX*	/h/ *HAVE*	/ɚ/ *FINGER*	/a/ *GOT*	/aɪ/ *KITE*
/d/ *DUCK*	/θ/ *THINK*	/tʃ/ *CHICKEN*	/ɝ/ *CHURCH*	/ɔ/ *TALK*	/ɔɪ/ *TOY*
/k/ *KEEP*	/ð/ *THIS*	/dʒ/ *JUMPING*	/i/ *SEE*	/o/ *GOAT*	/aʊ/ *OUT*
/g/ *GOAT*	/s/ *SEE*	/l/ *LAKE*	/ɪ/ *PIG*	/ʊ/ *BOOK*	
/m/ *ME*	/z/ *ZOO*	/j/ *YOU*	/eɪ, e/ *MAKE*	/u/ *GLUE*	

SR	fewer syllables than the adult target word, _____ has been applied.
	Recall that it is possible for more than one sound change to occur within a single production. For example, when TELEPHONE /tɛləfon/ → [dɛfon], the two sound
/t/ → [d] /lə/ → [ø]	changes are noted as /___/ → [___] and /___/ → [___].
	It is also possible for more than one process to be applied to one attempted word, as we saw in the previous section. The multiple processes may result in a single
sound changes	sound change or in several _____.
[tɛləfo]	If DFC is applied to /tɛləfon/, the resulting production is [_____].
[tɛfo]	If SR is also applied, for a total of two sound changes, then the child's production of /tɛləfon/ might be [_____].
unstressed	Notice that we assume that the stressed syllables remain while the _____ syllable has been deleted.
	The sound changes involved in this example (from left to right) would be
/lə/ → [ø]	/___/ → [___]
/n/ → [ø]	/___/ → [___]
two	A total of _____ sound changes have been made that account for the differences between TELEPHONE and [tɛfo].

Deletion of Final Consonant	DFC	Consonant Harmony	CH	Backing to Velars	BK
Prevocalic Voicing	PVV	Postvocalic Devoicing	PVD	Epenthesis	EPEN
Syllable Reduction	SR	Vocalization	VOC	Metathesis	METATH
Velar Fronting	VF	Palatal Fronting	PF	Coalescence	COAL
Stopping of Fricatives and Affricates	ST	Gliding of Liquids	GL	Palatalization	PAL
Cluster Reduction	CR	Deaffrication	DEAFF	Denasalization	DENAS
Stridency Deletion	STR	Deletion of Initial Consonant	DIC	Idiosyncratic Processes	
		Glottal Replacement	GR		

In general, the more sound changes, the more altered the production. [tɛfo] is more altered than [tɛləfo]. The former contains two sound changes, and the latter contains one. The fewer sound changes there are, the closer the production is to the _____.

attempted word, OR
adult form, OR
underlying form

One long-term effect of deletion processes is that they can mask the presence of other productive processes. A particular child may apply PVV to 100% of attempted words that provide the opportunity to be voiced. That is, he or she may apply it to 100% of word-initial, voiceless consonants. However, if the child deletes 100% of prevocalic consonants, there will be zero opportunity to apply the process of _____.

PVV

Once prevocalic consonants are no longer consistently deleted, the opportunities for PVV to be applied will increase. PVV will then increase from 0% to some higher proportion because of the increase in inclusion of _____ consonants.

word-initial

Examine the following words for the application of PREVOCALIC VOICING:

	Adult Form	Child's Form
CAT	/kæt/	→ [gæt]
TOE	/to/	→ [do]
PIE	/paɪ/	→ [baɪ]

/p/ PIG	/n/ NO	/ʃ/ SHE	/w/ WAGON	/ɛ/ BED	/ʌ/ GUN
/b/ BED	/ŋ/ STING	/ʒ/ ROUGE	/ʍ/ WHEEL	/æ/ CAT	/ə/ ABOUT
/t/ TOY	/f/ FOX	/h/ HAVE	/ɚ/ FINGER	/a/ GOT	/aɪ/ KITE
/d/ DUCK	/θ/ THINK	/tʃ/ CHICKEN	/ɝ/ CHURCH	/ɔ/ TALK	/ɔɪ/ TOY
/k/ KEEP	/ð/ THIS	/dʒ/ JUMPING	/i/ SEE	/o/ GOAT	/aʊ/ OUT
/g/ GOAT	/s/ SEE	/l/ LAKE	/ɪ/ PIG	/ʊ/ BOOK	
/m/ ME	/z/ ZOO	/j/ YOU	/eɪ, e/ MAKE	/u/ GLUE	

SEE	/si/	→	[i]
CHICKEN	/tʃɪkɪn/	→	[ɪkɪn]
SHOE	/ʃu/	→	[u]

three, 50

Of the six words listed, PVV has been applied a total of _____ times, or _____%.

three

However, only _____ of the child's productions provide an opportunity to apply PVV.

100

Since PVV has been applied to all of the possible contexts, it has actually been applied to _____% of potential contexts.

Thus, there is a discrepancy between the 100% and 50% proportions because of the difference in actual opportunity for the process of PVV to be applied. When this occurs, the process of PVV has been "blocked." Once the child includes a word-initial consonant, an additional opportunity becomes available. This has been referred to as "process blocking" (Weiner, 1979). In our example, the process of DELETION OF INITIAL CONSONANT blocked the potential application of

PVV

_____.

Any phonological process that results in the deletion of a segment (consonant, cluster, or syllable) has the potential for process blocking. The two processes covered thus far that have the potential for process blocking are

DFC, SR

_____ and _____.

Deletion of Final Consonant	DFC	Consonant Harmony	CH	Backing to Velars	BK
Prevocalic Voicing	PVV	Postvocalic Devoicing	PVD	Epenthesis	EPEN
Syllable Reduction	SR	Vocalization	VOC	Metathesis	METATH
Velar Fronting	VF	Palatal Fronting	PF	Coalescence	COAL
Stopping of Fricatives and Affricates	ST	Gliding of Liquids	GL	Palatalization	PAL
Cluster Reduction	CR	Deaffrication	DEAFF	Denasalization	DENAS
Stridency Deletion	STR	Deletion of Initial Consonant	DIC	Idiosyncratic Processes	
		Glottal Replacement	GR		

A child's speech production sample should be examined for the presence of process blocking. If there are frequent deletion processes, the analysis may be misleading. That is, some of the processes that are blocked and therefore appear to be infrequent may actually become more _____ when the blocking process has been suppressed by the child.

frequent

Using information about the processes DFC, PVV, and SR, list the sound changes and corresponding processes for the child's productions of the following attempted words. The first example has been done for you.

	Adult Form	Child's Form	Sound Change	Process	
TELEPHONE	/tɛləfon/ →	[dɛləfon]	/t/ → [d]	PVV	[d], PVV
GIRAFFE	/dʒəræf/ →	[ræ]	/dʒə/ → [__] /f/ → [__]	____ ____	[ø], SR [ø], DFC
PAJAMAS	/pədʒæməz/ →	[æməz]	/pədʒ/ → [__]	____	[ø], SR
BANANA	/bənænə/ →	[ænə]	/bən/ → [__]	____	[ø], SR
SCISSORS	/sɪzɚz/ →	[zɪzɚ]	/s/ → [__] /z/ → [__]	____ ____	[z], PVV [ø], DFC
ELEPHANT	/ɛləfənt/ →	[ɛfə]	/lə/ → [__] /nt/ → [__]	____ ____	[ø], SR [ø], DFC
UMBRELLA	/əmbrɛlə/ →	[brɛ]	/əm/ → [__] /lə/ → [__]	____ ____	[ø], SR [ø], SR
WAGON	/wægən/ →	[wæ]	/gən/ → [__]	____	[ø], SR

/p/ *PIG*	/n/ *NO*	/ʃ/ *SHE*	/w/ *WAGON*	/ɛ/ *BED*	/ʌ/ *GUN*
/b/ *BED*	/ŋ/ *STING*	/ʒ/ *ROUGE*	/ʍ/ *WHEEL*	/æ/ *CAT*	/ə/ *ABOUT*
/t/ *TOY*	/f/ *FOX*	/h/ *HAVE*	/ɚ/ *FINGER*	/a/ *GOT*	/aɪ/ *KITE*
/d/ *DUCK*	/θ/ *THINK*	/tʃ/ *CHICKEN*	/ɝ/ *CHURCH*	/ɔ/ *TALK*	/ɔɪ/ *TOY*
/k/ *KEEP*	/ð/ *THIS*	/dʒ/ *JUMPING*	/i/ *SEE*	/o/ *GOAT*	/aʊ/ *OUT*
/g/ *GOAT*	/s/ *SEE*	/l/ *LAKE*	/ɪ/ *PIG*	/ʊ/ *BOOK*	
/m/ *ME*	/z/ *ZOO*	/j/ *YOU*	/eɪ, e/ *MAKE*	/u/ *GLUE*	

SUMMARY
Syllable Reduction

1. SR is a process that results in a production with fewer syllables than the attempted word.
2. SR is noted by the use of the symbol [ø].
3. Speakers generally retain the stressed syllable(s) and delete the unstressed syllable(s).
4. Since children's perception of syllable boundaries may not match the adult system, we expect some children to divide a word in one place and some in another.
5. The deletion of a consonant, cluster, or syllable may block the occurrence of a second process. This is called process blocking.
6. The application of SR may result in process blocking.

Deletion of Final Consonant	DFC	Consonant Harmony	CH	Backing to Velars	BK
Prevocalic Voicing	PVV	Postvocalic Devoicing	PVD	Epenthesis	EPEN
Syllable Reduction	SR	Vocalization	VOC	Metathesis	METATH
Velar Fronting	VF	Palatal Fronting	PF	Coalescence	COAL
Stopping of Fricatives and Affricates	ST	Gliding of Liquids	GL	Palatalization	PAL
Cluster Reduction	CR	Deaffrication	DEAFF	Denasalization	DENAS
Stridency Deletion	STR	Deletion of Initial Consonant	DIC	Idiosyncratic Processes	
		Glottal Replacement	GR		

SECTION 4. VELAR FRONTING

VELAR FRONTING (VF) is a process that, when applied, results in the forward production of velar consonants. An example of VELAR FRONTING might be COOK /kʊk/ → [tʊt], where /k/ → [t]. RING /rɪŋ/ → [rɪn] is another example of VELAR FRONTING, or
_____.

| | VF |

The abbreviation for VELAR FRONTING is
_____.

| | VF |

The velar consonants are /k/, /g/, /ŋ/. They are generally fronted to alveolars when the process of _____ is applied.

| | VF |

Thus, /k/ → [t], /g/ → [d], and /ŋ/ → [n]. When any of these sound changes occur, the process of _____ is considered.

| | VF |

Another example of VF would be GO /go/ → [do], where /___/ → [d], an alveolar consonant.

| | /g/ |

List the productions that would result from the application of VF to the following adult forms:

Adult Form	Child's Form			
CAR	/kar/	→	/___/	[tar]
WAGON	/wægən/	→	/___/	[wædən]
RING	/rɪŋ/	→	/___/	[rɪn]

/p/ *PIG*	/n/ *NO*	/ʃ/ *SHE*	/w/ *WAGON*	/ɛ/ *BED*	/ʌ/ *GUN*
/b/ *BED*	/ŋ/ *STING*	/ʒ/ *ROUGE*	/ʍ/ *WHEEL*	/æ/ *CAT*	/ə/ *ABOUT*
/t/ *TOY*	/f/ *FOX*	/h/ *HAVE*	/ɚ/ *FINGER*	/a/ *GOT*	/aɪ/ *KITE*
/d/ *DUCK*	/θ/ *THINK*	/tʃ/ *CHICKEN*	/ɝ/ *CHURCH*	/ɔ/ *TALK*	/ɔɪ/ *TOY*
/k/ *KEEP*	/ð/ *THIS*	/dʒ/ *JUMPING*	/i/ *SEE*	/o/ *GOAT*	/aʊ/ *OUT*
/g/ *GOAT*	/s/ *SEE*	/l/ *LAKE*	/ɪ/ *PIG*	/ʊ/ *BOOK*	
/m/ *ME*	/z/ *ZOO*	/j/ *YOU*	/eɪ, e/ *MAKE*	/u/ *GLUE*	

[pɪd]   PIG   /pɪg/   →   /____/

List the sound changes that have resulted from the application of VF to the following words:

	Adult Form		Child's Form	Sound Change
/k/ → [t]	CAR	/kar/	→ [tar]	/___/ → [___]
/g/ → [d]	WAGON	/wægən/	→ [wædən]	/___/ → [___]
/ŋ/ → [n]	RING	/rɪŋ/	→ [rɪn]	/___/ → [___]
/k/ → [t]	COMB	/kom/	→ [tom]	/___/ → [___]
/g/ → [d]	PIG	/pɪg/	→ [pɪd]	/___/ → [___]

We recognize **VELAR FRONTING** as characteristic of very young children's speech. As adult listeners, we tend to "fill in" the velar consonants for the child. Thus we recognize [dev] as the verb _____ in, "He [dev] me it."

GAVE

Although the listener readily accommodates, the use of VF may produce many homonyms. Recall that _____ are words that sound alike but differ in underlying meaning. GUY and DIE become homonyms when VF is applied to GUY.

homonyms

Examine the following pairs of homonyms. Give the phonological process that was applied in order to create each homonym pair. The first example has been completed for you.

Deletion of Final Consonant — DFC	Consonant Harmony — CH	Backing to Velars — BK
Prevocalic Voicing — PVV	Postvocalic Devoicing — PVD	Epenthesis — EPEN
Syllable Reduction — SR	Vocalization — VOC	Metathesis — METATH
Velar Fronting — VF	Palatal Fronting — PF	Coalescence — COAL
Stopping of Fricatives and Affricates — ST	Gliding of Liquids — GL	Palatalization — PAL
Cluster Reduction — CR	Deaffrication — DEAFF	Denasalization — DENAS
Stridency Deletion — STR	Deletion of Initial Consonant — DIC	Idiosyncratic Processes
	Glottal Replacement — GR	

Homonyms	*Surface Form*	*Process*	
GAME			
DAME	[dem]	__VF__	
KEY			
KEEP	[ki]	_____	DFC
CAME			
GAME	[gem]	_____	PVV
WING			
WIN	[wɪn]	_____	VF
CUPCAKE			
CUP	[kʌp]	_____	SR

When a child uses several processes frequently, many _____ may result. ... **homonyms**

Velars that occur anywhere within a word may be fronted. _____ is not limited in its application to one position within a word, as are DFC and PVV. ... **VF**

Initially, when young children apply the process of **VELAR FRONTING**, it may apply to all velars. Later, the process may be applied _____ to velars that occur in certain positions within words. ... **optionally, OR selectively**

There is some evidence that word-final velars are the first to be produced correctly. That is, the process of _____ may be suppressed first in word-final position. ... **VF**

/p/ *PIG*	/n/ *NO*	/ʃ/ *SHE*	/w/ *WAGON*	/ɛ/ *BED*	/ʌ/ *GUN*
/b/ *BED*	/ŋ/ *STING*	/ʒ/ *ROUGE*	/ʍ/ *WHEEL*	/æ/ *CAT*	/ə/ *ABOUT*
/t/ *TOY*	/f/ *FOX*	/h/ *HAVE*	/ɚ/ *FINGER*	/a/ *GOT*	/aɪ/ *KITE*
/d/ *DUCK*	/θ/ *THINK*	/tʃ/ *CHICKEN*	/ɝ/ *CHURCH*	/ɔ/ *TALK*	/ɔɪ/ *TOY*
/k/ *KEEP*	/ð/ *THIS*	/dʒ/ *JUMPING*	/i/ *SEE*	/o/ *GOAT*	/aʊ/ *OUT*
/g/ *GOAT*	/s/ *SEE*	/l/ *LAKE*	/ɪ/ *PIG*	/ʊ/ *BOOK*	
/m/ *ME*	/z/ *ZOO*	/j/ *YOU*	/eɪ, e/ *MAKE*	/u/ *GLUE*	

selectively

For example, the words KEEP, MONKEY, CUP, ROCKET may be produced [tip], [mʌnti], [tʌp], [ratɪt] while the words DUCK, RUG, SING may include velars in their surface forms. This would happen if the process of VF were applied _____.

optional

In examining the speech sample of a young or disordered child, it is wise to note the overall occurrence of VF as well as the selective application of the process to position-specific velars. When a process is applied optionally, as in some positions but not others, it is called an _____ process for that child.

Examine the productions below and describe the specific pattern of VF that the child is using:

	Adult Form		Child's Form
CAR	/kar/	→	[tar]
CUP	/kʌp/	→	[tʌp]
COMB	/kom/	→	[tom]
PIG	/pɪg/	→	[pɪg]
BACK	/bæk/	→	[bæk]
RING	/rɪŋ/	→	[rɪŋ]

The child fronts velars prevocalically but not postvocalically.

Optional Process:

VF

Thus, the process of _____ is applied selectively, or is an optional process.

Examine the following productions and describe the optional pattern for VF:

Deletion of Final Consonant	DFC	Consonant Harmony	CH	Backing to Velars	BK
Prevocalic Voicing	PVV	Postvocalic Devoicing	PVD	Epenthesis	EPEN
Syllable Reduction	SR	Vocalization	VOC	Metathesis	METATH
Velar Fronting	VF	Palatal Fronting	PF	Coalescence	COAL
Stopping of Fricatives and Affricates	ST	Gliding of Liquids	GL	Palatalization	PAL
Cluster Reduction	CR	Deaffrication	DEAFF	Denasalization	DENAS
Stridency Deletion	STR	Deletion of Initial Consonant	DIC	Idiosyncratic Processes	
		Glottal Replacement	GR		

	Adult Form	*Child's Form*
DOG	/dɔg/	→ [dɔd]
BACK	/bæk/	→ [bæt]
COME	/kʌm/	→ [tʌm]
GO	/go/	→ [do]
DOGGIE	/dɔgi/	→ [dɔgi]
BECKY	/bɛki/	→ [bɛki]
ROCKET	/rakɪt/	→ [rakɪt]

Optional Process:

Velars are fronted when prevocalic or postvocalic, but not intervocalically.

VELAR FRONTING often occurs in words that already contain alveolar consonants. For example, DUCK /dʌk/ → [dʌt]. By the definition of VF, the velar consonant has been fronted to an alveolar. However, there is already an alveolar in the word DUCK. It is then possible that some type of assimilation occurred. This will be discussed in Section 8. On the basis of the information presented thus far, when a velar is fronted to an alveolar, the process of _____ has been applied.

VF

If velars are fronted inconsistently, then the possibility of an optional rule or some type of assimilation must be considered. When velars are fronted consistently, it is probable that _____ accounts for those sound changes.

VF

This text will cover one type of assimilation in depth. The term used is CONSONANT HARMONY. A word

---

/p/ *PIG*	/n/ *NO*	/ʃ/ *SHE*	/w/ *WAGON*	/ɛ/ *BED*	/ʌ/ *GUN*
/b/ *BED*	/ŋ/ *STING*	/ʒ/ *ROUGE*	/ʍ/ *WHEEL*	/æ/ *CAT*	/ə/ *ABOUT*
/t/ *TOY*	/f/ *FOX*	/h/ *HAVE*	/ɚ/ *FINGER*	/a/ *GOT*	/aɪ/ *KITE*
/d/ *DUCK*	/θ/ *THINK*	/tʃ/ *CHICKEN*	/ɝ/ *CHURCH*	/ɔ/ *TALK*	/ɔɪ/ *TOY*
/k/ *KEEP*	/ð/ *THIS*	/dʒ/ *JUMPING*	/i/ *SEE*	/o/ *GOAT*	/aʊ/ *OUT*
/g/ *GOAT*	/s/ *SEE*	/l/ *LAKE*	/ɪ/ *PIG*	/ʊ/ *BOOK*	
/m/ *ME*	/z/ *ZOO*	/j/ *YOU*	/eɪ, e/ *MAKE*	/u/ *GLUE*	

**CONSONANT
HARMONY**

like GO may be produced with the velar /g/ because there is not an alveolar consonant within the word. A word like GOT may become [dat] because of the assimilatory influence of the /t/. When this occurs, the process of _____ may have been applied.

CONSONANT HARMONY is covered in more detail later in this text (p.115). However, it should be noted here that velars are not always fronted as a result of VF; some may become alveolar because of the harmony with another alveolar _____ within the word.

consonant

As with other processes, if no contexts are attempted, no statement may be made about the application of the process. For VF to be applied, the target word must contain a _____ consonant.

velar

Indicate whether or not VF can be applied to the following attempted words:

yes, /k/	KISS	/kɪs/	_____
no velars	KNIFE	/naɪf/	_____
yes, /k/	BACK	/bæk/	_____
yes, /ŋ/	LIGHTNING	/laɪtnɪŋ/	_____
yes, /g/	RUG	/rʌg/	_____
no velars	DOUGH	/do/	_____
yes, /g/	WAGON	/wægən/	_____

Deletion of Final Consonant	DFC	Consonant Harmony	CH	Backing to Velars	BK
Prevocalic Voicing	PVV	Postvocalic Devoicing	PVD	Epenthesis	EPEN
Syllable Reduction	SR	Vocalization	VOC	Metathesis	METATH
Velar Fronting	VF	Palatal Fronting	PF	Coalescence	COAL
Stopping of Fricatives and Affricates	ST	Gliding of Liquids	GL	Palatalization	PAL
Cluster Reduction	CR	Deaffrication	DEAFF	Denasalization	DENAS
Stridency Deletion	STR	Deletion of Initial Consonant	DIC	Idiosyncratic Processes	
		Glottal Replacement	GR		

Of the seven attempted words, a total of
_____ provided the opportunity for VF to be
applied.

five

One particular child uses the process of VF
selectively. Specifically, she applies VF only to velars that
are adjacent to the vowels /u/ and /o/. How would she
produce the following target words?

	Adult Form		Child's Form	
COME	/kʌm/	→ [_____]		[kʌm]
COAT	/kot/	→ [_____]		[tot]
COWBOY	/kaʊbɔɪ/	→ [_____]		[kaʊbɔɪ]
AGO	/əgo/	→ [_____]		[ədo]
ROCKET	/rakɪt/	→ [_____]		[rakɪt]

Another child uses VF in all contexts and also uses
PVV in all contexts. How would the following target
words be produced?

	Adult Form		Child's Form	
TALK	/tɔk/	→ [_____]		[dɔt]
BOY	/bɔɪ/	→ [_____]		[bɔɪ]
GONE	/gɔn/	→ [_____]		[dɔn]
LEG	/lɛg/	→ [_____]		[lɛd]

/p/ *PIG*	/n/ *NO*	/ʃ/ *SHE*	/w/ *WAGON*	/ɛ/ *BED*	/ʌ/ *GUN*
/b/ *BED*	/ŋ/ *STING*	/ʒ/ *ROUGE*	/ʍ/ *WHEEL*	/æ/ *CAT*	/ə/ *ABOUT*
/t/ *TOY*	/f/ *FOX*	/h/ *HAVE*	/ɚ/ *FINGER*	/a/ *GOT*	/aɪ/ *KITE*
/d/ *DUCK*	/θ/ *THINK*	/tʃ/ *CHICKEN*	/ɝ/ *CHURCH*	/ɔ/ *TALK*	/ɔɪ/ *TOY*
/k/ *KEEP*	/ð/ *THIS*	/dʒ/ *JUMPING*	/i/ *SEE*	/o/ *GOAT*	/aʊ/ *OUT*
/g/ *GOAT*	/s/ *SEE*	/l/ *LAKE*	/ɪ/ *PIG*	/ʊ/ *BOOK*	
/m/ *ME*	/z/ *ZOO*	/j/ *YOU*	/eɪ, e/ *MAKE*	/u/ *GLUE*	

[dar]	CAR	/kar/	→ [_____]
[dɪtʃɪn]	KITCHEN	/kɪtʃɪn/	→ [_____]
[dlaʊn]	CLOWN	/klaʊn/	→ [_____]
[dip]	KEEP	/kip/	→ [_____]

Count the number of times that this child used VF and PVV. She used VF a total of _____ times and PVV a total of _____ times.

seven, five

A third child applies the processes of VF, PVV, and DFC consistently to all words. How would the following target words be produced by this child?

		Adult Form	Child's Form
[dɔ]	TALK	/tɔk/	→ [_____]
[bɔɪ]	BOY	/bɔɪ/	→ [_____]
[dɔ]	GONE	/gɔn/	→ [_____]
[lɛ]	LEG	/lɛg/	→ [_____]
[da]	CAR	/kar/	→ [_____]
[dɪtʃɪ]	KITCHEN	/kɪtʃɪn/	→ [_____]
[dlaʊ]	CLOWN	/klaʊn/	→ [_____]
[di]	KEEP	/kip/	→ [_____]

Deletion of Final Consonant	DFC	Consonant Harmony	CH	Backing to Velars	BK
Prevocalic Voicing	PVV	Postvocalic Devoicing	PVD	Epenthesis	EPEN
Syllable Reduction	SR	Vocalization	VOC	Metathesis	METATH
Velar Fronting	VF	Palatal Fronting	PF	Coalescence	COAL
Stopping of Fricatives and Affricates	ST	Gliding of Liquids	GL	Palatalization	PAL
		Deaffrication	DEAFF	Denasalization	DENAS
Cluster Reduction	CR	Deletion of Initial Consonant	DIC	Idiosyncratic Processes	
Stridency Deletion	STR	Glottal Replacement	GR		

Count the number of times that each process was applied. PVV was applied _____ times. DFC was applied _____ times. VF was applied _____ times.

five, seven, five

The previous child, attempting these same target words, also used VF consistently. Her total was seven. Compare with the total listed just above for VF, which is *five*. The reason that there are fewer applications of VF within the speech sample of the latter child is that _____ _____.

The process DFC effectively blocked the application of VF in word-final position.

Once postvocalic consonants are no longer deleted, the frequency of VF on these particular words (if the process continues to be applied consistently) will increase. That is, as DFC decreases, VF is likely to _____.

increase

Give the sound changes and the process(es) that account for those sound changes for the following productions:

	Adult Form	Child's Form	Sound Change(s)	Processes	
AIRPLANE	/ɛɪrplen/ →	[ble]	/ɛɪr/ → [ø]	_____	SR
			/n/ → [ø]	_____	DFC
CAT	/kæt/ →	[dæt]	/k/ → [___]	_____	[d], VF, PVV
KITCHEN	/kɪtʃɪn/ →	[gɪtʃɪ]	/k/ → [___]	_____	[g], PVV
			/n/ → [___]	_____	[ø], DFC
PIG	/pɪg/ →	[bɪd]	/p/ → [___]	_____	[b], PVV
			/g/ → [___]	_____	[d], VF
MONKEY	/mʌŋki/ →	[mʌnti]	/ŋk/ → [___]	_____	[nt], VF

/p/ *PIG*	/n/ *NO*	/ʃ/ *SHE*	/w/ *WAGON*	/ɛ/ *BED*	/ʌ/ *GUN*
/b/ *BED*	/ŋ/ *STING*	/ʒ/ *ROUGE*	/ʍ/ *WHEEL*	/æ/ *CAT*	/ə/ *ABOUT*
/t/ *TOY*	/f/ *FOX*	/h/ *HAVE*	/ɚ/ *FINGER*	/a/ *GOT*	/aɪ/ *KITE*
/d/ *DUCK*	/θ/ *THINK*	/tʃ/ *CHICKEN*	/ɝ/ *CHURCH*	/ɔ/ *TALK*	/ɔɪ/ *TOY*
/k/ *KEEP*	/ð/ *THIS*	/dʒ/ *JUMPING*	/i/ *SEE*	/o/ *GOAT*	/aʊ/ *OUT*
/g/ *GOAT*	/s/ *SEE*	/l/ *LAKE*	/ɪ/ *PIG*	/ʊ/ *BOOK*	
/m/ *ME*	/z/ *ZOO*	/j/ *YOU*	/eɪ, e/ *MAKE*	/u/ *GLUE*	

[dr], PVV	TRUCK	/trʌk/ → [drʌt]	/tr/ → [____] _____	
[t], VF			/k/ → [____] _____	
[t], VF	ROCKET	/rakɪt/ → [ratɪ]	/k/ → [____] _____	
[ø], DFC			/t/ → [____] _____	
[t], VF	BROKEN	/brokən/→ [brot]	/k/ → [____] _____	
[ø], SR			/ən/ → [____] _____	

Count the number of times that each process was used.

three	DFC: _____
four	PVV: _____
two	SR: _____
six	VF: _____
15	TOTAL: _____

SUMMARY
Velar Fronting

1. VF is a process that, when applied, results in the forward production of velar consonants.
2. Word-final velars may appear first.
3. The application of either VF or CONSONANT HARMONY may result in the alteration from a velar to an alveolar.

Deletion of Final		Consonant Harmony	CH	Backing to Velars	BK
Consonant	DFC	Postvocalic Devoicing	PVD	Epenthesis	EPEN
Prevocalic Voicing	PVV	Vocalization	VOC	Metathesis	METATH
Syllable Reduction	SR	Palatal Fronting	PF	Coalescence	COAL
Velar Fronting	VF	Gliding of Liquids	GL	Palatalization	PAL
Stopping of Fricatives		Deaffrication	DEAFF	Denasalization	DENAS
and Affricates	ST	Deletion of Initial		Idiosyncratic	
Cluster Reduction	CR	Consonant	DIC	Processes	
Stridency Deletion	STR	Glottal Replacement	GR		

SECTION 5. STOPPING OF FRICATIVES AND AFFRICATES

STOPPING OF FRICATIVES AND AFFRICATES (ST) is a process that results in the production of stops for fricatives and affricates. SUN /sʌn/ → [tʌn] is an example of _____.

STOPPING, or ST

The abbreviation for STOPPING OF FRICATIVES AND AFFRICATES is _____.

ST

Another example of ST would be FINGER /fɪŋgɚ/ → [pɪŋgɚ], where /___/ → [p] is the resulting sound change.

/f/

Since the effect is to *stop* a fricative or affricate, we recognize the process as _____.

STOPPING, or ST

STOPPING often results in a homorganic consonant. When a fricative or affricate is stopped by raising the tongue slightly to stop the airflow without changing the PLACE of articulation, a _____ stop consonant is produced.

homorganic

Thus, if /s/ is stopped by merely raising the tongue, the _____ stop consonant, /t/, will result.

homorganic

Give the homorganic stops for the following fricatives and affricates. Assume that the voicing is constant.

/s/ → [___]

[t]

/z/ → [___]

[d]

/p/ PIG	/n/ NO	/ʃ/ SHE	/w/ WAGON	/ɛ/ BED	/ʌ/ GUN
/b/ BED	/ŋ/ STING	/ʒ/ ROUGE	/ʍ/ WHEEL	/æ/ CAT	/ə/ ABOUT
/t/ TOY	/f/ FOX	/h/ HAVE	/ɚ/ FINGER	/a/ GOT	/aɪ/ KITE
/d/ DUCK	/θ/ THINK	/tʃ/ CHICKEN	/ɝ/ CHURCH	/ɔ/ TALK	/ɔɪ/ TOY
/k/ KEEP	/ð/ THIS	/dʒ/ JUMPING	/i/ SEE	/o/ GOAT	/aʊ/ OUT
/g/ GOAT	/s/ SEE	/l/ LAKE	/ɪ/ PIG	/ʊ/ BOOK	
/m/ ME	/z/ ZOO	/j/ YOU	/eɪ, e/ MAKE	/u/ GLUE	

[t], possibly palatal	/ʃ/ → [___]
[d], possibly palatal	/ʒ/ → [___]
[p], possibly labiodental	/f/ → [___]
[b], possibly labiodental	/v/ → /___/
[t], possibly palatal	/tʃ/ → /___/
[d], possibly palatal	/dʒ/ → /___/

Thus, the consonants most likely to be produced with the application of the process ST are _____ with the target consonants. That is, they are produced at the same *place* of articulation.

homorganic

List the productions that would result from the application of ST to the following attempted words:

		Adult Form		Child's Form
[ti]	SEE	/si/	→	[_____]
[lip]	LEAF	/lif/	→	[_____]
[tɛr]	CHAIR	/tʃɛr/	→	[_____]
[tu]	SHOE	/ʃu/	→	[_____]

Deletion of Final Consonant	DFC	Consonant Harmony	CH	Backing to Velars	BK
Prevocalic Voicing	PVV	Postvocalic Devoicing	PVD	Epenthesis	EPEN
Syllable Reduction	SR	Vocalization	VOC	Metathesis	METATH
Velar Fronting	VF	Palatal Fronting	PF	Coalescence	COAL
Stopping of Fricatives and Affricates	ST	Gliding of Liquids	GL	Palatalization	PAL
Cluster Reduction	CR	Deaffrication	DEAFF	Denasalization	DENAS
Stridency Deletion	STR	Deletion of Initial Consonant	DIC	Idiosyncratic Processes	
		Glottal Replacement	GR		

EASY	/izɪ/	→	[_____]	[idɪ]
JUMPING	/dʒʌmpɪŋ/	→	[_____]	[dʌmpɪŋ]
TREASURE	/trɛʒɚ/	→	[_____]	[trɛdɚ]
VACUUM	/vækjuəm/	→	[_____]	[bækjuəm]

The three other fricatives, which are non-strident, are /____/, /____/, and /____/.

/h/, /θ/, and /ð/

/θ/ and /ð/ are also interdental. When they are homorganically stopped, the result may be a dentalized /____/ and /____/.

/t̪/ and /d̪/

However, young children frequently produce the /t/ and /d/ at the alveolar ridge. We will also consider these to be the simple STOPPING OF FRICATIVES AND AFFRICATES resulting in _____ stop consonants.

homorganic

Thus, the productions resulting from ST (homorganic) for the following attempted words are as follows:

	Adult Form		Child's Form	
THUMB	/θʌm/	→	[_____]	[tʌm], OR [t̪ʌm]
THIS	/ðɪs/	→	[_____]	[dɪs], OR [d̪ɪs]
NOTHING	/nʌθɪŋ/	→	[_____]	[nʌtɪŋ], OR [nʌt̪ɪŋ]
BATH	/bæθ/	→	[_____]	[bæt], OR [bæt̪]
MOTHER	/mʌðɚ/	→	[_____]	[mʌdɚ], OR [mʌd̪ɚ]

/p/ *PIG*	/n/ *NO*	/ʃ/ *SHE*	/w/ *WAGON*	/ɛ/ *BED*	/ʌ/ *GUN*
/b/ *BED*	/ŋ/ *STING*	/ʒ/ *ROUGE*	/ʍ/ *WHEEL*	/æ/ *CAT*	/ə/ *ABOUT*
/t/ *TOY*	/f/ *FOX*	/h/ *HAVE*	/ɚ/ *FINGER*	/a/ *GOT*	/aɪ/ *KITE*
/d/ *DUCK*	/θ/ *THINK*	/tʃ/ *CHICKEN*	/ɝ/ *CHURCH*	/ɔ/ *TALK*	/ɔɪ/ *TOY*
/k/ *KEEP*	/ð/ *THIS*	/dʒ/ *JUMPING*	/i/ *SEE*	/o/ *GOAT*	/aʊ/ *OUT*
/g/ *GOAT*	/s/ *SEE*	/l/ *LAKE*	/ɪ/ *PIG*	/ʊ/ *BOOK*	
/m/ *ME*	/z/ *ZOO*	/j/ *YOU*	/eɪ, e/ *MAKE*	/u/ *GLUE*	

homorganic

A voiceless fricative or affricate may be stopped and also voiced. For example, SUN /sʌn/ → [tʌn] when ST is applied. If PVV is also applied, then /sʌn/ → [dʌn]. The [d] is still a _____ stop, but it has also been voiced.

The following words were produced by a child who applied both ST and PVV to fricatives and affricates. How would the following target words be produced by this child?

		Adult Form		Child's Form
[di]	SEE	/si/	→	[_____]
[baɪt]	FIGHT	/faɪt/	→	[_____]
[dɪŋk]	THINK	/θɪŋk/	→	[_____]
[did]	TEASE	/tiz/	→	[_____]
[dɛləpon]	TELEPHONE	/tɛləfon/	→	[_____]

The process of ST does not always result in production of a homorganic stop. Identify the non-homorganic sound changes that result from STOPPING in the following attempted words:

		Adult Form		Child's Form	Sound Change
[p]	SHOVEL	/ʃʌvəl/	→	[pʌvəl]	/ʃ/ → /___/
[t]	TELEPHONE	/tɛləfon/	→	[tɛton]	/f/ → /___/

Deletion of Final Consonant	DFC	Consonant Harmony	CH	Backing to Velars	BK
Prevocalic Voicing	PVV	Postvocalic Devoicing	PVD	Epenthesis	EPEN
Syllable Reduction	SR	Vocalization	VOC	Metathesis	METATH
Velar Fronting	VF	Palatal Fronting	PF	Coalescence	COAL
Stopping of Fricatives and Affricates	ST	Gliding of Liquids	GL	Palatalization	PAL
Cluster Reduction	CR	Deaffrication	DEAFF	Denasalization	DENAS
Stridency Deletion	STR	Deletion of Initial Consonant	DIC	Idiosyncratic Processes	
		Glottal Replacement	GR		

GLOVE /glʌv/ → [glʌg] /v/ → /___/ [g]

SOUP /sup/ → [bup] /s/ → /___/ [b]

BRUSH /brʌʃ/ → [brʌp] /ʃ/ → /___/ [p]

When the process of ST results in a non-homorganic stop consonant, there is usually at least one other _____ that has been applied.

> process

For example, when KNIFE /naɪf/ → [naɪt], the /f/ → [t] sound change results from both _____ and CONSONANT HARMONY (see p. 115). The alveolar placement for /n/ has influenced the articulatory placement from /f/ to [t].

> ST

The substitution of homorganic stops for fricatives or affricates is more natural and therefore more easily interpreted by the listener. The further removed the stop consonant is from the target continuant in place, manner, or voicing, the more _____ the child's production.

> unintelligible

Another way of stating the same principle is this: the more processes that contribute to a single sound change, the more _____ the word.

> unintelligible

A fricative may be stopped and result in an affricate. For example, when SHOE /ʃu/ → [tʃu], the /ʃ/ has been stopped to become the affricate [tʃ]. Another example might be ZEBRA /zibrə/ → [dʒibrə], where /z/ has been _____ to become [dʒ], an affricate.

> stopped

It seems that the use of an affricate to replace a fricative represents progress toward maintaining the

/p/ *PIG*	/n/ *NO*	/ʃ/ *SHE*	/w/ *WAGON*	/ɛ/ *BED*	/ʌ/ *GUN*
/b/ *BED*	/ŋ/ *STING*	/ʒ/ *ROUGE*	/ʍ/ *WHEEL*	/æ/ *CAT*	/ə/ *ABOUT*
/t/ *TOY*	/f/ *FOX*	/h/ *HAVE*	/ɚ/ *FINGER*	/a/ *GOT*	/aɪ/ *KITE*
/d/ *DUCK*	/θ/ *THINK*	/tʃ/ *CHICKEN*	/ɝ/ *CHURCH*	/ɔ/ *TALK*	/ɔɪ/ *TOY*
/k/ *KEEP*	/ð/ *THIS*	/dʒ/ *JUMPING*	/i/ *SEE*	/o/ *GOAT*	/aʊ/ *OUT*
/g/ *GOAT*	/s/ *SEE*	/l/ *LAKE*	/ɪ/ *PIG*	/ʊ/ *BOOK*	
/m/ *ME*	/z/ *ZOO*	/j/ *YOU*	/eɪ, e/ *MAKE*	/u/ *GLUE*	

fricative	continuancy. A stop consonant may be used initially, later becoming an affricate and finally a _____.
[t]	Thus, a child who produces the sound change /s/ → [tʃ] approximates the attempted word more closely than the child who produces the sound change /s/ → [____], which is a homorganic stop consonant.

For the following attempted words, write the productions that would result from STOPPING to (a) a homorganic stop consonant and (b) an affricate.

		Adult Form		Child's Forms (a)	(b)
[ti], [tʃi]	SEE	/si/	→	[_____]	[_____]
[tu], [tʃu]	SHOE	/ʃu/	→	[_____]	[_____]
[idɪ], idʒɪ]	EASY	/izɪ/	→	[_____]	[_____]
[dɪpɚ], [dʒɪpɚ]	ZIPPER	/zɪpɚ/	→	[_____]	[_____]
[trɛdɚ], [trɛdʒɚ]	TREASURE	/trɛʒɚ/	→	[_____]	[_____]
[maʊt], [maʊtʃ]	MOUSE	/maʊs/	→	[_____]	[_____]
[brʌt], [brʌtʃ]	BRUSH	/brʌʃ/	→	[_____]	[_____]

Indicate whether or not each production resulted from using the process of ST:

		Adult Form	Child's Form	YES/NO
YES, /θ/ → [t]	THUMB	/θʌm/	→ [tʌm]	_____

Deletion of Final Consonant	DFC	Consonant Harmony	CH	Backing to Velars	BK
Prevocalic Voicing	PVV	Postvocalic Devoicing	PVD	Epenthesis	EPEN
Syllable Reduction	SR	Vocalization	VOC	Metathesis	METATH
Velar Fronting	VF	Palatal Fronting	PF	Coalescence	COAL
Stopping of Fricatives and Affricates	ST	Gliding of Liquids	GL	Palatalization	PAL
Cluster Reduction	CR	Deaffrication	DEAFF	Denasalization	DENAS
Stridency Deletion	STR	Deletion of Initial Consonant	DIC	Idiosyncratic Processes	
		Glottal Replacement	GR		

MOTHER	/mʌðɚ/	→ [mʌvɚ]	_____	NO, /ð/ → [v]
MOTHER	/mʌðɚ/	→ [mʌdɚ]	_____	YES, /ð/ → [d]
ZIPPER	/zɪpɚ/	→ [dɪpɚ]	_____	YES, /z/ → [d]
CHAIR	/tʃɛr/	→ [ʃɛr]	_____	NO, /tʃ/ → [ʃ]
TELEPHONE	/tɛləfon/	→ [tɛləpon]	_____	YES, /f/ → [p]
VACUUM	/vækjuəm/	→ [gækjuəm]	_____	YES, /v/ → [g]

Of the seven words attempted, five, or 71%, involved _____ of a fricative or affricate.

ST, or STOPPING

ST may be applied to all occurrences of affricates and fricatives, or it may be applied selectively. If applied selectively, we say it is an _____ process.

optional

Examine the following list of attempted words and their productions. Determine how the process of ST is applied selectively, that is, describe the optional rule.

	Adult Form		Child's Form
BUS	/bʌs/	→	[bʌs]
SAND	/sænd/	→	[tʃænd]
BRUSH	/brʌʃ/	→	[brʌs]
SHOE	/ʃu/	→	[tʃu]
DOES	/dʌz/	→	[dʌz]
THING	/θɪŋ/	→	[tɪŋ]
ZOO	/zu/	→	[du]
WITH	/wɪθ/	→	[wɪθ]

/p/ PIG	/n/ NO	/ʃ/ SHE	/w/ WAGON	/ɛ/ BED	/ʌ/ GUN
/b/ BED	/ŋ/ STING	/ʒ/ ROUGE	/ʍ/ WHEEL	/æ/ CAT	/ə/ ABOUT
/t/ TOY	/f/ FOX	/h/ HAVE	/ɚ/ FINGER	/a/ GOT	/aɪ/ KITE
/d/ DUCK	/θ/ THINK	/tʃ/ CHICKEN	/ɝ/ CHURCH	/ɔ/ TALK	/ɔɪ/ TOY
/k/ KEEP	/ð/ THIS	/dʒ/ JUMPING	/i/ SEE	/o/ GOAT	/aʊ/ OUT
/g/ GOAT	/s/ SEE	/l/ LAKE	/ɪ/ PIG	/ʊ/ BOOK	
/m/ ME	/z/ ZOO	/j/ YOU	/eɪ, e/ MAKE	/u/ GLUE	

Word-initial fricatives only are stopped.	Optional Process:
stopped	ST is not limited to consonants occurring within certain positions in words. Wherever a fricative or affricate occurs, it can be _____.
stopped	There is, however, a tendency for fricatives to be stopped word-initially. Because they are followed by a phoneme (the vowel), the airflow is not continued but is _____.
stops	Thus, ZOO /zu/ → [du] because the /z/ is followed by /u/, which _____ the airflow.
stopped	When a fricative or affricate occurs in word-final position, the airflow can be continued and therefore is not as likely to be _____.
initial	Some clinicians have observed that fricatives and affricates (particularly voiceless) develop in word-final position prior to developing in word-_____ position.
fricatives, affricates	This is contrary to the concept that phonemes develop in a set order: Initial, Medial, Final. For _____ and _____, this established order does not necessarily apply.
stopped	When examining a child's speech sample, observe where the fricatives and affricates occur. When they are word-initial they are likely to be _____.
continued	When they occur word-finally, they are likely to be _____.

Deletion of Final Consonant	DFC	Consonant Harmony	CH	Backing to Velars	BK
Prevocalic Voicing	PVV	Postvocalic Devoicing	PVD	Epenthesis	EPEN
Syllable Reduction	SR	Vocalization	VOC	Metathesis	METATH
Velar Fronting	VF	Palatal Fronting	PF	Coalescence	COAL
Stopping of Fricatives and Affricates	ST	Gliding of Liquids	GL	Palatalization	PAL
Cluster Reduction	CR	Deaffrication	DEAFF	Denasalization	DENAS
Stridency Deletion	STR	Deletion of Initial Consonant	DIC	Idiosyncratic Processes	
		Glottal Replacement	GR		

Indicate whether the fricatives and affricates in the following words are likely to be STOPPED or CONTINUED.

CHAIR	/tʃɛr/	_____	STOPPED
WITCH	/wɪtʃ/	_____	CONTINUED
ICE	/aɪs/	_____	CONTINUED
FINGER	/fɪŋgɚ/	_____	STOPPED
ZIPPER	/zɪpɚ/	_____	STOPPED
KNIFE	/naɪf/	_____	CONTINUED
BRUSH	/brʌʃ/	_____	CONTINUED
SHIP	/ʃɪp/	_____	STOPPED
THAT	/ðæt/	_____	STOPPED

While it is less likely that word-final fricatives and affricates will be stopped, young children and disordered children do apply the process of _____ anywhere. It is important to examine the individual child's pattern.

ST

Additional processes may be applied to fricatives and affricates. When the word KNIFE /naɪf/ → [naɪs], the sound change is identified as /____/ → [____].

/f/ → [s]

Although the /f/ in the target word has not been articulated correctly, it has also *not* had the process of _____ applied to it.

ST

/p/ PIG	/n/ NO	/ʃ/ SHE	/w/ WAGON	/ɛ/ BED	/ʌ/ GUN
/b/ BED	/ŋ/ STING	/ʒ/ ROUGE	/ʍ/ WHEEL	/æ/ CAT	/ə/ ABOUT
/t/ TOY	/f/ FOX	/h/ HAVE	/ɚ/ FINGER	/a/ GOT	/aɪ/ KITE
/d/ DUCK	/θ/ THINK	/tʃ/ CHICKEN	/ɝ/ CHURCH	/ɔ/ TALK	/ɔɪ/ TOY
/k/ KEEP	/ð/ THIS	/dʒ/ JUMPING	/i/ SEE	/o/ GOAT	/aʊ/ OUT
/g/ GOAT	/s/ SEE	/l/ LAKE	/ɪ/ PIG	/ʊ/ BOOK	
/m/ ME	/z/ ZOO	/j/ YOU	/eɪ, e/ MAKE	/u/ GLUE	

Indicate which of the following sound changes resulted from the application of STOPPING (among other processes):

	Sound Change			YES/NO
NO	/s/	→	[f]	_____
YES	/f/	→	[p]	_____
YES	/ʃ/	→	[t]	_____
NO	/θ/	→	[f]	_____
NO	/tʃ/	→	[ʃ]	_____
YES	/ʒ/	→	[dʒ]	_____
NO	/dʒ/	→	[tʃ]	_____

In young and disordered children, the process of _____ is often applied concurrently with PVV (*Prevocalic Voicing*).

ST

Thus, words like SUN /sʌn/ and SAND /sænd/ become [dʌn] and [_____].

[dænd]

Give the altered forms for the following target words. Assume that the child applied both ST and PVV to these words.

		Adult Form	Child's Form
[dɪŋk]	SINK	/sɪŋk/	→ [_____]

Deletion of Final		Consonant Harmony	CH	Backing to Velars	BK
Consonant	DFC	Postvocalic Devoicing	PVD	Epenthesis	EPEN
Prevocalic Voicing	PVV	Vocalization	VOC	Metathesis	METATH
Syllable Reduction	SR	Palatal Fronting	PF	Coalescence	COAL
Velar Fronting	VF	Gliding of Liquids	GL	Palatalization	PAL
Stopping of Fricatives		Deaffrication	DEAFF	Denasalization	DENAS
and Affricates	ST	Deletion of Initial		Idiosyncratic	
Cluster Reduction	CR	Consonant	DIC	Processes	
Stridency Deletion	STR	Glottal Replacement	GR		

CHICKEN   /tʃɪkɪn/   → [_____]   [dɪkɪn]

SHEEP   /ʃip/   → [_____]   [dip] or [dʒip]

SOCK   /sak/   → [_____]   [dak]

FORK   /fork/   → [_____]   [bork]

STOPPING is a process that occurs frequently in the speech of young children and children with phonological disorders. When children attempt fricatives, they first produce _____, particularly in word-initial contexts.

stops

Some investigators (see, for example, Hodson, 1978) have observed that developmentally, children produce a fricative plus a homorganic stop (as in [st]) when attempting fricatives (in this case, /s/). When a fricative is followed by a stop consonant, it is most natural for that stop to be _____ with the fricative.

homorganic

Recall that fricatives tend to be _____ prevocalically. Thus, FIVE /faɪv/ → [paɪv] or [baɪv].

stopped

However, they may occur as fricatives in _____ position without being stopped.

word-final

As has just been stated, the most likely word position for successful production of a fricative or an affricate is _____.

word-final

Because of this tendency, the elimination of STOPPING may be facilitated by targeting fricatives in

---

/p/ PIG	/n/ NO	/ʃ/ SHE	/w/ WAGON	/ɛ/ BED	/ʌ/ GUN
/b/ BED	/ŋ/ STING	/ʒ/ ROUGE	/ʍ/ WHEEL	/æ/ CAT	/ə/ ABOUT
/t/ TOY	/f/ FOX	/h/ HAVE	/ɚ/ FINGER	/a/ GOT	/aɪ/ KITE
/d/ DUCK	/θ/ THINK	/tʃ/ CHICKEN	/ɝ/ CHURCH	/ɔ/ TALK	/ɔɪ/ TOY
/k/ KEEP	/ð/ THIS	/dʒ/ JUMPING	/i/ SEE	/o/ GOAT	/aʊ/ OUT
/g/ GOAT	/s/ SEE	/l/ LAKE	/ɪ/ PIG	/ʊ/ BOOK	
/m/ ME	/z/ ZOO	/j/ YOU	/eɪ, e/ MAKE	/u/ GLUE	

final | word-_____ position.

Examine the following target words and their productions..Give each sound change that occurs within each production and list the process(es) that accounted for that sound change. The first one has been done for you.

		Adult Form		Child's Form	Sound Change	Process(es)
	SUN	/sʌn/	→	[dʌn]	/s_/ → [d_]	ST, PVV
/f/ → [p], ST	LEAF	/lif/	→	[lip]	/__/ → [__]	_____
/z/ → [d], ST	EASY	/izɪ/	→	[idʒɪ]	/__/ → [__]	_____
/dʒ/ → [d], ST	JUMP	/dʒʌmp/	→	[dʌmp]	/__/ → [__]	_____
/θ/ → [d], ST, PVV	THUMB	/θʌm/	→	[dʌm]	/__/ → [__]	_____
/s/ → [ts], ST	BUS	/bʌs/	→	[bʌts]	/__/ → [__]	_____
/s/ → [d], ST, PVV /k/ → [t], VF	SOCK	/sak/	→	[dat]	/__/ → [__] /__/ → [__]	_____ _____
/tʃ/ → [dʒ], PVV /k/ → [t], VF	CHICK	/tʃɪk/	→	[dʒɪt]	/__/ → [__] /__/ → [__]	_____ _____

ST | The process of _____ may be blocked by the application of one of the deletion processes.

process blocking | For example, when BUS /bʌs/ → [bʌ], there is no opportunity for ST to be applied. The term used to describe this is _____.

Deletion of Final Consonant	DFC	Consonant Harmony	CH
Prevocalic Voicing	PVV	Postvocalic Devoicing	PVD
Syllable Reduction	SR	Vocalization	VOC
Velar Fronting	VF	Palatal Fronting	PF
Stopping of Fricatives and Affricates	ST	Gliding of Liquids Deaffrication	GL DEAFF
Cluster Reduction	CR	Deletion of Initial Consonant	DIC
Stridency Deletion	STR	Glottal Replacement	GR

Backing to Velars BK
Epenthesis EPEN
Metathesis METATH
Coalescence COAL
Palatalization PAL
Denasalization DENAS
Idiosyncratic Processes

For each of the following examples, indicate whether or not the process of ST has been blocked by one of the deletion processes already introduced (DFC, or SR).

	Adult Form		Child's Form	YES/NO
LEAF	/lif/	→	[li]	_____
SHOE	/ʃu/	→	[du]	_____
NOTHING	/nʌθɪŋ/	→	[nʌ]	_____
BATH	/bæθ/	→	[bæs]	_____
MOUSE	/maʊs/	→	[maʊ]	_____

YES, /f/ → [ø], DFC

NO, /ʃ/ → [d], ST

YES, /θɪŋ/ → [ø], SR

NO, /θ/ → [s]

YES, /s/ → [ø], DFC

The process of ST has been applied when a fricative becomes a stop consonant or an _____.

affricate

The process of ST has also been applied when an affricate becomes a _____ consonant.

stop

When a fricative or affricate becomes a stop consonant, the phoneme loses its STRIDENCY. The

---

/p/ *PIG*	/n/ *NO*	/ʃ/ *SHE*	/w/ *WAGON*	/ɛ/ *BED*	/ʌ/ *GUN*
/b/ *BED*	/ŋ/ *STING*	/ʒ/ *ROUGE*	/ʍ/ *WHEEL*	/æ/ *CAT*	/ə/ *ABOUT*
/t/ *TOY*	/f/ *FOX*	/h/ *HAVE*	/ɚ/ *FINGER*	/a/ *GOT*	/aɪ/ *KITE*
/d/ *DUCK*	/θ/ *THINK*	/tʃ/ *CHICKEN*	/ɝ/ *CHURCH*	/ɔ/ *TALK*	/ɔɪ/ *TOY*
/k/ *KEEP*	/ð/ *THIS*	/dʒ/ *JUMPING*	/i/ *SEE*	/o/ *GOAT*	/aʊ/ *OUT*
/g/ *GOAT*	/s/ *SEE*	/l/ *LAKE*	/ɪ/ *PIG*	/ʊ/ *BOOK*	
/m/ *ME*	/z/ *ZOO*	/j/ *YOU*	/eɪ, e/ *MAKE*	/u/ *GLUE*	

	process of STRIDENCY DELETION is covered in Section 7.
	Children may stop consonants other than fricatives and affricates; however, these processes are considered to be miscellaneous. One example would be stopping of a glide as in WAGON /wægən/ → [bægən], where the /w/ has been replaced by [b], which is a _____
stop	consonant.
	Another example would be the stopping of a nasal. Thus, MOUSE /maʊs/ → [baʊs] would be an example of this. This has also been called DENASALIZATION, which is covered later in the text.
fricatives, affricates	The process STOPPING OF FRICATIVES AND AFFRICATES (or ST) refers to the use of a stop consonant or affricate for _____ and _____ only.

Deletion of Final Consonant	DFC	Consonant Harmony	CH	Backing to Velars	BK
Prevocalic Voicing	PVV	Postvocalic Devoicing	PVD	Epenthesis	EPEN
Syllable Reduction	SR	Vocalization	VOC	Metathesis	METATH
Velar Fronting	VF	Palatal Fronting	PF	Coalescence	COAL
Stopping of Fricatives and Affricates	ST	Gliding of Liquids	GL	Palatalization	PAL
		Deaffrication	DEAFF	Denasalization	DENAS
Cluster Reduction	CR	Deletion of Initial Consonant	DIC	Idiosyncratic Processes	
Stridency Deletion	STR	Glottal Replacement	GR		

SUMMARY
Stopping of Fricatives and Affricates

1. ST is a process that results in the production of stops for fricatives and affricates.
2. The application of ST most often results in a homorganic production.
3. The application of ST to a fricative may result in the production of an affricate.
4. There is a tendency for word-initial fricatives and affricates to be stopped.
5. Fricatives and affricates may first emerge in word-final position.
6. Consonants other than fricatives and affricates may be stopped; these are not included under ST.

/p/ *PIG*	/n/ *NO*	/ʃ/ *SHE*	/w/ *WAGON*	/ɛ/ *BED*	/ʌ/ *GUN*
/b/ *BED*	/ŋ/ *STING*	/ʒ/ *ROUGE*	/ʍ/ *WHEEL*	/æ/ *CAT*	/ə/ *ABOUT*
/t/ *TOY*	/f/ *FOX*	/h/ *HAVE*	/ɚ/ *FINGER*	/a/ *GOT*	/aɪ/ *KITE*
/d/ *DUCK*	/θ/ *THINK*	/tʃ/ *CHICKEN*	/ɝ/ *CHURCH*	/ɔ/ *TALK*	/ɔɪ/ *TOY*
/k/ *KEEP*	/ð/ *THIS*	/dʒ/ *JUMPING*	/i/ *SEE*	/o/ *GOAT*	/aʊ/ *OUT*
/g/ *GOAT*	/s/ *SEE*	/l/ *LAKE*	/ɪ/ *PIG*	/ʊ/ *BOOK*	
/m/ *ME*	/z/ *ZOO*	/j/ *YOU*	/eɪ, e/ *MAKE*	/u/ *GLUE*	

SECTION 6. CLUSTER REDUCTION

CLUSTER REDUCTION, or CR

CLUSTER REDUCTION (CR) is a process that results in the deletion of one or two members of a two- or three-consonant cluster. DRUM /drʌm/ → [dʌm] is an example of _____.

CR

The abbreviation for CLUSTER REDUCTION is _____.

[k]

Another example of CR would be CLAP /klæp/ → [kæp], where /kl/ → [____] is the sound change that has occurred.

cluster

Recall that a sound change involving an entire cluster is noted as /cluster/ → [singleton] in order to represent the action upon the entire cluster. When a cluster is reduced by one member, the deletion of that member is not referred to outside of the context of the _____.

/kl/

Thus, when CLAP /klæp/ → [kæp], the SOUND CHANGE includes /____/ to the left of the arrow.

deleted

CLUSTER REDUCTION is a deletion process. That is, something from the attempted word has been _____ by the child.

cluster

Although a single consonant may have been deleted, we indicated that the entire _____ has been altered whenever we note the corresponding sound change.

Deletion of Final Consonant	DFC	Consonant Harmony	CH	Backing to Velars	BK
Prevocalic Voicing	PVV	Postvocalic Devoicing	PVD	Epenthesis	EPEN
Syllable Reduction	SR	Vocalization	VOC	Metathesis	METATH
Velar Fronting	VF	Palatal Fronting	PF	Coalescence	COAL
Stopping of Fricatives and Affricates	ST	Gliding of Liquids	GL	Palatalization	PAL
Cluster Reduction	CR	Deaffrication	DEAFF	Denasalization	DENAS
Stridency Deletion	STR	Deletion of Initial Consonant	DIC	Idiosyncratic Processes	
		Glottal Replacement	GR		

The young child or phonologically disordered child may change CLOWN /klaʊn/ → [kaʊn] and STOVE /stov/ → [tov]. Similarly, SNAIL /snel/ may change to [nel] with the application of _____.

CR

The capital letter C is used to indicate a "consonant" and the capital letter V is used to indicate a "vowel," so that "CCV" represents a word that begins with a consonant cluster and ends with a _____.

vowel

An example of a CCV word would be BLUE /blu/. The cluster contains two consonants (CC), which are _____.

/bl/

An example of a CCCV word would be STRAW /strɔ/. The cluster contains three consonants (CCC), which are _____.

/str/

Clusters also appear at the ends of words. For example, EAST /ist/ is a VCC word. The word-final cluster contains two consonants (CC), which are _____.

/st/

When a CC cluster (as in /kl/) remains a CC cluster even though it is not pronounced correctly, the process of _____ has not been applied.

CR

For example, when CLAP /klæp/ → [kwæp], the child's production is also a CCVC word just like /klæp/. There has been a sound change involving the cluster (namely, /kl/ → [kw]), but both the target word and the child's production contain a word-initial, two-consonant _____.

cluster

/p/ PIG	/n/ NO	/ʃ/ SHE	/w/ WAGON	/ɛ/ BED	/ʌ/ GUN
/b/ BED	/ŋ/ STING	/ʒ/ ROUGE	/ʍ/ WHEEL	/æ/ CAT	/ə/ ABOUT
/t/ TOY	/f/ FOX	/h/ HAVE	/ɚ/ FINGER	/a/ GOT	/aɪ/ KITE
/d/ DUCK	/θ/ THINK	/tʃ/ CHICKEN	/ɝ/ CHURCH	/ɔ/ TALK	/ɔɪ/ ˈTOY
/k/ KEEP	/ð/ THIS	/dʒ/ JUMPING	/i/ SEE	/o/ GOAT	/aʊ/ OUT
/g/ GOAT	/s/ SEE	/l/ LAKE	/ɪ/ PIG	/ʊ/ BOOK	
/m/ ME	/z/ ZOO	/j/ YOU	/eɪ, e/ MAKE	/u/ GLUE	

CR

C; CC, C

[kaʊn]

Thus, if CLOWN /klaʊn/ → [kwaʊn], _____ has not been applied. The sound change is /kl/ → [kw] and does not represent reduction of the cluster by one or more members.

For a cluster to be reduced, the production must contain fewer consonants in the cluster than the target word. Thus, CC → ____ and CCC → ____ or ____.

When clusters are reduced, children generally follow additional rules in determining which member(s) of the cluster to retain. When the cluster contains a liquid (/r/ or /l/), these are often deleted. Thus, TREE /tri/ → [ti] when CR is applied. Similarly, CLOWN /klaʊn/ → [_____] when CR is applied.

List the productions that would result from the application of CR to the following clusters, which contain liquids:

	Adult Form		Child's Form
[bu]	BLUE	/blu/	→ [_____]
[pɪtɪ]	PRETTY	/prɪtɪ/	→ [_____]
[gæs]	GLASS	/glæs/	→ [_____]
[sip]	SLEEP	/slip/	→ [_____]
[peɪ]	PLAY	/pleɪ/	→ [_____]
[dʌm]	DRUM	/drʌm/	→ [_____]

Deletion of Final Consonant	DFC	Consonant Harmony	CH	Backing to Velars	BK
Prevocalic Voicing	PVV	Postvocalic Devoicing	PVD	Epenthesis	EPEN
Syllable Reduction	SR	Vocalization	VOC	Metathesis	METATH
Velar Fronting	VF	Palatal Fronting	PF	Coalescence	COAL
Stopping of Fricatives and Affricates	ST	Gliding of Liquids	GL	Palatalization	PAL
		Deaffrication	DEAFF	Denasalization	DENAS
Cluster Reduction	CR	Deletion of Initial Consonant	DIC	Idiosyncratic Processes	
Stridency Deletion	STR	Glottal Replacement	GR		

Because most young children use this rule and tend to delete the _____ from the cluster, the adult listener is able to understand the child's forms quite easily.

liquid

The child who deletes the non-liquid from the cluster draws attention to herself or himself. For example, the word SLEEP /slip/ would be produced [_____] if the non-liquid member of the cluster were deleted.

[lip]

From the word list just given, indicate the productions that would result IF the liquid member of the cluster were retained:

	Adult Form		Child's Form	
BLUE	/blu/	→ [_____]		[lu]
PRETTY	/prɪtɪ/	→ [_____]		[rɪtɪ]
GLASS	/glæs/	→ [_____]		[læs]
SLEEP	/slip/	→ [_____]		[lip]
PLAY	/pleɪ/	→ [_____]		[leɪ]
DRUM	/drʌm/	→ [_____]		[rʌm]

Most adults recognize the clusters from the first of these two word lists as the most familiar. That is because children generally delete the _____ from clusters that contain liquids.

liquid

/p/ *PIG*	/n/ *NO*	/ʃ/ *SHE*	/w/ *WAGON*	/ɛ/ *BED*	/ʌ/ *GUN*
/b/ *BED*	/ŋ/ *STING*	/ʒ/ *ROUGE*	/ʍ/ *WHEEL*	/æ/ *CAT*	/ə/ *ABOUT*
/t/ *TOY*	/f/ *FOX*	/h/ *HAVE*	/ɚ/ *FINGER*	/a/ *GOT*	/aɪ/ *KITE*
/d/ *DUCK*	/θ/ *THINK*	/tʃ/ *CHICKEN*	/ɝ/ *CHURCH*	/ɔ/ *TALK*	/ɔɪ/ *TOY*
/k/ *KEEP*	/ð/ *THIS*	/dʒ/ *JUMPING*	/i/ *SEE*	/o/ *GOAT*	/aʊ/ *OUT*
/g/ *GOAT*	/s/ *SEE*	/l/ *LAKE*	/ɪ/ *PIG*	/ʊ/ *BOOK*	
/m/ *ME*	/z/ *ZOO*	/j/ *YOU*	/eɪ, e/ *MAKE*	/u/ *GLUE*	

liquid

It is unusual for children to retain the _____ in clusters which contain liquids. However, a good number of phonologically disordered children retain the liquid when reducing clusters. That is, the examples from the second of these word lists will occur within the speech samples of disordered children.

CR

Whether the liquid is deleted when the cluster is reduced, or whether the other member is deleted when the cluster is reduced, the process of _____ has been applied.

List the two possible productions that would result if the child reduced the clusters both ways. That is, with liquid deletion and with liquid retention.

	Adult Form	Child's Form Liquid	Child's Form No Liquid
[rʌm], [dʌm]	DRUM /drʌm/ →	[_____]	[_____]
[rin], [gin]	GREEN /grin/ →	[_____]	[_____]
[rʌk], [tʌk]	TRUCK /trʌk/ →	[_____]	[_____]
[læs],]kæs]	CLASS /klæs/ →	[_____]	[_____]
[laɪd], [saɪd]	SLIDE /slaɪd/ →	[_____]	[_____]

CR

All of the productions just listed in either the liquid-retained or the liquid-deleted columns are examples of the process of _____.

Children seem to use additional rules when simplifying clusters. When there is an /s/ cluster that

Deletion of Final Consonant	DFC	Consonant Harmony	CH	Backing to Velars	BK
Prevocalic Voicing	PVV	Postvocalic Devoicing	PVD	Epenthesis	EPEN
Syllable Reduction	SR	Vocalization	VOC	Metathesis	METATH
Velar Fronting	VF	Palatal Fronting	PF	Coalescence	COAL
Stopping of Fricatives and Affricates	ST	Gliding of Liquids	GL	Palatalization	PAL
Cluster Reduction	CR	Deaffrication	DEAFF	Denasalization	DENAS
Stridency Deletion	STR	Deletion of Initial Consonant	DIC	Idiosyncratic Processes	
		Glottal Replacement	GR		

contains a liquid (as in SLEEP), the /s/ is retained, and the liquid tends to be deleted from the cluster. However, when the /s/ cluster does NOT contain liquids, the /____/ is deleted.

/s/

For example, in the word SNAIL /snel/, when the cluster is reduced the word may become [_____]. The /s/ member of the cluster is deleted because the cluster does not contain a liquid.

[nel]

Similarly, when the /sm/ cluster in SMOKE /smok/ is reduced, the word becomes [_____].

[mok]

When /s/ forms a cluster with a non-liquid consonant, the /s/ is usually _____.

deleted

Use this cluster rule to form the productions that would occur with the application of CR to the following words:

	Adult Form		Child's Form	
STOP	/stap/	→	[_____]	[tap]
SMALL	/smɔl/	→	[_____]	[mɔl]
SKY	/skaɪ/	→	[_____]	[kaɪ]
SPOT	/spat/	→	[_____]	[pat]
SNAKE	/snek/	→	[_____]	[nek]

There are CCC clusters that contain both an /s/ and a liquid. For example, STRAW /strɔ/ contains both. A

/p/ *PIG*	/n/ *NO*	/ʃ/ *SHE*	/w/ *WAGON*	/ɛ/ *BED*	/ʌ/ *GUN*
/b/ *BED*	/ŋ/ *STING*	/ʒ/ *ROUGE*	/ʍ/ *WHEEL*	/æ/ *CAT*	/ə/ *ABOUT*
/t/ *TOY*	/f/ *FOX*	/h/ *HAVE*	/ɚ/ *FINGER*	/a/ *GOT*	/aɪ/ *KITE*
/d/ *DUCK*	/θ/ *THINK*	/tʃ/ *CHICKEN*	/ɝ/ *CHURCH*	/ɔ/ *TALK*	/ɔɪ/ *TOY*
/k/ *KEEP*	/ð/ *THIS*	/dʒ/ *JUMPING*	/i/ *SEE*	/o/ *GOAT*	/aʊ/ *OUT*
/g/ *GOAT*	/s/ *SEE*	/l/ *LAKE*	/ɪ/ *PIG*	/ʊ/ *BOOK*	
/m/ *ME*	/z/ *ZOO*	/j/ *YOU*	/eɪ, e/ *MAKE*	/u/ *GLUE*	

/s/ and /r/

child might reduce the cluster by deleting the /s/, or by deleting the /r/, or by deleting both. When a three-member cluster contains both an /s/ and a liquid, the remaining member will be retained if it is reduced to one member. For example, if STRAW /strɔ/ (CCCV) is reduced to a CV syllable, the child will most likely delete the _____ and the _____.

[tɔ]

Thus, the word STRAW /strɔ/ would become [_____] with the application of CR.

[stɔ], [trɔ]

If the cluster were reduced to two members from three members, then STRAW /strɔ/ might become either [_____] or [_____].

[pæʃ]

Similarly, when SPLASH /splæʃ/ (CCCVC) is reduced to a CVC, the child will most likely produce [_____], deleting the /s/ and the liquid.

[spæʃ], [plæʃ]

If two members of the cluster are retained, then the child might produce [_____] or [_____].

[pwæʃ]

Often, when the liquid is retained, it is produced as a glide. STRAW /strɔ/ might then be produced as [twɔ]. Similarly, SPLASH /splæʃ/ might be produced as [_____]. This will be covered in Section 12.

CR

Recall that when the child produces a cluster of the same size as that of the target word, the process of _____ has NOT been applied.

Deletion of Final Consonant	DFC	Consonant Harmony	CH	Backing to Velars	BK
Prevocalic Voicing	PVV	Postvocalic Devoicing	PVD	Epenthesis	EPEN
Syllable Reduction	SR	Vocalization	VOC	Metathesis	METATH
Velar Fronting	VF	Palatal Fronting	PF	Coalescence	COAL
Stopping of Fricatives and Affricates	ST	Gliding of Liquids	GL	Palatalization	PAL
Cluster Reduction	CR	Deaffrication	DEAFF	Denasalization	DENAS
Stridency Deletion	STR	Deletion of Initial Consonant	DIC	Idiosyncratic Processes	
		Glottal Replacement	GR		

Indicate whether or not the following productions were the result of the application of CR:

	Adult Form		Child's Form	YES/NO		
CLOWN	/klaʊn/	→	[kwaʊn]	_____	NO, /kl/ → [kw]
TREE	/tri/	→	[twi]	_____	NO, /tr/ → [tw]
SMILE	/smaɪl/	→	[maɪl]	_____	YES, /sm/ → [m]
SKI	/ski/	→	[sti]	_____	NO, /sk/ → [st]
GREEN	/grin/	→	[gin]	_____	YES, /gr/ → [g]
PLAY	/pleɪ/	→	[beɪ]	_____	YES, /pl/ → [b]
SKATE	/sket/	→	[get]	_____	YES, /sk/ → [g]

Clusters, because they contain more than one consonant, provide the opportunity for several processes to be applied simultaneously. Often, _____ is applied in conjunction with another process, such as PVV, PREVOCALIC VOICING.

CR

Since many clusters contain liquids (/l/ and /r/), they are subject to GLIDING (which is discussed in a later section). Therefore, they may become [w] or [j]. The word CLOWN /klaʊn/ may be produced several ways. Determine which combinations of the following processes were applied to result in each of the productions of CLOWN listed below.

/p/ PIG	/n/ NO	/ʃ/ SHE	/w/ WAGON	/ɛ/ BED	/ʌ/ GUN
/b/ BED	/ŋ/ STING	/ʒ/ ROUGE	/ʍ/ WHEEL	/æ/ CAT	/ə/ ABOUT
/t/ TOY	/f/ FOX	/h/ HAVE	/ɚ/ FINGER	/a/ GOT	/aɪ/ KITE
/d/ DUCK	/θ/ THINK	/tʃ/ CHICKEN	/ɝ/ CHURCH	/ɔ/ TALK	/ɔɪ/ TOY
/k/ KEEP	/ð/ THIS	/dʒ/ JUMPING	/i/ SEE	/o/ GOAT	/aʊ/ OUT
/g/ GOAT	/s/ SEE	/l/ LAKE	/ɪ/ PIG	/ʊ/ BOOK	
/m/ ME	/z/ ZOO	/j/ YOU	/eɪ, e/ MAKE	/u/ GLUE	

	Processes:	CR	PVV	GLIDING	VF
	Productions:				
CR, PVV	[gaʊn]			_____	
CR with retention of the liquid	[laʊn]			_____	
GLIDING of the /l/	[kwaʊn]			_____	
CR, GLIDING of the /l/	[waʊn]			_____	
GLIDING of the /l/	[kjaʊn]			_____	
CR, GLIDING of the /l/	[jaʊn]			_____	
CR, VF	[taʊn]			_____	
CR, VF, PVV	[daʊn]			_____	
PVV, GLIDING of the /l/	[gwaʊn]			_____	
VF, GLIDING of the /l/	[twaʊn]			_____	
VF, PVV, GLIDING of the /l/	[dwaʊn]			_____	
VF, GLIDING of the /l/	[tjaʊn]			_____	

Deletion of Final Consonant	DFC	Consonant Harmony	CH	Backing to Velars	BK		
Prevocalic Voicing	PVV	Postvocalic Devoicing	PVD	Epenthesis	EPEN		
Syllable Reduction	SR	Vocalization	VOC	Metathesis	METATH		
Velar Fronting	VF	Palatal Fronting	PF	Coalescence	COAL		
Stopping of Fricatives and Affricates	ST	Gliding of Liquids	GL	Palatalization	PAL		
		Deaffrication	DEAFF	Denasalization	DENAS		
Cluster Reduction	CR	Deletion of Initial Consonant	DIC	Idiosyncratic Processes			
Stridency Deletion	STR	Glottal Replacement	GR				

[djaʊn] _____ | VF, PVV, GLIDING of the /l/

[gjaʊn] _____ | PVV, GLIDING of the /l/

Clusters that occur in word-final position may also be reduced. For example, NEST /nɛst/ → [nɛs] has resulted from the application of CR. Similarly, LAMP /læmp/ → [_____] when CR is applied. | [læm]; OR [læp]

Either member of the cluster may be retained. List the possible productions that would result if each word-final cluster were reduced to one member.

	Adult Form		Child's Form(s)	
MASK	/mæsk/	→	[_____] [_____]	[mæs], [mæk]
LEFT	/lɛft/	→	[_____] [_____]	[lɛf], [lɛt]
TENT	/tɛnt/	→	[_____] [_____]	[tɛn], [tɛt]
CARD	/kard/	→	[_____] [_____]	[kar], [kad]
SINK	/sɪŋk/	→	[_____] [_____]	[sɪŋ], [sɪk]

Children follow general patterns for reducing word-final clusters. For example, when a fricative is followed by a stop, the fricative is retained, and the stop is deleted from the cluster. For example, NEST /nɛst/ would become [_____] if the child applied this specific rule within the process of CR. | [nɛs]

/p/ PIG	/n/ NO	/ʃ/ SHE	/w/ WAGON	/ɛ/ BED	/ʌ/ GUN
/b/ BED	/ŋ/ STING	/ʒ/ ROUGE	/ʍ/ WHEEL	/æ/ CAT	/ə/ ABOUT
/t/ TOY	/f/ FOX	/h/ HAVE	/ɚ/ FINGER	/a/ GOT	/aɪ/ KITE
/d/ DUCK	/θ/ THINK	/tʃ/ CHICKEN	/ɝ/ CHURCH	/ɔ/ TALK	/ɔɪ/ TOY
/k/ KEEP	/ð/ THIS	/dʒ/ JUMPING	/i/ SEE	/o/ GOAT	/aʊ/ OUT
/g/ GOAT	/s/ SEE	/l/ LAKE	/ɪ/ PIG	/ʊ/ BOOK	
/m/ ME	/z/ ZOO	/j/ YOU	/eɪ, e/ MAKE	/u/ GLUE	

[mæs]

Similarly, MASK /mæsk/ would become [_____].

[lɛf]

Verbs such as LEFT /lɛft/ could have the same rule applied and would then be produced as [_____].

Regular past tense verbs are also subject to this rule if they end in a consonant cluster. For example, KISSED /kɪst/ ends with the cluster /st/. The /t/ marks the past tense. If the child applies the process of CR to this word as well as others that end with /s/ clusters, then the production that would result might be [_____].

[kɪs]

[waʃ]

Similarly, the verb WASHED /waʃt/ would be produced as [_____] if this CR rule applied.

It is sometimes a challenge to determine whether the child is deleting stop consonants from word-final clusters only in past tense verbs, or in all words that end with a _____.

fricative + stop cluster

Intervocalic clusters may be reduced by the child. As clusters, they are subject to reduction in the same manner that word-initial and word-final clusters are reduced. If the intervocalic cluster is reduced to fewer remaining members, then _____ has been applied.

CR

Sometimes clusters occur at syllable boundaries. For the purposes of phonological analysis in this text, they are still considered to behave like clusters. There are no broadly accepted rules for dividing English words into _____ by identification of established syllable boundaries. When multisyllabic words are divided, the intervocalic cluster may be a postvocalic cluster within the first syllable (/bæsk-ɪt/), or a prevocalic cluster within the

Deletion of Final		Consonant Harmony	CH	Backing to Velars	BK
Consonant	DFC	Postvocalic Devoicing	PVD	Epenthesis	EPEN
Prevocalic Voicing	PVV	Vocalization	VOC	Metathesis	METATH
Syllable Reduction	SR	Palatal Fronting	PF	Coalescence	COAL
Velar Fronting	VF	Gliding of Liquids	GL	Palatalization	PAL
Stopping of Fricatives		Deaffrication	DEAFF	Denasalization	DENAS
and Affricates	ST	Deletion of Initial		Idiosyncratic	
Cluster Reduction	CR	Consonant	DIC	Processes	
Stridency Deletion	STR	Glottal Replacement	GR		

second syllable (/bæ-skɪt/); or each member of the cluster may belong to its adjacent syllable (/bæs-kɪt/).

syllables

Guidelines have been suggested for dividing words into syllables (Pulgram, 1970; Paden, 1971). When completing a phonological analysis, it is necessary to choose a method of syllabification, especially with regard to intervocalic clusters. The assignment of phonological processes to sound changes is influenced by this choice. Consult Appendix IV for further information on Syllabification Issues.

As clusters, they are subject to reduction in the same manner that pre- and post-vocalic clusters can be reduced. If the intervocalic cluster is reduced to one member, then _____ has been applied.

CR

For the following sample productions, indicate whether or not CR has been applied to the intervocalic clusters.

	Adult Form		*Child's Form*	*YES/NO*		
BASKET	/bæskɪt/	→	[bæsɪt]	_____	YES, /sk/ → [s]
TRACTOR	/træktɚ/	→	[trækɚ]	_____	YES, /kt/ → [k]
ROOSTER	/rustɚ/	→	[ruftɚ]	_____	NO, /st/ → [ft]
VACUUM	/vakjuəm/	→	[vakwuəm]	_____	NO, /kj/ → [kw]
BATHTUB	/bæθtəb/	→	[bætəb]	_____	YES, /θt/ → [t]

/p/ *PIG*	/n/ *NO*	/ʃ/ *SHE*	/w/ *WAGON*	/ɛ/ *BED*	/ʌ/ *GUN*
/b/ *BED*	/ŋ/ *STING*	/ʒ/ *ROUGE*	/ʍ/ *WHEEL*	/æ/ *CAT*	/ə/ *ABOUT*
/t/ *TOY*	/f/ *FOX*	/h/ *HAVE*	/ɚ/ *FINGER*	/a/ *GOT*	/aɪ/ *KITE*
/d/ *DUCK*	/θ/ *THINK*	/tʃ/ *CHICKEN*	/ɝ/ *CHURCH*	/ɔ/ *TALK*	/ɔɪ/ *TOY*
/k/ *KEEP*	/ð/ *THIS*	/dʒ/ *JUMPING*	/i/ *SEE*	/o/ *GOAT*	/aʊ/ *OUT*
/g/ *GOAT*	/s/ *SEE*	/l/ *LAKE*	/ɪ/ *PIG*	/ʊ/ *BOOK*	
/m/ *ME*	/z/ *ZOO*	/j/ *YOU*	/eɪ, e/ *MAKE*	/u/ *GLUE*	

CR

As with other processes, if no clusters are attempted by the child, _____ cannot be applied.

Indicate whether each of the following words provides an opportunity for CR to be applied:

NO

BANANA /bənænə/ _____

NO, /dʒ/ is not a cluster.

GIRAFFE /dʒəræf/ _____

YES, /ŋg/

FINGER /fɪŋgɚ/ _____

YES, /nt/; PH is not a cluster.

ELEPHANT /ɛləfənt/ _____

NO, /tʃ/ is not a cluster.

MATCHES /mætʃɪz/ _____

YES, /tn/

LIGHTNING /laɪtnɪŋ/ _____

NO

APPLE /æpl̩/ _____

CR

Sometimes a cluster is reduced to one member that has characteristics of both members of the cluster. For example, when SWING /swɪŋ/ → [fɪŋ], the [f] is a voiceless fricative like the /s/ and is labial like the /w/. To produce this, both _____ and CONSONANT HARMONY are applied to the target word.

/m/

Similarly, when SMOKE /smok/ → [fok], the processes of CR and CONSONANT HARMONY have been applied. The /f/ again shares characteristics with the /s/ and the bilabial _____.

Deletion of Final Consonant	DFC	Consonant Harmony	CH	Backing to Velars	BK
Prevocalic Voicing	PVV	Postvocalic Devoicing	PVD	Epenthesis	EPEN
Syllable Reduction	SR	Vocalization	VOC	Metathesis	METATH
Velar Fronting	VF	Palatal Fronting	PF	Coalescence	COAL
Stopping of Fricatives and Affricates	ST	Gliding of Liquids	GL	Palatalization	PAL
Cluster Reduction	CR	Deaffrication	DEAFF	Denasalization	DENAS
Stridency Deletion	STR	Deletion of Initial Consonant	DIC	Idiosyncratic Processes	
		Glottal Replacement	GR		

Some investigators describe this process as COALESCENCE (see Section 19) because the phoneme that replaces the cluster retains characteristics of both original members of the cluster. Others view it as the application of a combination of the processes _____ and _____, where the CONSONANT HARMONY is applied prior to the deletion process.

CR, CONSONANT HARMONY

For example, SMOKE /smok/ → [fmok] by CONSONANT HARMONY (see Section 8), and then the cluster is reduced from /fm/ to [___].

[f]

This latter treatment has implications for remediation that COALESCENCE does not imply. If we consider that the cluster is altered prior to its reduction, then treatment would proceed in exactly the reverse. That is, first we would target _____ for suppression, and then CONSONANT HARMONY would be suppressed.

CR

Thus, if the child produced [fok] in the example just given, once CR had been suppressed, the child would produce [fmok]. Only after both members of the _____ were present would CONSONANT HARMONY be included as a target.

cluster

The inclusion of all members of a cluster (or two of three) adds greatly to overall intelligibility. Evidence is growing to suggest that young speakers produce CC forms very early, although they tend to substitute phonemes for one or both members of the _____.

cluster

For example, a three year old may produce the target word GREEN /grin/ as [dwin]. Here, the sound change

/p/ *PIG*	/n/ *NO*	/ʃ/ *SHE*	/w/ *WAGON*	/ɛ/ *BED*	/ʌ/ *GUN*	
/b/ *BED*	/ŋ/ *STING*	/ʒ/ *ROUGE*	/ʍ/ *WHEEL*	/æ/ *CAT*	/ə/ *ABOUT*	
/t/ *TOY*	/f/ *FOX*	/h/ *HAVE*	/ɚ/ *FINGER*	/a/ *GOT*	/aɪ/ *KITE*	
/d/ *DUCK*	/θ/ *THINK*	/tʃ/ *CHICKEN*	/ɝ/ *CHURCH*	/ɔ/ *TALK*	/ɔɪ/ *TOY*	
/k/ *KEEP*	/ð/ *THIS*	/dʒ/ *JUMPING*	/i/ *SEE*	/o/ *GOAT*	/aʊ/ *OUT*	
/g/ *GOAT*	/s/ *SEE*	/l/ *LAKE*	/ɪ/ *PIG*	/ʊ/ *BOOK*		
/m/ *ME*	/z/ *ZOO*	/j/ *YOU*	/eɪ, e/ *MAKE*	/u/ *GLUE*		

VF	/g/ → [d] has resulted from the application of _____.
CR	The sound change /r/ → [w] has resulted from the application of GLIDING. However, since both members of the cluster have been retained, the process of _____ has NOT been applied.
CR	Although the cluster is still altered (just as it would be through CR) the child who alters a cluster but retains the cluster is more intelligible than the child who applies the process of _____ to clusters.
deletion	In general, deletions affect intelligibility relatively more than substitutions or substitution processes, and CR is one of the _____ processes.
CR, DFC	When a cluster is deleted, it is assumed that CR occurred prior to the deletion. Thus, if the cluster /st/ is deleted from the word NEST /nɛst/, resulting in [nɛ], two processes have been applied: _____ and _____.
cluster	The implications for treatment are important. If the child deletes clusters pre- or post-vocalically, facilitate the production of a consonant to mark the cluster prior to facilitating the production of both members of the _____.
final	For example, if the child produces [nɛ] for /nest/, the first goal would be to facilitate the production of a word-_____ consonant. This would result in a CVC production rather than a CV production.

Deletion of Final Consonant	DFC	Consonant Harmony	CH	Backing to Velars	BK
Prevocalic Voicing	PVV	Postvocalic Devoicing	PVD	Epenthesis	EPEN
Syllable Reduction	SR	Vocalization	VOC	Metathesis	METATH
Velar Fronting	VF	Palatal Fronting	PF	Coalescence	COAL
Stopping of Fricatives and Affricates	ST	Gliding of Liquids	GL	Palatalization	PAL
Cluster Reduction	CR	Deaffrication	DEAFF	Denasalization	DENAS
Stridency Deletion	STR	Deletion of Initial Consonant	DIC	Idiosyncratic Processes	
		Glottal Replacement	GR		

The next step would be to facilitate the production of a CC word-finally. If the child then produced [nesk], we would recognize this as retention of the _____ even though the word was mispronounced.

cluster

Although both deletion of a cluster and deletion of a singleton can result from DFC, deletion of a cluster is regarded as a combination of two steps. First, the cluster is reduced to a singleton, as in DESK /dɛsk/ → [dɛs]. Second, the remaining singleton is deleted, as in /dɛs/ → [dɛ]. Thus, when a cluster is deleted, there are actually _____ steps involved.

two

This is called a *derivation*. When a child's production results from the application of more than one process, the _____ lists the intermediate steps (Edwards and Shriberg, 1983).

derivation

Derivations can play an important part in determining the order of processes to target in treatment. In the example just given, the _____ lists the intermediate steps as CLUSTER REDUCTION and then DELETION OF FINAL CONSONANT. In treatment, we would work backwards: target DFC first and then CLUSTER REDUCTION.

derivation

List the sound changes and their corresponding processes for the following words. Recall that when DFC has been applied, it is assumed that CR has also been applied.

/p/ *PIG*	/n/ *NO*	/ʃ/ *SHE*	/w/ *WAGON*	/ɛ/ *BED*	/ʌ/ *GUN*
/b/ *BED*	/ŋ/ *STING*	/ʒ/ *ROUGE*	/ʍ/ *WHEEL*	/æ/ *CAT*	/ə/ *ABOUT*
/t/ *TOY*	/f/ *FOX*	/h/ *HAVE*	/ɚ/ *FINGER*	/a/ *GOT*	/aɪ/ *KITE*
/d/ *DUCK*	/θ/ *THINK*	/tʃ/ *CHICKEN*	/ɝ/ *CHURCH*	/ɔ/ *TALK*	/ɔɪ/ *TOY*
/k/ *KEEP*	/ð/ *THIS*	/dʒ/ *JUMPING*	/i/ *SEE*	/ʊ/ *GOAT*	/aʊ/ *OUT*
/g/ *GOAT*	/s/ *SEE*	/l/ *LAKE*	/ɪ/ *PIG*	/ʊ/ *BOOK*	
/m/ *ME*	/z/ *ZOO*	/j/ *YOU*	/eɪ, e/ *MAKE*	/u/ *GLUE*	

		Adult Form	Child's Form		Sound Changes	Processes

/kl/ → [dl]
VF, PVV

CLASS /klæs/ → [dlæs]   /___/ → [___] _____

/st/ → [d]
CR, PVV

STOP /stap/ → [dap]   /___/ → [___] _____

/sl/ → [t]
CR, ST

SLEEP /slip/ → [tip]   /___/ → [___] _____

/mp/ → [ø]
CR, DFC

LAMP /læmp/ → [læ]   /___/ → [___] _____

/fl/ → [p]
ST, CR

FLAG /flæg/ → [pæg]   /___/ → [___] _____

/tr/ → [dr]
PVV

TREE /tri/ → [dri]   /___/ → [___] _____

/sk/ → [g]
CR, PVV

SKATE /sket/ → [get]   /___/ → [___] _____

/nt/ → [n]
CR

TENT /tɛnt/ → [tɛn]   /___/ → [___] _____

/sk/ → [st]
VF

DESK /dɛsk/ → [dɛst]   /___/ → [___] _____

/lk/ → [ø]
CR, DFC

MILK /mɪlk/ → [mɪ]   /___/ → [___] _____

Deletion of Final Consonant	DFC	Consonant Harmony	CH	Backing to Velars	BK
Prevocalic Voicing	PVV	Postvocalic Devoicing	PVD	Epenthesis	EPEN
Syllable Reduction	SR	Vocalization	VOC	Metathesis	METATH
Velar Fronting	VF	Palatal Fronting	PF	Coalescence	COAL
Stopping of Fricatives and Affricates	ST	Gliding of Liquids	GL	Palatalization	PAL
		Deaffrication	DEAFF	Denasalization	DENAS
Cluster Reduction	CR	Deletion of Initial Consonant	DIC	Idiosyncratic Processes	
Stridency Deletion	STR	Glottal Replacement	GR		

SUMMARY
Cluster Reduction

1. CR is a process that results in the deletion of one or two members of a two- or three-consonant cluster.
2. The entire cluster is included within the sound change notation.
3. The liquid within a cluster is often deleted.
4. The /s/ within an s-cluster (with the exception of s + liquid) is usually the deleted member.
5. Word-final fricative + stop clusters are commonly reduced to the fricative.
6. CR may be applied to word-final past tense morphemes.
7. Intervocalic clusters are considered herein to be clusters. Refer to Appendix IV.
8. When a cluster is deleted, it is assumed that CR occurred prior to the deletion.
9. A derivation outlines the intermediate steps between a target and production when more than one process has been applied.

/p/ *PIG*	/n/ *NO*	/ʃ/ *SHE*	/w/ *WAGON*	/ɛ/ *BED*	/ʌ/ *GUN*
/b/ *BED*	/ŋ/ *STING*	/ʒ/ *ROUGE*	/ʍ/ *WHEEL*	/æ/ *CAT*	/ə/ *ABOUT*
/t/ *TOY*	/f/ *FOX*	/h/ *HAVE*	/ɚ/ *FINGER*	/a/ *GOT*	/aɪ/ *KITE*
/d/ *DUCK*	/θ/ *THINK*	/tʃ/ *CHICKEN*	/ɝ/ *CHURCH*	/ɔ/ *TALK*	/ɔɪ/ *TOY*
/k/ *KEEP*	/ð/ *THIS*	/dʒ/ *JUMPING*	/i/ *SEE*	/o/ *GOAT*	/aʊ/ *OUT*
/g/ *GOAT*	/s/ *SEE*	/l/ *LAKE*	/ɪ/ *PIG*	/ʊ/ *BOOK*	
/m/ *ME*	/z/ *ZOO*	/j/ *YOU*	/eɪ, e/ *MAKE*	/u/ *GLUE*	

SECTION 7. STRIDENCY DELETION

STRIDENCY DELETION (STR) is a process that results from the replacement of a strident consonant with a non-strident consonant. SUN /sʌn/ → [tʌn] is an example of _____.

STRIDENCY DELETION, or STR

Another example of STR would be FINGER /fɪŋgɚ/ → [pɪŋgɚ], where the /f/ becomes [____].

[p]

The English consonants that are considered to be strident (Edwards and Shriberg, 1983, p. 34) are /s/, /z/, /ʃ/, /ʒ/, /tʃ/, /dʒ/, /f/, and /v/. These consonants are either _____ or affricates.

fricatives

They are strident because of the aperiodic acoustic energy produced during their articulation. Of these, /s/ and /z/ are the most _____.

strident

/f/ and /v/ are the least _____. The amount of acoustic energy present during their production falls between that of /ʃ/ and /ʒ/ and /θ/ and /ð/.

strident

/θ/ and /ð/ are NOT stridents because of the relatively lower energy level acoustically and because children appear to alter them differently than other fricatives and affricates. When /θ/ and /ð/ are stopped, deleted, or replaced by other consonants, the process of _____ has *not* been applied.

STR

STR may also result from the deletion of a strident consonant. BUS /bʌs/ → [bʌ] is an example of the application of _____, as well as DFC.

STR

Deletion of Final Consonant	DFC	Consonant Harmony	CH	Backing to Velars	BK
Prevocalic Voicing	PVV	Postvocalic Devoicing	PVD	Epenthesis	EPEN
Syllable Reduction	SR	Vocalization	VOC	Metathesis	METATH
Velar Fronting	VF	Palatal Fronting	PF	Coalescence	COAL
Stopping of Fricatives and Affricates	ST	Gliding of Liquids	GL	Palatalization	PAL
Cluster Reduction	CR	Deaffrication	DEAFF	Denasalization	DENAS
Stridency Deletion	STR	Deletion of Initial Consonant	DIC	Idiosyncratic Processes	
		Glottal Replacement	GR		

Stridency may be deleted through either the deletion of an entire consonant ([ʌn]) or the substitution of a non-_____ consonant ([tʌn]).

strident

STR occurs mainly as a result of the application of another process. For example, FROG /frɔg] as a result of the application of _____ and STR.

ST

/f/ will become non-strident only if it is stopped ([p]), or deleted, or replaced by a non-strident consonant. It is not possible to delete the _____ from /f/ without also doing one of these three things.

stridency

Write YES beside each of the following words that contains a strident consonant phoneme:

FIGHT	/faɪt/	_____	YES, /f/
SOAP	/sop/	_____	YES, /s/
THINK	/θɪŋk/	_____	NO, /θ/ is not strident.
ZOO	/zu/	_____	YES, /z/
WATCH	/watʃ/	_____	YES, /tʃ/
THIS	/ðɪs/	_____	YES, /s/; /ð/ is not strident.
NOTHING	/nʌθɪŋ/	_____	NO, /θ/ is not strident.

/p/ *PIG*	/n/ *NO*	/ʃ/ *SHE*	/w/ *WAGON*	/ɛ/ *BED*	/ʌ/ *GUN*
/b/ *BED*	/ŋ/ *STING*	/ʒ/ *ROUGE*	/ʍ/ *WHEEL*	/æ/ *CAT*	/ə/ *ABOUT*
/t/ *TOY*	/f/ *FOX*	/h/ *HAVE*	/ɚ/ *FINGER*	/a/ *GOT*	/aɪ/ *KITE*
/d/ *DUCK*	/θ/ *THINK*	/tʃ/ *CHICKEN*	/ɝ/ *CHURCH*	/ɔ/ *TALK*	/ɔɪ/ *TOY*
/k/ *KEEP*	/ð/ *THIS*	/dʒ/ *JUMPING*	/i/ *SEE*	/o/ *GOAT*	/aʊ/ *OUT*
/g/ *GOAT*	/s/ *SEE*	/l/ *LAKE*	/ɪ/ *PIG*	/ʊ/ *BOOK*	
/m/ *ME*	/z/ *ZOO*	/j/ *YOU*	/eɪ, e/ *MAKE*	/u/ *GLUE*	

YES, /f/; /ð/ is not strident.	FEATHER	/fɛðɚ/	_____
NO	DRINK	/drɪŋk/	_____
YES, /z/	TOYS	/tɔɪz/	_____

There are 10 words in the list just given. _____ of them contain strident phonemes. Therefore, _____ of them provide the opportunity for STR to be applied.

seven, seven

If all stridents were deleted, how would the child's productions look?

		Adult Form		Child's Form
[aɪt]	FIGHT	/faɪt/	→ [	_____]
[op]	SOAP	/sop/	→ [	_____]
[θɪŋk], /θ/ is not a strident!	THINK	/θɪŋk/	→ [	_____]
[u]	ZOO	/zu/	→ [	_____]
[wa]	WATCH	/watʃ/	→ [	_____]
[ðɪ], /ð/ is not a strident!	THIS	/ðɪs/	→ [	_____]
[nʌθɪŋ], /θ/ is not a strident.	NOTHING	/nʌθɪŋ/	→ [	_____]

Deletion of Final Consonant	DFC	Consonant Harmony	CH	Backing to Velars	BK
Prevocalic Voicing	PVV	Postvocalic Devoicing	PVD	Epenthesis	EPEN
Syllable Reduction	SR	Vocalization	VOC	Metathesis	METATH
Velar Fronting	VF	Palatal Fronting	PF	Coalescence	COAL
Stopping of Fricatives and Affricates	ST	Gliding of Liquids	GL	Palatalization	PAL
		Deaffrication	DEAFF	Denasalization	DENAS
Cluster Reduction	CR	Deletion of Initial Consonant	DIC	Idiosyncratic Processes	
Stridency Deletion	STR	Glottal Replacement	GR		

FEATHER   /fɛðɚ/   → [_____]

[ɛðɚ], /ð/ is not a strident.

DRINK   /drɪŋk/   → [_____]

[drɪŋk], there are no stridents.

TOYS   /tɔɪz/   → [_____]

[tɔɪ]

Note that with a plural (such as TOYS), the deletion of the plural marker can result from the application of _____ and _____.

DFC, STR

Since the child has deleted strident consonants from all seven words containing them, the productivity of STR is _____ out of _____, or _____%.

seven, seven, 100

Using the same list of words, a second child stops (ST) all prevocalic stridents. Give the resulting productions for each words:

	Adult Form	Child's Form
FIGHT	/faɪt/	→ [_____]

[paɪt]

| SOAP | /sop/ | → [_____] |

[top]

| THINK | /θɪŋk/ | → [_____] |

[θɪŋk], /θ/ is not a strident.

| ZOO | /zu/ | → [_____] |

[du]

| WATCH | /watʃ/ | → [_____] |

[watʃ]

/p/ PIG	/n/ NO	/ʃ/ SHE	/w/ WAGON	/ɛ/ BED	/ʌ/ GUN
/b/ BED	/ŋ/ STING	/ʒ/ ROUGE	/ʍ/ WHEEL	/æ/ CAT	/ə/ ABOUT
/t/ TOY	/f/ FOX	/h/ HAVE	/ɚ/ FINGER	/a/ GOT	/aɪ/ KITE
/d/ DUCK	/θ/ THINK	/tʃ/ CHICKEN	/ɝ/ CHURCH	/ɔ/ TALK	/ɔɪ/ TOY
/k/ KEEP	/ð/ THIS	/dʒ/ JUMPING	/i/ SEE	/o/ GOAT	/aʊ/ OUT
/g/ GOAT	/s/ SEE	/l/ LAKE	/ɪ/ PIG	/ʊ/ BOOK	
/m/ ME	/z/ ZOO	/j/ YOU	/eɪ, e/ MAKE	/u/ GLUE	

[ðɪs], /ð/ is not a strident.

THIS   /ðɪs/   → [_____]

[drɪŋk], there are no stridents.

DRINK   /drɪŋk/   → [_____]

[tɔɪz]

TOYS   /tɔɪz/   → [_____]

three

How many previously strident phonemes have become non-strident because of the application of ST? _____

A third child stops all prevocalic consonants (ST) and deletes all postvocalic consonants (DFC). Give the resulting productions for each of the target words.

		Adult Form	*Child's Form*
[paɪ]	FIGHT	/faɪt/	→ [_____]
[to]	SOAP	/sop/	→ [_____]
[tɪ]	THINK	/θɪŋk/	→ [_____]
[du]	ZOO	/zu/	→ [_____]
[wa]	WATCH	/watʃ/	→ [_____]
[dɪ]	THIS	/ðɪs/	→ [_____]

Deletion of Final Consonant	DFC	Consonant Harmony	CH	Backing to Velars	BK
Prevocalic Voicing	PVV	Postvocalic Devoicing	PVD	Epenthesis	EPEN
Syllable Reduction	SR	Vocalization	VOC	Metathesis	METATH
Velar Fronting	VF	Palatal Fronting	PF	Coalescence	COAL
Stopping of Fricatives and Affricates	ST	Gliding of Liquids	GL	Palatalization	PAL
Cluster Reduction	CR	Deaffrication	DEAFF	Denasalization	DENAS
Stridency Deletion	STR	Deletion of Initial Consonant	DIC	Idiosyncratic Processes	
		Glottal Replacement	GR		

NOTHING	/nʌθɪŋ/	→ [＿＿＿]		[nʌθɪ]
FEATHER	/fɛðɚ/	→ [＿＿＿]		[pɛðə]
DRINK	/drɪŋk/	→ [＿＿＿]		[drɪ]
TOYS	/tɔɪz/	→ [＿＿＿]		[tɔɪ]

There are now ＿＿＿＿＿ phonemes that were previously strident and are no longer strident through deletion or another sound change.

seven

Notice that when DFC is applied to the word DRINK /drɪŋk/, which contains a word-final *cluster*, the entire ＿＿＿＿＿ is deleted.

cluster

Thus, both the /ŋ/ and the /k/ are deleted, and the process of ＿＿＿＿＿ has been applied in addition to DFC.

CR

List the sound changes for the following productions. IN ALL CASES, STR has been applied.

	Adult Form		Child's Form	Sound Change	
BRIDGE	/brɪdʒ/	→	[brɪd]	/＿＿/ → [＿＿]	/dʒ/ → [d]
BRUSH	/brʌʃ/	→	[brʌ]	/＿＿/ → [＿＿]	/ʃ/ → [ø]
CALF	/kæf/	→	[kæp]	/＿＿/ → [＿＿]	/f/ → [p]
CHICKEN	/tʃɪkɪn/	→	[dɪkɪn]	/＿＿/ → [＿＿]	/tʃ/ → [d]
GAS	/gæs/	→	[gæθ]	/＿＿/ → [＿＿]	/s/ → [θ]

/p/ *PIG*	/n/ *NO*	/ʃ/ *SHE*	/w/ *WAGON*	/ɛ/ *BED*	/ʌ/ *GUN*
/b/ *BED*	/ŋ/ *STING*	/ʒ/ *ROUGE*	/ʍ/ *WHEEL*	/æ/ *CAT*	/ə/ *ABOUT*
/t/ *TOY*	/f/ *FOX*	/h/ *HAVE*	/ɚ/ *FINGER*	/a/ *GOT*	/aɪ/ *KITE*
/d/ *DUCK*	/θ/ *THINK*	/tʃ/ *CHICKEN*	/ɝ/ *CHURCH*	/ɔ/ *TALK*	/ɔɪ/ *TOY*
/k/ *KEEP*	/ð/ *THIS*	/dʒ/ *JUMPING*	/i/ *SEE*	/o/ *GOAT*	/aʊ/ *OUT*
/g/ *GOAT*	/s/ *SEE*	/l/ *LAKE*	/ɪ/ *PIG*	/ʊ/ *BOOK*	
/m/ *ME*	/z/ *ZOO*	/j/ *YOU*	/eɪ, e/ *MAKE*	/u/ *GLUE*	

/skr/ → [kr]	ICE CREAM /aɪskrim/ → [aɪkrim]	/___/ → [___]
/f/ → [θ]	FEATHER /fɛðɚ/ → [θɛðɚ]	/___/ → [___]
/ʃ/ → [θ]	FISH /fɪʃ/ → [fɪθ]	/___/ → [___]
/z/ → [ø]	NOSE /noz/ → [no]	/___/ → [___]
/v/ → [b]	VANILLA /vənɪlə/ → [bənɪlə]	/___/ → [___]

It is apparent that _____ will apply whenever
STR DFC is applied to strident fricatives and affricates.

STR will generally apply when ST is applied to
strident fricatives and affricates. However, when ST is
applied to a fricative and it results in the production of an
affricate (as in SOAP /sop/ → [tʃop]), then _____
STR has NOT been applied.

/f/, /v/, /s/, /z/, Name the eight strident English consonants: /___/,
/ʃ/, /ʒ/, /tʃ/, /dʒ/ /___/, /___/, /___/, /___/, /___/, /___/, /___/

Indicate whether each of the following altered forms
has resulted from the application of STR (other processes
may also have been applied):

		Adult Form	Child's Form	YES/NO
YES, /tʃ/ → [t]	CHAIR	/tʃɛr/	→ [tɛr]	_____
YES, /v/ → [b]	OVER	/ovɚ/	→ [obɚ]	_____
NO, /θ/ is not strident.	NOTHING	/nʌθɪŋ/	→ [nʌtɪŋ]	_____

Deletion of Final Consonant	DFC	Consonant Harmony	CH	Backing to Velars	BK
Prevocalic Voicing	PVV	Postvocalic Devoicing	PVD	Epenthesis	EPEN
Syllable Reduction	SR	Vocalization	VOC	Metathesis	METATH
Velar Fronting	VF	Palatal Fronting	PF	Coalescence	COAL
Stopping of Fricatives and Affricates	ST	Gliding of Liquids	GL	Palatalization	PAL
Cluster Reduction	CR	Deaffrication	DEAFF	Denasalization	DENAS
Stridency Deletion	STR	Deletion of Initial Consonant	DIC	Idiosyncratic Processes	
		Glottal Replacement	GR		

SAY	/seɪ/	→ [deɪ]	_____	YES, /s/ → [d]
BUS	/bʌs/	→ [bʌtʃ]	_____	NO, /tʃ/ is also strident.
SHUT	/ʃʌt/	→ [tʌt]	_____	YES, /ʃ/ → [t]
SHOE	/ʃu/	→ [su]	_____	NO, /s/ is also strident.
THIS	/ðɪs/	→ [dɪs]	_____	NO, /ð/ is not strident.
TELEPHONE	/tɛləfon/	→ [tɛləpon]	_____	YES, /f/ → [p]
WISH	/wɪʃ/	→ [wɪtʃ]	_____	NO, /tʃ/ is also strident.

Recall that when a fricative becomes an affricate, the process of _____ does not apply because the affricates are also strident.

STR

For example, when WASH /waʃ/ → [watʃ], the /ʃ/ → [tʃ] and the _____ is retained.

stridency

Similarly, when SUN /sʌn/ → [tsʌn], the stridency is retained. [ts] is a strident alveolar affricate here and not the addition of a word-initial ____. In any case, the child's production contains a strident to mark the word-initial strident /s/.

[t]

The consonant /ʃ/ is sometimes fronted to /s/ by young children. This process is called PALATAL FRONTING and will be covered in Section 11. The sound

/p/ PIG	/n/ NO	/ʃ/ SHE	/w/ WAGON	/ɛ/ BED	/ʌ/ GUN
/b/ BED	/ŋ/ STING	/ʒ/ ROUGE	/ʍ/ WHEEL	/æ/ CAT	/ə/ ABOUT
/t/ TOY	/f/ FOX	/h/ HAVE	/ɚ/ FINGER	/a/ GOT	/aɪ/ KITE
/d/ DUCK	/θ/ THINK	/tʃ/ CHICKEN	/ɝ/ CHURCH	/ɔ/ TALK	/ɔɪ/ TOY
/k/ KEEP	/ð/ THIS	/dʒ/ JUMPING	/i/ SEE	/o/ GOAT	/aʊ/ OUT
/g/ GOAT	/s/ SEE	/l/ LAKE	/ɪ/ PIG	/ʊ/ BOOK	
/m/ ME	/z/ ZOO	/j/ YOU	/eɪ, e/ MAKE	/u/ GLUE	

PALATAL FRONTING

change /tʃ/ → [ts], from the palatal affricate to the alveolar affricate, is an example of _____.

affricates.

For now, it is sufficient to recognize that the /ts/ and /tʃ/ are both _____.

The process of CR, CLUSTER REDUCTION, may result in STR. For example, when STOP /stap/ → [tap], the child's production no longer contains the strident consonant, /___/.

/s/

/st/ → [t]

The corresponding sound change is /___/ → [___].

clusters

Recall that clusters are always recorded as _____ in sound change notation. Thus, the /s/ is not considered as a singleton.

Write YES or NO beside each of the following to indicate whether STR has been applied:

	Adult Form		Child's Form	YES/NO
YES, /ft/ → [pt]	AFTER	/æftɚ/	→ [æptɚ]	_____
YES, /ns/ → [nθ]	ANSWER	/ænsɚ/	→ [ænθɚ]	_____
YES, /ks/ → [k]	BOX	/baks/	→ [bak]	_____
NO, /sm/ → [sm]	CHRISTMAS	/krɪsməs/	→ [kɪsməs]	_____
NO, /zp/ → [fp]	NEWSPAPER	/nuzpepɚ/	→ [nufpepɚ]	_____
YES, /skr/ → [gr]	SCRATCH	/skrætʃ/	→ [grætʃ]	_____

Deletion of Final Consonant	DFC	Consonant Harmony	CH	Backing to Velars	BK
Prevocalic Voicing	PVV	Postvocalic Devoicing	PVD	Epenthesis	EPEN
Syllable Reduction	SR	Vocalization	VOC	Metathesis	METATH
Velar Fronting	VF	Palatal Fronting	PF	Coalescence	COAL
Stopping of Fricatives and Affricates	ST	Gliding of Liquids	GL	Palatalization	PAL
Cluster Reduction	CR	Deaffrication	DEAFF	Denasalization	DENAS
Stridency Deletion	STR	Deletion of Initial Consonant	DIC	Idiosyncratic Processes	
		Glottal Replacement	GR		

SHRINK /ʃrɪŋk/ → [srɪŋk] _____ NO, /ʃr/ → [sr]

SLEEP /slip/ → [wip] _____ YES, /sl/ → [w]

SMOKE /smok/ → [fok] _____ NO, /sm/ → [f]

SPIDER /spaɪdɚ/ → [baɪdɚ] _____ YES, /sp/ → [b]

STR will accompany _____ whenever the altered production does not include a strident consonant to replace one or more members of the affected cluster.

CR

There are thus far four processes that, when applied to strident consonants, may also result in STR. They are _____ _____ _____ _____

DFC, ST, CR, SR

/p/ PIG	/n/ NO	/ʃ/ SHE	/w/ WAGON	/ɛ/ BED	/ʌ/ GUN
/b/ BED	/ŋ/ STING	/ʒ/ ROUGE	/ʍ/ WHEEL	/æ/ CAT	/ə/ ABOUT
/t/ TOY	/f/ FOX	/h/ HAVE	/ɚ/ FINGER	/a/ GOT	/aɪ/ KITE
/d/ DUCK	/θ/ THINK	/tʃ/ CHICKEN	/ɝ/ CHURCH	/ɔ/ TALK	/ɔɪ/ TOY
/k/ KEEP	/ð/ THIS	/dʒ/ JUMPING	/i/ SEE	/o/ GOAT	/aʊ/ OUT
/g/ GOAT	/s/ SEE	/l/ LAKE	/ɪ/ PIG	/ʊ/ BOOK	
/m/ ME	/z/ ZOO	/j/ YOU	/eɪ, e/ MAKE	/u/ GLUE	

SUMMARY
Stridency Deletion

1. STR is a process that results from the replacement of a strident consonant with a non-strident consonant or the deletion of a strident consonant.
2. Stridency is the aperiodic acoustic energy produced during the articulation of /s/, /z/, /ʃ/, /ʒ/, /tʃ/, /dʒ/, /f/, and /v/.
3. /θ/ and /ð/ are not strident because of the relatively lower energy level acoustically and because children appear to alter them differently than other fricatives and affricates.
4. STR cannot occur by itself.
5. The processes that may result in STR include DFC, ST, CR, and SR.

Deletion of Final Consonant	DFC	Consonant Harmony	CH	Backing to Velars	BK
Prevocalic Voicing	PVV	Postvocalic Devoicing	PVD	Epenthesis	EPEN
Syllable Reduction	SR	Vocalization	VOC	Metathesis	METATH
Velar Fronting	VF	Palatal Fronting	PF	Coalescence	COAL
Stopping of Fricatives and Affricates	ST	Gliding of Liquids	GL	Palatalization	PAL
Cluster Reduction	CR	Deaffrication	DEAFF	Denasalization	DENAS
Stridency Deletion	STR	Deletion of Initial Consonant	DIC	Idiosyncratic Processes	
		Glottal Replacement	GR		

SECTION 8. CONSONANT HARMONY

CONSONANT HARMONY (CH) is a process that results in one consonant becoming more like another within a word. One consonant seems to "pull" the other in its direction. DOG /dɔg/ → [gɔg] is an example of _____.

> CONSONANT HARMONY, or CH

The abbreviation for CONSONANT HARMONY is _____.

> CH

Another example of CH would be KNIFE /naɪf/ → [naɪs], where the alveolar /n/ has "_____" the /f/ in its direction, resulting in the alveolar [s].

> pulled

The labiodental /f/ was pulled toward the alveolar place of articulation through the application of _____.

> CH

Similarly, TELEPHONE /tɛləfon/ may become [tɛləson] because the alveolar consonants have "_____" the /f/ in their direction.

> pulled

This process is called _____ because one consonant has become quite like another within the same word.

> CONSONANT HARMONY

CONSONANT HARMONY involves a change in PLACE of articulation. Although voicing and manner may be affected, place of articulation is the characteristic considered in the process _____ (Ingram, 1981).

> CH

/p/ *PIG*	/n/ *NO*	/ʃ/ *SHE*	/w/ *WAGON*	/ɛ/ *BED*	/ʌ/ *GUN*
/b/ *BED*	/ŋ/ *STING*	/ʒ/ *ROUGE*	/ʍ/ *WHEEL*	/æ/ *CAT*	/ə/ *ABOUT*
/t/ *TOY*	/f/ *FOX*	/h/ *HAVE*	/ɚ/ *FINGER*	/a/ *GOT*	/aɪ/ *KITE*
/d/ *DUCK*	/θ/ *THINK*	/tʃ/ *CHICKEN*	/ɝ/ *CHURCH*	/ɔ/ *TALK*	/ɔɪ/ *TOY*
/k/ *KEEP*	/ð/ *THIS*	/dʒ/ *JUMPING*	/i/ *SEE*	/o/ *GOAT*	/aʊ/ *OUT*
/g/ *GOAT*	/s/ *SEE*	/l/ *LAKE*	/ɪ/ *PIG*	/ʊ/ *BOOK*	
/m/ *ME*	/z/ *ZOO*	/j/ *YOU*	/eɪ, e/ *MAKE*	/u/ *GLUE*	

CH

Differences in manner and voicing can often be attributed to the application of additional processes. For example, if CAP /kæp/ → [bæp], the process of PVV has also been applied to the word in addition to CONSONANT HARMONY. _____ has resulted in the /k/ moving to the bilabial [p], and PVV has resulted in the addition of voicing.

CH

_____ interferes with intelligibility by preventing easy prediction by the listener. For example, the child may attempt to say YES /jɛs/, but produce [dɛs]. In general, the listener would have less difficulty comprehending [ɛs] or [jɛ] or [jɛθ] than [dɛs].

intelligibility

As with deletion processes, CH interferes extensively with _____.

CH

The young child or phonologically disordered child may change CHICKEN /tʃɪkɪn/ → [tʃɪtʃɪn] or [kɪkɪn] through the application of _____.

[kʌk], [pʌp]

Similarly, ZIPPER /zɪpɚ/ → [bɪpɚ] or [zɪdɚ]. The child may also change CUP /kʌp/ → [_____] or [_____] through CH.

pulled

In each case, one consonant has _____ another toward its place of articulation.

[t]

When /k/ is pulled toward the alveolar ridge, it becomes [___].

[p]

When /k/ is pulled toward a bilabial, it becomes [___].

Deletion of Final Consonant	DFC	Consonant Harmony	CH	Backing to Velars	BK
Prevocalic Voicing	PVV	Postvocalic Devoicing	PVD	Epenthesis	EPEN
Syllable Reduction	SR	Vocalization	VOC	Metathesis	METATH
Velar Fronting	VF	Palatal Fronting	PF	Coalescence	COAL
Stopping of Fricatives and Affricates	ST	Gliding of Liquids	GL	Palatalization	PAL
Cluster Reduction	CR	Deaffrication	DEAFF	Denasalization	DENAS
Stridency Deletion	STR	Deletion of Initial Consonant	DIC	Idiosyncratic Processes	
		Glottal Replacement	GR		

Additional processes may contribute to the sound change. For example, when /k/ is pulled toward the alveolar /s/, it may become /t/ or /s/ or /d/ or /z/ because other processes in addition to _____ have been applied.

CH

When /k/ → [d], in the word KISS /kɪs/, _____ has been applied, drawing the /k/ to the alveolar ridge. If this were the only process applied, then the production would be [tɪs].

CH

The other process that has been applied is _____. When this is added to CH, the /k/ → /t/ → [d].

PVV

When a consonant has been pulled in the direction of another with no additional processes being applied, the production will be more similar to the attempted word. For example, [tɪs] is more similar to /kɪs/ than is [dɪs], to which another _____ has been applied.

process

Another example of CH is FEATHER /fɛðɚ/ → [θɛðɚ], where the /ð/ pulled the /f/ in its direction. Similarly, /fɛðɚ/ might become [fɛvɚ] with the application of _____.

CH

For each of the following words, write the sound change that corresponds with the child's production. In each case, CH has been applied to the target word.

	Adult Form	*Child's Form*	*Sound Change*	
CUP	/kʌp/	→ [kʌk]	/___/ → [___]	/p/ → [k]

/p/ PIG	/n/ NO	/ʃ/ SHE	/w/ WAGON	/ɛ/ BED	/ʌ/ GUN
/b/ BED	/ŋ/ STING	/ʒ/ ROUGE	/ʍ/ WHEEL	/æ/ CAT	/ə/ ABOUT
/t/ TOY	/f/ FOX	/h/ HAVE	/ɚ/ FINGER	/a/ GOT	/aɪ/ KITE
/d/ DUCK	/θ/ THINK	/tʃ/ CHICKEN	/ɝ/ CHURCH	/ɔ/ TALK	/ɔɪ/ TOY
/k/ KEEP	/ð/ THIS	/dʒ/ JUMPING	/i/ SEE	/o/ GOAT	/aʊ/ OUT
/g/ GOAT	/s/ SEE	/l/ LAKE	/ɪ/ PIG	/ʊ/ BOOK	
/m/ ME	/z/ ZOO	/j/ YOU	/eɪ, e/ MAKE	/u/ GLUE	

/k/ → [t]	KISS	/kɪs/	→ [tɪs]	/___/ → [___]
/f/ → [ʃ]	FISH	/fɪʃ/	→ [ʃɪʃ]	/___/ → [___]
/z/ → [ʒ]	SHOES	/ʃuz/	→ [ʃuʒ]	/___/ → [___]
/f/ → [s]	KNIFE	/naɪf/	→ [naɪs]	/___/ → [___]
/p/ → [t]	SOAP	/sop/	→ [sot]	/___/ → [___]
/f/ → [s]	FIGHT	/faɪt/	→ [saɪt]	/___/ → [___]
/ð/ → [z]	THIS	/ðɪs/	→ [zɪs]	/___/ → [___]
/θ/ → [s]	NOTHING	/nʌθɪŋ/	→ [nʌsɪŋ]	/___/ → [___]
/t/ → [p]	TELEPHONE	/tɛləfon/	→ [pɛləfon]	/___/ → [___]

PROGRESSIVE ASSIMILATION

Another name that has been used for CONSONANT HARMONY is ASSIMILATION. The principle is similar; one consonant has been influenced by another in the word. Sometimes an early consonant in the word will affect a later consonant. This is called PROGRESSIVE ASSIMILATION (Shriberg and Kwiatkowski, 1980). For example, CUP /kʌp/ → [kʌk] would result from the application of _____.

REGRESSIVE ASSIMILATION

Or, a later consonant could affect an earlier-occurring consonant within a word. This is called REGRESSIVE ASSIMILATION. For example, CUP /kʌp/ → [pʌp] would be an example of _____.

Type of assimilation has also been categorized by place of articulation. ASSIMILATION has been described

Deletion of Final Consonant	DFC	Consonant Harmony	CH	Backing to Velars	BK
Prevocalic Voicing	PVV	Postvocalic Devoicing	PVD	Epenthesis	EPEN
Syllable Reduction	SR	Vocalization	VOC	Metathesis	METATH
Velar Fronting	VF	Palatal Fronting	PF	Coalescence	COAL
Stopping of Fricatives and Affricates	ST	Gliding of Liquids	GL	Palatalization	PAL
Cluster Reduction	CR	Deaffrication	DEAFF	Denasalization	DENAS
Stridency Deletion	STR	Deletion of Initial Consonant	DIC	Idiosyncratic Processes	
		Glottal Replacement	GR		

as either labial, alveolar, or velar (Weiner, 1979). For example, CUP /kʌp/ → [kʌk] would be an example of _____ ASSIMILATION.

VELAR

If CUP /kʌp/ → [pʌp], this would be an example of _____ ASSIMILATION.

LABIAL

If DRAGON /drægən/ → [grægən], this would be an example of VELAR ASSIMILATION. If it became [drædən], it would be an example of _____ ASSIMILATION.

ALVEOLAR

CONSONANT HARMONY has been introduced as a process that affects primarily PLACE of articulation. Some would include other types of assimilation within this category. For example, when KISS /kɪs/ → [sɪs], not only has the /k/ been pulled toward the alveolar /s/, but it has also taken on the characteristics of continuancy and stridency. This is another type of _____.

ASSIMILATION, or CONSONANT HARMONY

When completing a phonological analysis that has been developed by someone other than yourself, it is important to determine from the manual the breadth of the process that includes ASSIMILATION, or _____.

CONSONANT HARMONY

For the following list of words, give the productions that would result from both alveolar and velar assimilation. These will be examples of the application of CONSONANT HARMONY as just described, and should not include changes other than in place of articulation. The first example has been done for you.

/p/ *PIG*	/n/ *NO*	/ʃ/ *SHE*	/w/ *WAGON*	/ɛ/ *BED*	/ʌ/ *GUN*
/b/ *BED*	/ŋ/ *STING*	/ʒ/ *ROUGE*	/ʍ/ *WHEEL*	/æ/ *CAT*	/ə/ *ABOUT*
/t/ *TOY*	/f/ *FOX*	/h/ *HAVE*	/ɚ/ *FINGER*	/a/ *GOT*	/aɪ/ *KITE*
/d/ *DUCK*	/θ/ *THINK*	/tʃ/ *CHICKEN*	/ɝ/ *CHURCH*	/ɔ/ *TALK*	/ɔɪ/ *TOY*
/k/ *KEEP*	/ð/ *THIS*	/dʒ/ *JUMPING*	/i/ *SEE*	/o/ *GOAT*	/aʊ/ *OUT*
/g/ *GOAT*	/s/ *SEE*	/l/ *LAKE*	/ɪ/ *PIG*	/ʊ/ *BOOK*	
/m/ *ME*	/z/ *ZOO*	/j/ *YOU*	/eɪ, e/ *MAKE*	/u/ *GLUE*	

		Adult Form		Alveolar Assimilation	Velar Assimilation
	DUCK	/dʌk/	→	[dʌt]	[gʌk]
[tet], [kek]	TAKE	/tek/	→	[_____]	[_____]
[tæd], [kæg]	TAG	/tæg/	→	[_____]	[_____]
[dɔn], [gɔŋ]	GONE	/gɔn/	→	[_____]	[_____]
[tʌn], [kʌŋ]	TONGUE	/tʌŋ/	→	[_____]	[_____]
[tot], [kok]	COAT	/kot/	→	[_____]	[_____]
[dot], [gok]	GOAT	/got/	→	[_____]	[_____]
[taɪnd], [kaɪŋg]	KIND	/kaɪnd/	→	[_____]	[_____]
[tɪtn̩], [kɪtŋ̩]	KITTEN	/kɪtn̩/	→	[_____]	[_____]
[tæt], [kæk]	CAT	/kæt/	→	[_____]	[_____]

alveolars

CH

From the words listed above, all of the productions in the ALVEOLAR ASSIMILATION column could have resulted from the application of VF. That is, all of the words in that column have velars that have been fronted to _____.

It is important to determine whether a given child is primarily applying VF to all words containing velars, or whether only some velars become alveolar as a result of applying the process _____.

Deletion of Final Consonant	DFC	Consonant Harmony	CH	Backing to Velars	BK
Prevocalic Voicing	PVV	Postvocalic Devoicing	PVD	Epenthesis	EPEN
Syllable Reduction	SR	Vocalization	VOC	Metathesis	METATH
Velar Fronting	VF	Palatal Fronting	PF	Coalescence	COAL
Stopping of Fricatives and Affricates	ST	Gliding of Liquids	GL	Palatalization	PAL
Cluster Reduction	CR	Deaffrication	DEAFF	Denasalization	DENAS
Stridency Deletion	STR	Deletion of Initial Consonant	DIC	Idiosyncratic Processes	
		Glottal Replacement	GR		

One method of making this determination is to examine the child's speech sample for the presence of target words containing velars. If the child produces velars in some words but not in others, then it is probable that the child is applying _____.

CH

The following productions from one child illustrate this point.

	Adult Form	*Child's Form*
DUCK	/dʌk/	→ [dʌt]
GREEN	/grin/	→ [drin]
GO	/go/	→ [do]
KEY	/ki/	→ [ti]
FROG	/frɔg/	→ [frɔd]
BUG	/bʌg/	→ [bʌd]
PICK	/pɪk/	→ [pɪt]

In each of these words, regardless of the presence or absence of an alveolar within the word, all velars are fronted to /t/ or /d/. It is most probable that the process of _____ accounts for these altered productions.

VF

A second child, producing the same seven words, has a different pattern of velar fronting:

/p/ *PIG*	/n/ *NO*	/ʃ/ *SHE*	/w/ *WAGON*	/ɛ/ *BED*	/ʌ/ *GUN*
/b/ *BED*	/ŋ/ *STING*	/ʒ/ *ROUGE*	/ʍ/ *WHEEL*	/æ/ *CAT*	/ə/ *ABOUT*
/t/ *TOY*	/f/ *FOX*	/h/ *HAVE*	/ɚ/ *FINGER*	/a/ *GOT*	/aɪ/ *KITE*
/d/ *DUCK*	/θ/ *THINK*	/tʃ/ *CHICKEN*	/ɝ/ *CHURCH*	/ɔ/ *TALK*	/ɔɪ/ *TOY*
/k/ *KEEP*	/ð/ *THIS*	/dʒ/ *JUMPING*	/i/ *SEE*	/o/ *GOAT*	/aʊ/ *OUT*
/g/ *GOAT*	/s/ *SEE*	/l/ *LAKE*	/ɪ/ *PIG*	/ʊ/ *BOOK*	
/m/ *ME*	/z/ *ZOO*	/j/ *YOU*	/eɪ, e/ *MAKE*	/u/ *GLUE*	

	Adult Form	Child's Form
DUCK	/dʌk/	→ [dʌt]
GREEN	/grin/	→ [drin]
GO	/go/	→ [go]
KEY	/ki/	→ [ki]
FROG	/frɔg/	→ [frɔg]
BUG	/bʌg/	→ [bʌg]
PICK	/pɪk/	→ [pɪk]

CH

This child "fronts" velars only when there is an alveolar consonant within the word. Therefore, it is probable that the process of _____ accounts for the altered forms.

pulls

That is, the only time that /k/ and /g/ (and possibly /ŋ/) become alveolar is when there is an alveolar consonant within the word that _____ the velar in its direction.

CONSONANT HARMONY

VELAR FRONTING will tend to be applied across contexts. _____ (between velars and alveolars) will tend to be applied only when both places of articulation are represented in the target word.

Deletion of Final Consonant	DFC	Consonant Harmony	CH	Backing to Velars	BK
Prevocalic Voicing	PVV	Postvocalic Devoicing	PVD	Epenthesis	EPEN
Syllable Reduction	SR	Vocalization	VOC	Metathesis	METATH
Velar Fronting	VF	Palatal Fronting	PF	Coalescence	COAL
Stopping of Fricatives and Affricates	ST	Gliding of Liquids	GL	Palatalization	PAL
Cluster Reduction	CR	Deaffrication	DEAFF	Denasalization	DENAS
Stridency Deletion	STR	Deletion of Initial Consonant	DIC	Idiosyncratic Processes	
		Glottal Replacement	GR		

Recall that CH can be one of several processes that are applied to a sound change or word. For example, if TELEPHONE /tɛləfon/ → [dɛləton], several processes have been applied. The sound change /t/ → [d] results from _____.

PVV

The sound change /f/ → [t] results from the application of two processes: _____ and ST. The /f/ → [s] through the application of CH; and then /s/ → [t] through the application of ST.

CH

Give the processes that accounted for the following sound changes within each word:

	Adult Form		Child's Form	Sound Change(s)		Process(es)	
CUP	/kʌp/	→	[bʌp]	/k/	→ [b]	_____	CH, PVV
KISS	/kɪs/	→	[dɪs]	/k/	→ [d]	_____	CH or VF, PVV
DUCK	/dʌk/	→	[dʌt]	/k/	→ [t]	_____	CH or VF
TAKE	/tek/	→	[gek]	/t/	→ [g]	_____	CH, PVV
SICK	/sɪk/	→	[kɪk]	/s/	→ [k]	_____	CH, ST, STR
ZIPPER	/zɪpɚ/	→	[bɪpɚ]	/z/	→ [b]	_____	CH, ST, STR,
MONKEY	/mʌŋki/	→	[mʌnti]	/ŋk/	→ [nt]	_____	VF
FIGHT	/faɪt/	→	[taɪt]	/f/	→ [t]	_____	CH, ST, STR
TAG	/tæg/	→	[dæ]	/t/	→ [d]	_____	PVV
				/g/	→ [ø]	_____	DFC

/p/ PIG	/n/ NO	/ʃ/ SHE	/w/ WAGON	/ɛ/ BED	/ʌ/ GUN
/b/ BED	/ŋ/ STING	/ʒ/ ROUGE	/ʍ/ WHEEL	/æ/ CAT	/ə/ ABOUT
/t/ TOY	/f/ FOX	/h/ HAVE	/ɚ/ FINGER	/a/ GOT	/aɪ/ KITE
/d/ DUCK	/θ/ THINK	/tʃ/ CHICKEN	/ɝ/ CHURCH	/ɔ/ TALK	/ɔɪ/ TOY
/k/ KEEP	/ð/ THIS	/dʒ/ JUMPING	/i/ SEE	/o/ GOAT	/aʊ/ OUT
/g/ GOAT	/s/ SEE	/l/ LAKE	/ɪ/ PIG	/ʊ/ BOOK	
/m/ ME	/z/ ZOO	/j/ YOU	/eɪ, e/ MAKE	/u/ GLUE	

CH **DFC**	BAG /bæg/ → [gæ] /b/ → [g] _____ /g/ → [ø] _____

Notice that CH can occur even when the influential consonant has been deleted from the target word. For example, when BAG /bæg/ → [gæ], the /g/ has influenced the /b/ so that it has become velar, even though the /g/ has been affected by the process

DFC _____.

Determine which deleted consonant influenced the affected consonant in the following examples of CH:

		Adult *Form*	*Child's* *Form*	*Influential* *Consonant*
/k/	DUCK	/dʌk/ →	[gʌ]	/___/
/b/	BANANA	/bənænə/ →	[mæmə]	/___/
/k/	BASKET	/bæskɪt/ →	[bæsɪk]	/___/
/dʒ/	GIRAFFE	/dʒəræf/ →	[ərætʃ]	/___/
/mp/	LAMP	/læmp/ →	[mæ]	/___/

Note that CH can be applied even when the influential consonant is deleted from the child's surface form. It is assumed that CH occurred prior to the

deletion _____ process.

When CONSONANT HARMONY occurs in both directions, the process applied is called METATHESIS. This will be covered in Section 18. An example of METATHESIS would be the change from FISH /fɪʃ/ to

---

Deletion of Final Consonant	DFC	Consonant Harmony Postvocalic Devoicing	CH PVD	Backing to Velars Epenthesis	BK EPEN
Prevocalic Voicing	PVV	Vocalization	VOC	Metathesis	METATH
Syllable Reduction	SR	Palatal Fronting	PF	Coalescence	COAL
Velar Fronting	VF	Gliding of Liquids	GL	Palatalization	PAL
Stopping of Fricatives and Affricates	ST	Deaffrication Deletion of Initial	DEAFF	Denasalization Idiosyncratic	DENAS
Cluster Reduction	CR	Consonant	DIC	Processes	
Stridency Deletion	STR	Glottal Replacement	GR		

[ʃif]. The /f/ has influenced the /ʃ/, and the /ʃ/ has influenced the /f/. When CH occurs in both directions, the process that has been applied is called _____.

METATHESIS

Indicate whether each of the following words provides an opportunity for CH to be applied:

	Adult Form	YES/NO	
BATHTUB	/bæθtəb/	_____	YES
BOY	/bɔɪ/	_____	NO
GIRAFFE	/dʒəræf/	_____	YES
COWBOY	/kaʊbɔɪ/	_____	YES
COOK	/kʊk/	_____	NO
PAJAMAS	/pədʒæməz/	_____	YES
PIE	/paɪ/	_____	NO
RABBIT	/ræbɪt/	_____	YES
TELEPHONE	/tɛləfon/	_____	YES
TEA	/ti/	_____	NO

CH can be applied to any word that has more than one consonant if the consonants are not all produced at the same point of articulation. Thus, CAT, CAB, CAN are available for the application of CH; but TAN, BABY, COOKIE are not, because consonants within each word are produced at _____.

the same point of articulation

/p/ *PIG*	/n/ *NO*	/ʃ/ *SHE*	/w/ *WAGON*	/ɛ/ *BED*	/ʌ/ *GUN*
/b/ *BED*	/ŋ/ *STING*	/ʒ/ *ROUGE*	/ʍ/ *WHEEL*	/æ/ *CAT*	/ə/ *ABOUT*
/t/ *TOY*	/f/ *FOX*	/h/ *HAVE*	/ɝ/ *FINGER*	/a/ *GOT*	/aɪ/ *KITE*
/d/ *DUCK*	/θ/ *THINK*	/tʃ/ *CHICKEN*	/ɝ/ *CHURCH*	/ɔ/ *TALK*	/ɔɪ/ *TOY*
/k/ *KEEP*	/ð/ *THIS*	/dʒ/ *JUMPING*	/i/ *SEE*	/o/ *GOAT*	/aʊ/ *OUT*
/g/ *GOAT*	/s/ *SEE*	/l/ *LAKE*	/ɪ/ *PIG*	/ʊ/ *BOOK*	
/m/ *ME*	/z/ *ZOO*	/j/ *YOU*	/eɪ, e/ *MAKE*	/u/ *GLUE*	

SUMMARY
Consonant Harmony

1. CH is a process that results in one consonant being produced at the same place of articulation as another consonant within the same word.
2. The term ASSIMILATION is also used to describe CH.
3. When CH results in velar → alveolar sound changes, the process of VF must be considered.
4. CH can occur even when the influential consonant has been deleted from the target word.

Deletion of Final Consonant	DFC	Consonant Harmony	CH	Backing to Velars	BK
		Postvocalic Devoicing	PVD	Epenthesis	EPEN
Prevocalic Voicing	PVV	Vocalization	VOC	Metathesis	METATH
Syllable Reduction	SR	Palatal Fronting	PF	Coalescence	COAL
Velar Fronting	VF	Gliding of Liquids	GL	Palatalization	PAL
Stopping of Fricatives and Affricates	ST	Deaffrication	DEAFF	Denasalization	DENAS
Cluster Reduction	CR	Deletion of Initial Consonant	DIC	Idiosyncratic Processes	
Stridency Deletion	STR	Glottal Replacement	GR		

SECTION 9. POSTVOCALIC DEVOICING

POSTVOCALIC DEVOICING (PVD) is the name of the process that indicates that the child's production of a word-final voiced consonant is devoiced. DOG /dɔg/ → [dɔk] is an example of _____.

POSTVOCALIC
DEVOICING

The abbreviation for POSTVOCALIC DEVOICING is _____.

PVD

Another example of PVD would be BED /bɛd/ → [bɛt], where the word-final /d/ has become _____.

[t], OR devoiced

Since the devoicing occurs word-finally, the term _____ devoicing is used.

postvocalic

When /z/ becomes completely devoiced, it becomes [___].

[s]

Give the devoiced forms of the following voiced consonants:

Voiced		Devoiced	
/b/	→	[___]	[p]
/d/	→	[___]	[t]
/g/	→	[___]	[k]
/v/	→	[___]	[f]
/ð/	→	[___]	[θ]
/z/	→	[___]	[s]

/p/ *PIG*	/n/ *NO*	/ʃ/ *SHE*	/w/ *WAGON*	/ɛ/ *BED*	/ʌ/ *GUN*
/b/ *BED*	/ŋ/ *STING*	/ʒ/ *ROUGE*	/ʍ/ *WHEEL*	/æ/ *CAT*	/ə/ *ABOUT*
/t/ *TOY*	/f/ *FOX*	/h/ *HAVE*	/ɚ/ *FINGER*	/a/ *GOT*	/aɪ/ *KITE*
/d/ *DUCK*	/θ/ *THINK*	/tʃ/ *CHICKEN*	/ɝ/ *CHURCH*	/ɔ/ *TALK*	/ɔɪ/ *TOY*
/k/ *KEEP*	/ð/ *THIS*	/dʒ/ *JUMPING*	/i/ *SEE*	/o/ *GOAT*	/aʊ/ *OUT*
/g/ *GOAT*	/s/ *SEE*	/l/ *LAKE*	/ɪ/ *PIG*	/ʊ/ *BOOK*	
/m/ *ME*	/z/ *ZOO*	/j/ *YOU*	/eɪ, e/ *MAKE*	/u/ *GLUE*	

[ʃ]	/ʒ/	→	[___]
[tʃ]	/dʒ/	→	[___]

silence

POSTVOCALIC DEVOICING is said to occur because the speaker terminates voicing prematurely in anticipation of the silence that will follow the word. This is a type of ASSIMILATION. The assimilation occurs because of the influence of the _____ following the word.

PVV

This is similar to the premature voice onset for consonants occurring word-initially. That is, the speaker initiates voicing prematurely in anticipation of the vowel in a CV sequence. When word-initial voiceless consonants are voiced, the process _____ has been applied.

PVD, PVV

Recall that this is also a type of ASSIMILATION with the vowel's voicing. Both _____ and _____ are examples of assimilation with voice features.

Complete the following sounds for the target words and their productions. Assume that the word-final consonants have been completely devoiced.

		Adult Form	Child's Form	Sound Change
[t]	BED	/bɛd/	→ [bɛt]	/d/ → [___]
[k]	DOG	/dɔg/	→ [dɔk]	/g/ → [___]
[p]	CRIB	/krɪb/	→ [krɪp]	/b/ → [___]

Deletion of Final Consonant	DFC	Consonant Harmony	CH	Backing to Velars	BK
Prevocalic Voicing	PVV	Postvocalic Devoicing	PVD	Epenthesis	EPEN
Syllable Reduction	SR	Vocalization	VOC	Metathesis	METATH
Velar Fronting	VF	Palatal Fronting	PF	Coalescence	COAL
Stopping of Fricatives and Affricates	ST	Gliding of Liquids	GL	Palatalization	PAL
Cluster Reduction	CR	Deaffrication	DEAFF	Denasalization	DENAS
Stridency Deletion	STR	Deletion of Initial Consonant	DIC	Idiosyncratic Processes	
		Glottal Replacement	GR		

CAGE	/keʤ/	→ [ketʃ]	/ʤ/ → [___]	[tʃ]
PLEASE	/pliz/	→ [plis]	/z/ → [___]	[s]
HAVE	/hæv/	→ [hæf]	/v/ → [___]	[f]
BATHTUB	/bæθtəb/	→ [bæθtəp]	/b/ → [___]	[p]

There are two homonym pairs that were created as a result of the application of PVD. List them here:

1. _____   BED/BET

2. _____   HAVE/HALF

The process of PVD creates a number of _____ by creating one surface form for two or more underlying forms.   homonyms

In order for PVD to be applied to a word, there must be a word-final voiced consonant. Indicate which of the following words provides an opportunity for PVD to be applied:

	Adult Form	*YES/NO*	
BLACK	/blæk/	___	NO, /k/ is already voiceless.
STOVE	/stov/	___	YES, /v/ is voiced.
FLAG	/flæg/	___	YES, /g/ is voiced.
SOUP	/sup/	___	NO, /p/ is voiceless.

/p/ *PIG*	/n/ *NO*	/ʃ/ *SHE*	/w/ *WAGON*	/ɛ/ *BED*	/ʌ/ *GUN*
/b/ *BED*	/ŋ/ *STING*	/ʒ/ *ROUGE*	/ʍ/ *WHEEL*	/æ/ *CAT*	/ə/ *ABOUT*
/t/ *TOY*	/f/ *FOX*	/h/ *HAVE*	/ɚ/ *FINGER*	/a/ *GOT*	/aɪ/ *KITE*
/d/ *DUCK*	/θ/ *THINK*	/tʃ/ *CHICKEN*	/ɝ/ *CHURCH*	/ɔ/ *TALK*	/ɔɪ/ *TOY*
/k/ *KEEP*	/ð/ *THIS*	/ʤ/ *JUMPING*	/i/ *SEE*	/o/ *GOAT*	/aʊ/ *OUT*
/g/ *GOAT*	/s/ *SEE*	/l/ *LAKE*	/ɪ/ *PIG*	/ʊ/ *BOOK*	
/m/ *ME*	/z/ *ZOO*	/j/ *YOU*	/eɪ, e/ *MAKE*	/u/ *GLUE*	

YES, /dʒ/ is voiced.

NO, /s/ is voiceless.

YES, /b/ is voiced.

PAGE	/pedʒ/	_____
HOUSE	/haʊs/	_____
TUB	/tʌb/	_____

Word-final nasal clusters and word-final nasals can be devoiced. When PVD is applied to word-final nasal clusters, the final consonant is devoiced. For example, WAND /wand/ ends with a /d/; the voiceless counterpart is [_____].

[want], or [t]

Similarly, when PENS /pɛnz/ is devoiced, it becomes [_____].

[pɛns]

THING /θɪŋ/ ends with a nasal. When it is devoiced, it appears that a voiceless cognate has been added. When the word-final consonant in /θɪŋ/ is devoiced, it becomes [θɪŋk]. Similarly, when MAN /mæn/ has PVD applied to it, the production that results is [_____].

[mænt]

Nasal consonants can be devoiced by STOPPING and then devoicing them. For example, RUN /rʌn/ → [rʌd] by a type of stopping called DENASALIZATION (See Section 21). If it is then devoiced, it becomes [rʌt]. Similarly, HAM /hæm/ → [_____] when both STOPPING (DENASALIZATION) and PVD are applied.

[hæp]

Nasals are rarely stopped and then devoiced. More often, the speaker appears to begin the devoicing prematurely, resulting in a cluster which includes a voiceless homorganic consonant. Thus, HAM /hæm/ → [hæmp]; RUN /rʌn/ → [rʌnt]; WING /wɪŋ/ → [_____].

[wɪŋk]

Deletion of Final Consonant	DFC	Consonant Harmony	CH	Backing to Velars	BK
Prevocalic Voicing	PVV	Postvocalic Devoicing	PVD	Epenthesis	EPEN
Syllable Reduction	SR	Vocalization	VOC	Metathesis	METATH
Velar Fronting	VF	Palatal Fronting	PF	Coalescence	COAL
Stopping of Fricatives and Affricates	ST	Gliding of Liquids	GL	Palatalization	PAL
		Deaffrication	DEAFF	Denasalization	DENAS
Cluster Reduction	CR	Deletion of Initial Consonant	DIC	Idiosyncratic Processes	
Stridency Deletion	STR	Glottal Replacement	GR		

Give the productions for the following target words, all of which end in nasals or nasal clusters. Assume that the child has applied only PVD to these words.

	Adult Form	*Child's Form*	
BROKEN	/brokən/ → [_____]		[brokənt]
BANG	/bæŋ/ → [_____]		[bæŋk]
MIND	/maɪnd/ → [_____]		[maɪnt]
LAMB	/læm/ → [_____]		[læmp]
MOON	/mun/ → [_____]		[munt]

This premature devoicing may result in *partial* devoicing. This is noted by the use of a small empty circle beneath the affected consonant. For example, if /v/ is partially devoiced, it is narrowly transcribed as: ʏ. When there is so much devoicing that the consonant sounds voiceless, the process of _____ has been applied.

PVD

The degree of devoicing of word-final consonants by children or adults varies considerably. The degree of voicing maintained influences the listener's perception of whether the consonant is voiced or voiceless. Young children do not stay within the perceptual category for [+ voiced], even though there is some evidence that their word-final devoiced consonants contain more _____ than their word-final voiceless consonants.

voicing

All of the examples given above indicate that all voicing from the target consonant had been deleted (as in

/p/ *PIG*	/n/ *NO*	/ʃ/ *SHE*	/w/ *WAGON*	/ɛ/ *BED*	/ʌ/ *GUN*
/b/ *BED*	/ŋ/ *STING*	/ʒ/ *ROUGE*	/ʍ/ *WHEEL*	/æ/ *CAT*	/ə/ *ABOUT*
/t/ *TOY*	/f/ *FOX*	/h/ *HAVE*	/ɚ/ *FINGER*	/a/ *GOT*	/aɪ/ *KITE*
/d/ *DUCK*	/θ/ *THINK*	/tʃ/ *CHICKEN*	/ɝ/ *CHURCH*	/ɔ/ *TALK*	/ɔɪ/ *TOY*
/k/ *KEEP*	/ð/ *THIS*	/dʒ/ *JUMPING*	/i/ *SEE*	/o/ *GOAT*	/aʊ/ *OUT*
/g/ *GOAT*	/s/ *SEE*	/l/ *LAKE*	/ɪ/ *PIG*	/ʊ/ *BOOK*	
/m/ *ME*	/z/ *ZOO*	/j/ *YOU*	/eɪ, e/ *MAKE*	/u/ *GLUE*	

| voicing | BED /bɛd/ → [bɛt]). If only PVD is applied to a word, the word retains the correct word-final consonant minus its _____. |

A portion of the voicing may be deleted as explained above for /v̥/. Similarly, [d̥] indicates that partial devoicing occurred, but the consonant retained much of the _____.

voicing (second margin label)

The process of PVD may be applied to a production if the word-final consonant has been substantially devoiced. Thus, if the voiceless cognate of the consonant has been transcribed, the process of _____ will have been applied.

PVD

Or, if partial voicing is retained, but the production is primarily voiceless (for example, [t̬]), the process of _____ has probably been applied.

PVD

Indicate whether each of the following is or is not an example of the application of PVD:

		Adult Form		Child's Form	YES/NO
YES	BED	/bɛd/	→	[bɛt]	_____
YES	BRIDGE	/brɪdʒ/	→	[brɪtʃ]	_____
NO	CAGE	/kedʒ/	→	[ked]	_____
NO	FROG	/frɔg/	→	[frɔg]	_____
YES	NOSE	/noz/	→	[nos]	_____
YES	PIG	/pɪg/	→	[pɪk]	_____

Deletion of Final Consonant	DFC	Consonant Harmony	CH	Backing to Velars	BK
Prevocalic Voicing	PVV	Postvocalic Devoicing	PVD	Epenthesis	EPEN
Syllable Reduction	SR	Vocalization	VOC	Metathesis	METATH
Velar Fronting	VF	Palatal Fronting	PF	Coalescence	COAL
Stopping of Fricatives and Affricates	ST	Gliding of Liquids	GL	Palatalization	PAL
		Deaffrication	DEAFF	Denasalization	DENAS
Cluster Reduction	CR	Deletion of Initial Consonant	DIC	Idiosyncratic Processes	
Stridency Deletion	STR	Glottal Replacement	GR		

STOVE	/stov/	→ [stov]	_____	NO

Of these seven productions, _____ were examples of the application of PVD.

four

The frequency-to-opportunity ratio was therefore 4/7, or _____%.

57

Recall that word-final clusters can also be devoiced. For example, HAND /hænd/ → [hænt] when PVD is applied. Similarly, SAND /sænd/ → [_____] when PVD is applied.

[sænt]

Apply PVD to the following words, which contain word-final clusters:

	Adult Form	Child's Form	
AROUND	/əraʊnd/	→ [_____]	[əraʊnt]
HUMMED	/hʌmd/	→ [_____]	[hʌmt]
BUZZED	/bʌzd/	→ [_____]	[bʌst], or [bʌzt]
FOUND	/faʊnd/	→ [_____]	[faʊnt]

Many word-final clusters to which PVD can be applied are bound morphemes. For example, BUZZED /bʌzd/ includes the regular past tense morpheme /d/. When PVD is applied, it becomes [bʌzt] or [bʌst], both of which may be perceived as nouns. Similarly, HUMMED /hʌmd/ → [_____] when PVD is applied and may be confused with another word (HUMPED).

[hʌmt]

/p/ PIG	/n/ NO	/ʃ/ SHE	/w/ WAGON	/ɛ/ BED	/ʌ/ GUN
/b/ BED	/ŋ/ STING	/ʒ/ ROUGE	/ʍ/ WHEEL	/æ/ CAT	/ə/ ABOUT
/t/ TOY	/f/ FOX	/h/ HAVE	/ɚ/ FINGER	/a/ GOT	/aɪ/ KITE
/d/ DUCK	/θ/ THINK	/tʃ/ CHICKEN	/ɝ/ CHURCH	/ɔ/ TALK	/ɔɪ/ TOY
/k/ KEEP	/ð/ THIS	/dʒ/ JUMPING	/i/ SEE	/o/ GOAT	/aʊ/ OUT
/g/ GOAT	/s/ SEE	/l/ LAKE	/ɪ/ PIG	/ʊ/ BOOK	
/m/ ME	/z/ ZOO	/j/ YOU	/eɪ, e/ MAKE	/u/ GLUE	

Morphemes that may undergo PVD include the following: regular past tense /d/ and /əd/, plural /z/ and /əz/, possessive /z/ and /əz/, regular third person singular /z/ and /əz/. Apply PVD to the following words, which end with bound morphemes:

		Adult Form		*Child's Form*
[ʃʌvəlt]	SHOVELED	/ʃʌvəld/	→	[_____]
[ʃus]	SHOES	/ʃuz/	→	[_____]
[pentɪt]	PAINTED	/pentɪd/	→	[_____]
[taɪt]	TIED	/taɪd/	→	[_____]
[dɔks], OR [dɔgs]	DOG'S	/dɔgz/	→	[_____]
[sis]	SEES	/siz/	→	[_____]
[plet]	PLAYED	/pled/	→	[_____]

The influence of PVD on intelligibility is variable. It appears that it is factor (McDade, Khan, and Seay, 1982). However, since it is a process that occurs in normal adult speech, it should not influence intelligibility greatly. That is, since adult speakers characteristically devoice word-final consonants, intelligibility should not be affected by

PVD _____ when it is the only process applied.

When it is the only process that affects a child's production, intelligibility does not appear to be affected. But when other processes are applied in addition to

PVD _____, intelligibility can be reduced significantly.

Deletion of Final		Consonant Harmony	CH	Backing to Velars	BK
Consonant	DFC	Postvocalic Devoicing	PVD	Epenthesis	EPEN
Prevocalic Voicing	PVV	Vocalization	VOC	Metathesis	METATH
Syllable Reduction	SR	Palatal Fronting	PF	Coalescence	COAL
Velar Fronting	VF	Gliding of Liquids	GL	Palatalization	PAL
Stopping of Fricatives		Deaffrication	DEAFF	Denasalization	DENAS
and Affricates	ST	Deletion of Initial		Idiosyncratic	
Cluster Reduction	CR	Consonant	DIC	Processes	
Stridency Deletion	STR	Glottal Replacement	GR		

To illustrate this point, apply PVD, ST, PVV, and VF to the following target words. Give the child's form for each one.

	Adult Form		*Child's Form*	
JACK	/dʒæk/	→	[_____]	[dæt]
SAD	/sæd/	→	[_____]	[dæt]
SHACK	/ʃæk/	→	[_____]	[dæt]
TACK	/tæk/	→	[_____]	[dæt]
DASH	/dæʃ/	→	[_____]	[dæt], OR [dætʃ]
CHAD	/tʃæd/	→	[_____]	[dæt]
CHAT	/tʃæt/	→	[_____]	[dæt]

It is obvious that when PVD is applied in addition to other processes, homonymy occurs. When one surface form is used to represent several underlying or adult words, these words become _____.

homonyms

The greater the homonymy, the less _____ the child's speech.

intelligible

When CLUSTER REDUCTION is also applied (and it frequently is), the number of homonyms doubles or triples. Clearly, PVD makes little difference to the listener when it is the only process applied or when its application does not result in a homonym. But when it is combined with other processes, intelligibility is _____.

decreased, OR affected

/p/ PIG	/n/ NO	/ʃ/ SHE	/w/ WAGON	/ɛ/ BED	/ʌ/ GUN
/b/ BED	/ŋ/ STING	/ʒ/ ROUGE	/ʍ/ WHEEL	/æ/ CAT	/ə/ ABOUT
/t/ TOY	/f/ FOX	/h/ HAVE	/ɚ/ FINGER	/a/ GOT	/aɪ/ KITE
/d/ DUCK	/θ/ THINK	/tʃ/ CHICKEN	/ɝ/ CHURCH	/ɔ/ TALK	/ɔɪ/ TOY
/k/ KEEP	/ð/ THIS	/dʒ/ JUMPING	/i/ SEE	/o/ GOAT	/aʊ/ OUT
/g/ GOAT	/s/ SEE	/l/ LAKE	/ɪ/ PIG	/ʊ/ BOOK	
/m/ ME	/z/ ZOO	/j/ YOU	/eɪ, e/ MAKE	/u/ GLUE	

Apply PVD to the following target words and give the child's form for each one:

		Adult Form		Child's Form
[kæp]	CAB	/kæb/	→	[_____]
[hæt]	HAD	/hæd/	→	[_____]
[ros]	ROSE	/roz/	→	[_____]
[hænt]	HAND	/hænd/	→	[_____]
[glʌf]	GLOVE	/glʌv/	→	[_____]
[hæŋk]	HANG	/hæŋ/	→	[_____]
[petʃ]	PAGE	/pedʒ/	→	[_____]

Give the sound changes for each of the following words and identify the multiple processes that have been applied to each. Assume the application of VF rather than CH when velars become alveolars.

		Adult Form	Child's Form	Sound Change	Process (es)
/ə/ → [ø], SR	AFRAID	/əfred/	→ [ped]	/___/ → [___] ___	
/fr/ → [p], ST, CR, STR				/___/ → [___] ___	
/br/ → [b], CR	BROKE	/brok/	→ [bot]	/___/ → [___] ___	
/k/ → [t], VF				/___/ → [___] ___	
/f/ → [p], ST, STR	FEED	/fid/	→ [pit]	/___/ → [___] ___	
/d/ → [t], PVD				/___/ → [___] ___	

Deletion of Final Consonant	DFC	Consonant Harmony	CH	Backing to Velars	BK
Prevocalic Voicing	PVV	Postvocalic Devoicing	PVD	Epenthesis	EPEN
Syllable Reduction	SR	Vocalization	VOC	Metathesis	METATH
Velar Fronting	VF	Palatal Fronting	PF	Coalescence	COAL
Stopping of Fricatives and Affricates	ST	Gliding of Liquids	GL	Palatalization	PAL
Cluster Reduction	CR	Deaffrication	DEAFF	Denasalization	DENAS
Stridency Deletion	STR	Deletion of Initial Consonant	DIC	Idiosyncratic Processes	
		Glottal Replacement	GR		

LAMP   /læmp/   → [læm]   /___/ → [___] _____   /mp/ → [m], CR

LEG   /lɛg/   → [lɛk]   /___/ → [___] _____   /g/ → [k], PVD

PANCAKE /pænkek/ → [pætet] /___/ → [___] _____   /nk/ → [t], CR,
                                                          VF
                            /___/ → [___] _____   /k/ → [t], VF

READ   /rid/   → [rid]   /___/ → [___] _____   no process applied

RANG   /ræŋ/   → [ræŋk] /___/ → [___] _____   /ŋ/ → [ŋk], PVD

SCHOOL   /skul/   → [kul]   /___/ → [___] _____   /sk/ → [k], CR,
                                                          STR

STEP   /stɛp/   → [dɛ]   /___/ → [___] _____   /st/ → [d], CR,
                                                          PVV, STR
                            /___/ → [___] _____   /p/ → [ø], DFC

Name the productions that were homonyms in the preceding exercise. For example, BUG /bʌg/ → [bʌk], and [bʌk] may represent both BUG and BUCK.

Production	Homonyms
[bʌk]	BUG/BUCK
[bot]	_____
[pit]	_____
[læm]	_____
[ræŋk]	_____
[kul]	_____

BROKE/BOAT

FEED/PETE

LAMP/LAMB

RANG/RANK

SCHOOL/COOL

/p/ *PIG*	/n/ *NO*	/ʃ/ *SHE*	/w/ *WAGON*	/ɛ/ *BED*	/ʌ/ *GUN*
/b/ *BED*	/ŋ/ *STING*	/ʒ/ *ROUGE*	/ʍ/ *WHEEL*	/æ/ *CAT*	/ə/ *ABOUT*
/t/ *TOY*	/f/ *FOX*	/h/ *HAVE*	/ɚ/ *FINGER*	/a/ *GOT*	/aɪ/ *KITE*
/d/ *DUCK*	/θ/ *THINK*	/tʃ/ *CHICKEN*	/ɝ/ *CHURCH*	/ɔ/ *TALK*	/ɔɪ/ *TOY*
/k/ *KEEP*	/ð/ *THIS*	/dʒ/ *JUMPING*	/i/ *SEE*	/o/ *GOAT*	/aʊ/ *OUT*
/g/ *GOAT*	/s/ *SEE*	/l/ *LAKE*	/ɪ/ *PIG*	/ʊ/ *BOOK*	
/m/ *ME*	/z/ *ZOO*	/j/ *YOU*	/eɪ, e/ *MAKE*	/u/ *GLUE*	

PVD

_____ may not affect intelligibility greatly when it is the only process applied.

However, when it is used in conjunction with other processes, it results in an increase in the number of homonyms produced and a consequent decrease in

intelligibility

_____.

PVD is not the only phonological process that results in homonyms. The application of any process can produce a homonym pair. The more processes the child uses productively, the greater the number of potential

homonyms

_____.

SUMMARY
Postvocalic Devoicing

1. PVD is the name of the process that indicates that the child's production of a word-final voiced consonant is devoiced.
2. Both PVD and PVV have been described as assimilations with the adjacent silence and vowel.
3. When word-final nasals are devoiced, the addition of a voiceless homorganic stop consonant is often perceived.
4. The devoicing may be partial or complete.
5. Adults regularly use the process of PVD in connected speech.

Deletion of Final Consonant	DFC	Consonant Harmony	CH	Backing to Velars	BK
Prevocalic Voicing	PVV	Postvocalic Devoicing	PVD	Epenthesis	EPEN
Syllable Reduction	SR	Vocalization	VOC	Metathesis	METATH
Velar Fronting	VF	Palatal Fronting	PF	Coalescence	COAL
Stopping of Fricatives and Affricates	ST	Gliding of Liquids	GL	Palatalization	PAL
Cluster Reduction	CR	Deaffrication	DEAFF	Denasalization	DENAS
Stridency Deletion	STR	Deletion of Initial Consonant	DIC	Idiosyncratic Processes	
		Glottal Replacement	GR		

SECTION 10. VOCALIZATION

VOCALIZATION (VOC) is the name of the process that results in the child's production of a word-final full vowel for a syllabic /əl/ or /ɚ/. TIGER /taɪgɚ/ → [taɪgʊ] is an example of _____.

VOCALIZATION

The abbreviation for VOCALIZATION is

_____.

VOC

Another example of VOC would be FINGER /fɪŋgɚ/ → [fɪŋgʊ], where the syllabic /ɚ/ has become [_____].

[ʊ]

VOC can occur in any position within a word. For example, when EARLY /ɝlɪ/ → [ʊlɪ], the process of _____ has been applied to the word-initial /ɝ/.

VOC

VOC can affect both /ɚ/ and /ɝ/ syllabics as well as /əl/. When TABLE /tebəl/ → [tebo], _____ has been applied.

VOC

The symbol for a syllabic /əl/ can also be represented by /l̩/. Because an entire syllable is represented by either notation, VOC can be applied to reduce the schwa-/l/ or /l̩/ to a _____.

vowel

It is important to assume that even when the schwa is not included in the transcription (as in /l̩/), there is a schwa-element. That is, the /əl/ represents an entire syllable, and so does the syllabic /___/.

/l̩/

Similarly, the symbol /ɚ/, which is a schwa + /r/, is

/p/ *PIG*	/n/ *NO*	/ʃ/ *SHE*	/w/ *WAGON*	/ɛ/ *BED*	/ʌ/ *GUN*
/b/ *BED*	/ŋ/ *STING*	/ʒ/ *ROUGE*	/ʍ/ *WHEEL*	/æ/ *CAT*	/ə/ *ABOUT*
/t/ *TOY*	/f/ *FOX*	/h/ *HAVE*	/ɚ/ *FINGER*	/a/ *GOT*	/aɪ/ *KITE*
/d/ *DUCK*	/θ/ *THINK*	/tʃ/ *CHICKEN*	/ɝ/ *CHURCH*	/ɔ/ *TALK*	/ɔɪ/ *TOY*
/k/ *KEEP*	/ð/ *THIS*	/dʒ/ *JUMPING*	/i/ *SEE*	/o/ *GOAT*	/aʊ/ *OUT*
/g/ *GOAT*	/s/ *SEE*	/l/ *LAKE*	/ɪ/ *PIG*	/ʊ/ *BOOK*	
/m/ *ME*	/z/ *ZOO*	/j/ *YOU*	/eɪ, e/ *MAKE*	/u/ *GLUE*	

syllable	sometimes written /ɾ/. Both symbols represent an entire _____.
VOC	If any one of these syllabic liquids becomes a non-schwa vowel, as in TABLE /tebl̩/ or MOTHER /mʌðɚ/ becoming [tebo] and [mʌðʊ], the process of _____ has been applied.
DFC	If any one of these syllabics (/ɚ/, /ɝ/, /ɾ/, /əl/, /l̩/) becomes a schwa, as in TABLE /tebl̩/ or MOTHER /mʌðɚ/ becoming [tebə] and [mʌðə], then the final liquid has been deleted from the schwa-liquid syllable. Since this results in the deletion of a word-final consonant, the process applied may be _____ rather than VOC.

Another example of the application of DFC versus VOC can be illustrated by examination of the following targets and the two types of productions:

	Adult Form	VOC Applied	DFC Applied
TABLE	/tebl̩/	[tebo]	[tebə]
WATER	/waɾɚ/	[waɾʊ]	[waɾə]
SHOVEL	/ʃʌvəl/	[ʃʌvo]	[ʃʌvə]
DOCTOR	/daktɚ/	[daktʊ]	[daktə]

VOC, DFC	From these examples, it is evident that the entire vowel element is altered when _____ is applied, but the liquid consonant alone is deleted when _____ is applied.
VOC	Some common vowels to which syllabic liquids change are [o] and [ʊ]. When a syllabic becomes one of these vowels, the process _____ has been applied.

Deletion of Final Consonant	DFC	Consonant Harmony	CH	Backing to Velars	BK
Prevocalic Voicing	PVV	Postvocalic Devoicing	PVD	Epenthesis	EPEN
Syllable Reduction	SR	Vocalization	VOC	Metathesis	METATH
Velar Fronting	VF	Palatal Fronting	PF	Coalescence	COAL
Stopping of Fricatives and Affricates	ST	Gliding of Liquids	GL	Palatalization	PAL
Cluster Reduction	CR	Deaffrication	DEAFF	Denasalization	DENAS
Stridency Deletion	STR	Deletion of Initial Consonant	DIC	Idiosyncratic Processes	
		Glottal Replacement	GR		

When the vowel remains a schwa at the end of a word, DFC may have been applied rather than _____.

VOC

For example, when FATHER /faðɚ/ → [faðə], the /r/ portion of the /ɚ/ has been deleted and the schwa has been retained. This is more similar to DFC than to _____.

VOC

VOCALIZATION usually results in a full vowel production, rather than a schwa. Researchers differ about whether the retained schwa is sufficient to justify assigning the process of _____.

VOC

We will consider _____ to have been applied when there is a full vowel representing the liquid. That is, either the schwa plus liquid has changed to a full vowel, or a vowel has been added to the schwa to represent the liquid.

VOC

For example, when FATHER /faðɚ/ → either [faðo] or [faðəʊ], _____ has been applied.

VOC

However, when FATHER /faðɚ/ → [faðə], _____ has been applied.

DFC

VOCALIZATION (VOC) has also been applied when PENCIL /pɛnsl̩/ → [_____]

[pɛnso], OR [pɛnsʊ]

Although the vowels vary, some are more common than others. In addition to [_____] and [_____], [ɔ] is commonly used.

[o], [ʊ]

Thus, PENCIL /pɛnsl̩/ could become [_____], [_____], or [_____] by the application of VOC.

[pɛnso], [pɛnsʊ], [pɛnsɔ] (in any order)

/p/ *PIG*	/n/ *NO*	/ʃ/ *SHE*	/w/ *WAGON*	/ɛ/ *BED*	/ʌ/ *GUN*
/b/ *BED*	/ŋ/ *STING*	/ʒ/ *ROUGE*	/ʍ/ *WHEEL*	/æ/ *CAT*	/ə/ *ABOUT*
/t/ *TOY*	/f/ *FOX*	/h/ *HAVE*	/ɚ/ *FINGER*	/a/ *GOT*	/aɪ/ *KITE*
/d/ *DUCK*	/θ/ *THINK*	/tʃ/ *CHICKEN*	/ɝ/ *CHURCH*	/ɔ/ *TALK*	/ɔɪ/ *TOY*
/k/ *KEEP*	/ð/ *THIS*	/dʒ/ *JUMPING*	/i/ *SEE*	/o/ *GOAT*	/aʊ/ *OUT*
/g/ *GOAT*	/s/ *SEE*	/l/ *LAKE*	/ɪ/ *PIG*	/ʊ/ *BOOK*	
/m/ *ME*	/z/ *ZOO*	/j/ *YOU*	/eɪ, e/ *MAKE*	/u/ *GLUE*	

VOC	Some children use [ɛ] to replace the entire syllabic. This is also an example of _____.
syllabic	Some word-final /l/s and /r/s are not syllabic. For example, CAR /kar/ does not end in syllabic /ɚ/ or /ɝ/; BALL /bal/ does not end in syllabic /əl/ or /l̩/. These are consonantal /l/ and /r/ rather than _____.
VOC	Consonantal /r/ and /l/ can be vocalized. For example, when CAR /kar/ → [kaʊ], _____ has been applied.
VOC	Similarly, when BALL /bal/ → [bao], _____ has been applied.
DFC	However, when CAR /kar/ → [ka], VOC has not been applied. Rather, /r/ as a postvocalic consonant has been deleted. This process is not VOC but _____.
DFC	Similarly, when BALL /bal/ → [ba], the process _____ has been applied, not VOC.
consonant, OR liquid	The difference between the two is that VOC results in some alteration of the vowel, by changing it to a diphthong or full vowel; whereas DFC results in only the deletion of the word-final _____.
	Give the productions that result when VOC is applied to the following attempted words. (For this section, any of the following vowels are acceptable as replacements for the syllabics: [o], [ʊ], [ɔ], [ɛ].)

Deletion of Final		Consonant Harmony	CH	Backing to Velars	BK
Consonant	DFC	Postvocalic Devoicing	PVD	Epenthesis	EPEN
Prevocalic Voicing	PVV	Vocalization	VOC	Metathesis	METATH
Syllable Reduction	SR	Palatal Fronting	PF	Coalescence	COAL
Velar Fronting	VF	Gliding of Liquids	GL	Palatalization	PAL
Stopping of Fricatives		Deaffrication	DEAFF	Denasalization	DENAS
and Affricates	ST	Deletion of Initial		Idiosyncratic	
Cluster Reduction	CR	Consonant	DIC	Processes	
Stridency Deletion	STR	Glottal Replacement	GR		

	Adult Form	*Child's Form*	
FEATHER	/fɛðɚ/	→ [_____]	[fɛðʊ]
TABLE	/tebḷ/	→ [_____]	[tebo]
SISTER	/sɪstɚ/	→ [_____]	[sɪstʊ]
AIRPLANE	/ɛɪrplen/	→ [_____]	[ɛʊplen]
APPLE	/æpḷ/	→ [_____]	[æpo]
BULLDOZER	/bʊldozɚ/	→ [_____]	[bʊldozʊ]
ANSWER	/ænsɚ/	→ [_____]	[ænsɔ]
CHAIR	/tʃɛr/	→ [_____]	[tʃɛʊ]
DOCTOR	/daktɚ/	→ [_____]	[daktɛ]
SHOVEL	/ʃʌvəl/	→ [_____]	[ʃʌvo]

VOCALIZATION is the name for the process that results in /ɚ/, /ɝ/, /ɾ/, /r/, /əl/, /ḷ/, or /l/ becoming a vowel. This is a phonological process. However, in some areas of the Northeast this is not _____ from normal adult production. As with any articulation/phonology assessment, children's productions must be compared with the local adult population for dialectical differences.

different, OR deviant

We have seen that the word-medial, or stressed, /ɝ/ can be vocalized. For example, when WORK /wɝk/ → [wʊk], _____ has been applied.

VOC

/p/ *PIG*	/n/ *NO*	/ʃ/ *SHE*	/w/ *WAGON*	/ɛ/ *BED*	/ʌ/ *GUN*
/b/ *BED*	/ŋ/ *STING*	/ʒ/ *ROUGE*	/ʍ/ *WHEEL*	/æ/ *CAT*	/ə/ *ABOUT*
/t/ *TOY*	/f/ *FOX*	/h/ *HAVE*	/ɚ/ *FINGER*	/a/ *GOT*	/aɪ/ *KITE*
/d/ *DUCK*	/θ/ *THINK*	/tʃ/ *CHICKEN*	/ɝ/ *CHURCH*	/ɔ/ *TALK*	/ɔɪ/ *TOY*
/k/ *KEEP*	/ð/ *THIS*	/dʒ/ *JUMPING*	/i/ *SEE*	/o/ *GOAT*	/aʊ/ *OUT*
/g/ *GOAT*	/s/ *SEE*	/l/ *LAKE*	/ɪ/ *PIG*	/ʊ/ *BOOK*	
/m/ *ME*	/z/ *ZOO*	/j/ *YOU*	/eɪ, e/ *MAKE*	/u/ *GLUE*	

List the sound changes for the following attempted words containing stressed /ɝ/ and their productions:

	Adult Form		Child's Form	Sound Change
/ɝ/ → [ʊ]	BIRD	/bɝd/	→ [bʊd]	/___/ → [___]
/ɝ/ → [ɔ]	FERN	/fɝn/	→ [fɔn]	/___/ → [___]
/ɝ/ → [ɔ]	GIRL	/gɝl/	→ [gɔl]	/___/ → [___]
/ɝ/ → [ʊ]	HEARD	/hɝd/	→ [hʊd]	/___/ → [___]
/ɝ/ → [ʊ]	PERSON	/pɝsn̩/	→ [pʊsn̩]	/___/ → [___]
/ɝ/ → [ɔ]	SERVE	/sɝv/	→ [sɔv]	/___/ → [___]
/ɝ/ → [ɔ]	WORK	/wɝk/	→ [wɔk]	/___/ → [___]

VOC

Consonantal /r/ and /l/ can also be vocalized within clusters. For example, CARD /kard/ → [kaʊd], when _____ has been applied. The /rd/ is a cluster and remains a cluster.

CR

When CARD /kard/ → [kad], the process of _____ has been applied. This is NOT an example of VOC.

Indicate whether VOC or CR has been applied to each of the following attempted words and their productions:

		Adult Form	Child's Form	Process
VOC	CALLED	/kɔld/	→ [kɔod]	_____

Deletion of Final Consonant	DFC	Consonant Harmony	CH	Backing to Velars	BK
Prevocalic Voicing	PVV	Postvocalic Devoicing	PVD	Epenthesis	EPEN
Syllable Reduction	SR	Vocalization	VOC	Metathesis	METATH
Velar Fronting	VF	Palatal Fronting	PF	Coalescence	COAL
Stopping of Fricatives and Affricates	ST	Gliding of Liquids	GL	Palatalization	PAL
Cluster Reduction	CR	Deaffrication	DEAFF	Denasalization	DENAS
Stridency Deletion	STR	Deletion of Initial Consonant	DIC	Idiosyncratic Processes	
		Glottal Replacement	GR		

HARM	/harm/	→ [haɔm]	_____		VOC
HOLD	/hold/	→ [hod]	_____		CR
SMART	/smart/	→ [smaʊt]	_____		VOC
TOLD	/told/	→ [toʊd]	_____		VOC
YARD	/jard/	→ [jaʊd]	_____		VOC
YARN	/jarn/	→ [jan]	_____		CR

Consonantal and syllabic /r/ and /l/ are not always handled separately. Some prefer to use the process category LIQUID SIMPLIFICATION to include VOCALIZATION and GLIDING (covered in Section 12). There does, however, appear to be a difference between the ways in which children simplify syllabic and consonantal forms. In general, they tend to apply VOC to the _____ forms and _____ to the consonantal forms.

syllabic, GL

Or, when these sounds appear in word-final position, children tend to delete the consonantal /l/ or /r/ and may even elongate the preceding _____, as in CAR /kar/ → [ka:].

vowel

When a syllabic appears in word-final position, children tend to alter the _____ rather than elongate it. For example, FATHER /faðɚ/ → [faðo] is an example of an altered vowel (from schwa to [o]).

vowel

Give the process that has accounted for the following sound changes:

		Adult Form		Child's Form	Sound Change	Process
VOC	DOCTOR	/daktɚ/	→	[daktɔ]	/ɚ/ → [ɔ]	_____
GL	CARRY	/kærɪ/	→	[kæwɪ]	/r/ → [w]	_____
VOC	FEATHER	/fɛðɚ/	→	[fɛðʊ]	/ɚ/ → [ʊ]	_____
VOC	BIRD	/bɝd/	→	[bʊd]	/ɝ/ → [ʊ]	_____
CR	GARDEN	/gardn̩/	→	[gadn̩]	/r/ → [ø]	_____
VOC	CAR	/kar/	→	[kao]	/r/ → [o]	_____
DFC	FAR	/far/	→	[fa:]	/r/ → [ø]	_____
VOC	MILK	/mɪlk/	→	[mɪʊk]	/lk/ → [ʊk]	_____
CR	BUILD	/bɪld/	→	[bɪd]	/ld/ → [d]	_____
CR, GL	EARLY	/ɝlɪ/	→	[ʊwɪ]	/ɝl/ → [ʊw]	_____

Indicate whether each of the following words provides an opportunity for VOC to be applied:

		Adult Form	YES/NO
YES, /ɚ/	MOTHER	/mʌðɚ/	_____
YES, /l/	WILL	/wɪl/	_____
YES, /ld/	BUILD	/bɪld/	_____
YES, /ɝ/	HER	/hɝ/	_____

Deletion of Final Consonant	DFC	Consonant Harmony	CH
Prevocalic Voicing	PVV	Postvocalic Devoicing	PVD
Syllable Reduction	SR	Vocalization	VOC
Velar Fronting	VF	Palatal Fronting	PF
Stopping of Fricatives and Affricates	ST	Gliding of Liquids	GL
Cluster Reduction	CR	Deaffrication	DEAFF
Stridency Deletion	STR	Deletion of Initial Consonant	DIC
		Glottal Replacement	GR

Backing to Velars	BK
Epenthesis	EPEN
Metathesis	METATH
Coalescence	COAL
Palatalization	PAL
Denasalization	DENAS
Idiosyncratic Processes	

PERSON	/pɝsn̩/	_____	YES, /ɝ/
SEAGULL	/sigəl/	_____	YES, /l/
TAR	/tar/	_____	YES, /r/
BEAR	/bɛr/	_____	YES, /r/
GARDEN	/gardn̩/	_____	YES, /r/
BATTLE	/bærl̩/	_____	YES, /l̩/

Even though children tend to alter the vowel to replace the syllabic in word-final position, recall that it is possible to delete the word-final /l/ or /r/ from the syllabic by retaining the schwa element and deleting the liquid element from the syllable. For example, when FATHER /faðɝ/ → [faðʊ], VOC has been applied. However, when it becomes [faðə], it may be the result of _____.   DFC

Similarly, when LEADER /lidɝ/ → [lidə], so that the schwa is unaltered, the process of _____ has been applied.   DFC

For each of the following target words, give the production which would result from applying DFC and VOC. For VOCALIZATION, you may use any of the vowels listed earlier. Try to "hear" young children pronounce these words when VOC is applied, and try to choose a vowel accordingly.

	Adult Form	Apply DFC	Apply VOC	
ANSWER	/ænsɝ/ →	[_____]	[_____]	[ænsə], [ænsɔ]

/p/ *PIG*	/n/ *NO*	/ʃ/ *SHE*	/w/ *WAGON*	/ɛ/ *BED*	/ʌ/ *GUN*
/b/ *BED*	/ŋ/ *STING*	/ʒ/ *ROUGE*	/ʍ/ *WHEEL*	/æ/ *CAT*	/ə/ *ABOUT*
/t/ *TOY*	/f/ *FOX*	/h/ *HAVE*	/ɚ/ *FINGER*	/a/ *GOT*	/aɪ/ *KITE*
/d/ *DUCK*	/θ/ *THINK*	/tʃ/ *CHICKEN*	/ɝ/ *CHURCH*	/ɔ/ *TALK*	/ɔɪ/ *TOY*
/k/ *KEEP*	/ð/ *THIS*	/dʒ/ *JUMPING*	/i/ *SEE*	/o/ *GOAT*	/aʊ/ *OUT*
/g/ *GOAT*	/s/ *SEE*	/l/ *LAKE*	/ɪ/ *PIG*	/ʊ/ *BOOK*	
/m/ *ME*	/z/ *ZOO*	/j/ *YOU*	/eɪ, e/ *MAKE*	/u/ *GLUE*	

[æpə], [æpo]	APPLE	/æpl̩/	→ [_____]	[_____]
[bʊldozə], [bʊldozʊ]	BULLDOZER	/bʊldozɚ/	→ [_____]	[_____]
[hi], [hio]	HEEL	/hil/	→ [_____]	[_____]
[mɪdə], [mɪdo]	MIDDLE	/mɪdl̩/	→ [_____]	[_____]
[morə], [moɾʊ]	MOTOR	/moɾɚ/	→ [_____]	[_____]
[nɪkə], [nɪko]	NICKEL	/nɪkl̩/	→ [_____]	[_____]
[pɛbə], [pɛbo]	PEBBLE	/pɛbl̩/	→ [_____]	[_____]
[θʌndə], [θʌndʊ]	THUNDER	/θʌndɚ/	→ [_____]	[_____]
[waɾə], [waɾʊ]	WATER	/waɾɚ/	→ [_____]	[_____]

LIQUID SIMPLIFICATION

Sometimes the process category LIQUID SIMPLIFICATION is used. Then it is appropriate to group all of the sound changes affecting liquids within this single process category. DFC, VOC, and GLIDING OF LIQUIDS (GL) are each treated separately in this text so that the clinician will be familiar with all three. However, any simplification of one of the liquids (syllabic or consonantal) can be included under the broader process category _____.

processes

VOCALIZATION is a common phonological process and continues to be productive after most other _____ have been suppressed.

Thus far, we have limited the application of VOC to syllabic liquids or liquids in postvocalic position. It is also

Deletion of Final Consonant	DFC	Consonant Harmony	CH	Backing to Velars	BK
Prevocalic Voicing	PVV	Postvocalic Devoicing	PVD	Epenthesis	EPEN
Syllable Reduction	SR	Vocalization	VOC	Metathesis	METATH
Velar Fronting	VF	Palatal Fronting	PF	Coalescence	COAL
Stopping of Fricatives and Affricates	ST	Gliding of Liquids	GL	Palatalization	PAL
Cluster Reduction	CR	Deaffrication	DEAFF	Denasalization	DENAS
Stridency Deletion	STR	Deletion of Initial Consonant	DIC	Idiosyncratic Processes	
		Glottal Replacement	GR		

possible to replace a prevocalic or intervocalic liquid with a vowel. For example, RABBIT /ræbɪt/ → [ʊæbɪt] with the application of VOCALIZATION. Similarly, LAMP /læmp/ → [_____] with the application of VOCALIZATION.

[ʊæmp]

Often, the vowel replacement will sound similar to a /w/. [wæbɪt] and [ʊæbɪt] sound very much alike. The lip rounding may be absent from the vocalized production. Although VOC will primarily affect syllabic liquids, it may also be used by a child to replace other _____ in various within-word positions.

liquids

When BERRY /bɛrɪ/ → [bɛʊɪ], the process of _____ has been applied.

VOC

When BERRY /bɛrɪ/ → [bɛwɪ], the process of _____ has been applied.

GL

VOC may be blocked by deletion processes. For example, if the prevocalic consonant is deleted in a word like RAIN, then there is no opportunity for the /r/ to be either glided or vocalized. DFC may also affect the number of opportunities to apply VOC, as in the word WHEEL /wil/ → [wi]. When there is a liquid syllabic (as in /pipl̩/ or /pipəl/), the process of _____ may block the occurrence of one of these processes by eliminating the entire syllable.

SR

For each of the following words, indicate which process has blocked the process of VOC from occurring.

	Adult Form	Child's Form	Process
FEATHER	/fɛðɚ/	→ [fɛ]	_____

SR

/p/ *PIG*	/n/ *NO*	/ʃ/ *SHE*	/w/ *WAGON*	/ɛ/ *BED*	/ʌ/ *GUN*
/b/ *BED*	/ŋ/ *STING*	/ʒ/ *ROUGE*	/ʍ/ *WHEEL*	/æ/ *CAT*	/ə/ *ABOUT*
/t/ *TOY*	/f/ *FOX*	/h/ *HAVE*	/ɚ/ *FINGER*	/a/ *GOT*	/aɪ/ *KITE*
/d/ *DUCK*	/θ/ *THINK*	/tʃ/ *CHICKEN*	/ɝ/ *CHURCH*	/ɔ/ *TALK*	/ɔɪ/ *TOY*
/k/ *KEEP*	/ð/ *THIS*	/dʒ/ *JUMPING*	/i/ *SEE*	/o/ *GOAT*	/aʊ/ *OUT*
/g/ *GOAT*	/s/ *SEE*	/l/ *LAKE*	/ɪ/ *PIG*	/ʊ/ *BOOK*	
/m/ *ME*	/z/ *ZOO*	/j/ *YOU*	/eɪ, e̞/ *MAKE*	/u/ *GLUE*	

DFC	TABLE	/tebl̩/	→ [tebə]	_____
SR	SISTER	/sistɚ/	→ [sɪs]	_____
DFC	APPLE	/æpl̩/	→ [æpə]	_____
CR	DRESS	/drɛs/	→ [dɛs]	_____
CR	CARD	/kard/	→ [kad]	_____

After application of the processes of SR, DFC, and CR, there remain no opportunities for VOC to be applied. Of the target words, there are six liquids that could be glided or vocalized. The productivity of GL and VOC would seem to be very low if all six were considered to be potential opportunities. If the blocked opportunities are eliminated, then the productivity will be as high as

100 _____%.

VOC may be used in conjunction with other processes. For example, if TREE /tri/ → [ʊi], where the /tr/ → [ʊ], then the processes of VOC and _____

CR have been applied

Give the single and multiple processes involved in each sound change within each of the following productions:

	Adult Form	Child's Form	Sound Change	Process (es)
ST, STR CHAIR	/tʃɛr/	→ [tɛɔ]	/tʃ/ → [t]	_____
VOC			/r/ → [ɔ]	_____

Deletion of Final Consonant	DFC	Consonant Harmony	CH
Prevocalic Voicing	PVV	Postvocalic Devoicing	PVD
Syllable Reduction	SR	Vocalization	VOC
Velar Fronting	VF	Palatal Fronting	PF
Stopping of Fricatives and Affricates	ST	Gliding of Liquids	GL
Cluster Reduction	CR	Deaffrication	DEAFF
Stridency Deletion	STR	Deletion of Initial Consonant	DIC
		Glottal Replacement	GR

Backing to Velars	BK
Epenthesis	EPEN
Metathesis	METATH
Coalescence	COAL
Palatalization	PAL
Denasalization	DENAS
Idiosyncratic Processes	

TRAFFIC	/træfɪk/	→ [tʊæfɪt]	/tr/ → [tʊ] _____		VOC
			/k/ → [t] _____		VF
PEPPER	/pɛpɚ/	→ [bɛpə]	/p/ → [b] _____		PVV
			/ɚ/ → [ə] _____		DFC
LAUGH	/læf/	→ [læp]	/f/ → [p] _____		ST, STR
ALL GONE	/ɔlgɔn/	→ [ɔʊdɔn]	/lg/ → [ʊd] _____		VOC, VF
CARD	/kard/	→ [kaɔ]	/rd/ → [ɔ] _____		VOC, CR
CALENDAR	/kæləndɚ/	→ [kæwəndɔ]	/l/ → [w] _____		GL
			/ɚ/ → [ɔ] _____		VOC
PARK	/park/	→ [paɔk]	/rk/ → [ɔk] _____		VOC

VOCALIZATION has also been used to describe the change from syllabic nasals (/əm/ and /ən/, or /m̩/ and /n̩/) to altered vowels. For example, WELCOME /wɛlkəm/ → [wɛlkɛ] is an example of VOC applied to the syllabic _____.

/əm/

While children will vocalize /ɚ/, /ɝ/, /l/, and /əl/ into one of the vowels listed above, they treat syllabic /əm/ and /ən/ more like consonant deletion. For example, BACON /bekən/ → [bekə], which is more like _____ than VOC.

DFC

Similarly, WELCOME /wɛlkəm/ → [wɛlkə] with the application of _____.

DFC

This is referred to by some as NASAL OMISSION (Hodson, 1980). For our purposes, if the nasal itself does

---

/p/ *PIG*	/n/ *NO*	/ʃ/ *SHE*	/w/ *WAGON*	/ɛ/ *BED*	/ʌ/ *GUN*
/b/ *BED*	/ŋ/ *STING*	/ʒ/ *ROUGE*	/ʍ/ *WHEEL*	/æ/ *CAT*	/ə/ *ABOUT*
/t/ *TOY*	/f/ *FOX*	/h/ *HAVE*	/ɚ/ *FINGER*	/a/ *GOT*	/aɪ/ *KITE*
/d/ *DUCK*	/θ/ *THINK*	/tʃ/ *CHICKEN*	/ɝ/ *CHURCH*	/ɔ/ *TALK*	/ɔɪ/ *TOY*
/k/ *KEEP*	/ð/ *THIS*	/dʒ/ *JUMPING*	/i/ *SEE*	/o/ *GOAT*	/aʊ/ *OUT*
/g/ *GOAT*	/s/ *SEE*	/l/ *LAKE*	/ɪ/ *PIG*	/ʊ/ *BOOK*	
/m/ *ME*	/z/ *ZOO*	/j/ *YOU*	/eɪ, e/ *MAKE*	/u/ *GLUE*	

DFC

not become a vowel, but rather is deleted with the schwa /ə/ remaining, we will consider this to be a result of the application of _____ .

Assign to each of the following words the process that best describes the sound change that the child made:

		Adult Form		Child's Form	Process
VOC	LESSON	/lɛsn̩/	→	[lɛsɛ]	_____
DFC	DRAGON	/dræɡən/	→	[dræɡə]	_____
VOC	OFTEN	/ɔfən/	→	[ɔfɛ]	_____
VOC	PERSON	/pɝsn̩/	→	[pɝso]	_____
DFC	COUSIN	/kʌzn̩/	→	[kʌzə]	_____
DFC	BOTTOM	/barm̩/	→	[barə]	_____

DFC

Children may retain the naslity of the word-final nasal consonant even though they delete or vocalize the final nasal. For example, BACON /bekən/ → [bekə̃] indicates that the nasality on the vowel has been retained. Since the word-final consonant has been deleted, we still assume that the child has applied the process of _____ .

nasality

However, retention of the nasal aspect of the vowel is more similar to the adult model than deletion of the nasal with production of the non-nasal vowel. Among the words just listed, no _____ was retained in the vowels.

Deletion of Final Consonant	DFC	Consonant Harmony	CH	Backing to Velars	BK
Prevocalic Voicing	PVV	Postvocalic Devoicing	PVD	Epenthesis	EPEN
Syllable Reduction	SR	Vocalization	VOC	Metathesis	METATH
Velar Fronting	VF	Palatal Fronting	PF	Coalescence	COAL
Stopping of Fricatives and Affricates	ST	Gliding of Liquids	GL	Palatalization	PAL
Cluster Reduction	CR	Deaffrication	DEAFF	Denasalization	DENAS
Stridency Deletion	STR	Deletion of Initial Consonant	DIC	Idiosyncratic Processes	
		Glottal Replacement	GR		

Vowels that are adjacent to nasal consonants are themselves _____.

nasal

The velo-pharyngeal port is somewhat open preceding and succeeding the production of a nasal consonant. This gives the adjacent vowels a _____ quality.

nasal

When the nasality is retained in the vowel even when the nasal has been deleted or vocalized, the child is marking the presence of the word-final _____.

nasal consonant

However, since there is usually nasality on adjacent vowels, we treat this DFC no differently from deletion of non-nasal postvocalic consonants. While we assume that the process _____ has been applied, the experienced clinician will note whether or not the vowel nasality was retained.

DFC

The child who retains the _____ approaches the adult form more closely than the child who does not.

nasality

For example, LISTEN /lɪsn̩/ → [lɪsə̃] is more similar to the _____ than [lɪsə], which has no retained nasality.

adult form

The retention of nasality in the vowel, when the nasal consonant itself has been deleted, has also been described as a type of COALESCENCE (Edwards and Shriberg 1983, p. 95). That is, the essence of one phoneme has been incorporated into another. In this case, the nasality of the nasal consonant has been incorporated into the _____.

vowel

/p/ *PIG*	/n/ *NO*	/ʃ/ *SHE*	/w/ *WAGON*	/ɛ/ *BED*	/ʌ/ *GUN*
/b/ *BED*	/ŋ/ *STING*	/ʒ/ *ROUGE*	/ʍ/ *WHEEL*	/æ/ *CAT*	/ə/ *ABOUT*
/t/ *TOY*	/f/ *FOX*	/h/ *HAVE*	/ɚ/ *FINGER*	/a/ *GOT*	/aɪ/ *KITE*
/d/ *DUCK*	/θ/ *THINK*	/tʃ/ *CHICKEN*	/ɝ/ *CHURCH*	/ɔ/ *TALK*	/ɔɪ/ *TOY*
/k/ *KEEP*	/ð/ *THIS*	/dʒ/ *JUMPING*	/i/ *SEE*	/o/ *GOAT*	/aʊ/ *OUT*
/g/ *GOAT*	/s/ *SEE*	/l/ *LAKE*	/ɪ/ *PIG*	/ʊ/ *BOOK*	
/m/ *ME*	/z/ *ZOO*	/j/ *YOU*	/eɪ, e/ *MAKE*	/u/ *GLUE*	

DFC

For the purposes of this text, whether the vowel's nasality is retained or not, if the postvocalic nasal has been deleted, the process of _____ has been applied.

VOC

Furthermore, if the remaining schwa has been altered to a different vowel, as in OFTEN /ɔfən/ → [ɔfʊ], then the process of _____ has been applied.

SUMMARY
Vocalization

1. VOC is the name of the process that results in the child's production of a word-final full vowel for the syllabics /l̩/, /r̩/, /m̩/, or /n̩/.
2. Liquid syllabics are represented in the following ways: /əl/ or /l̩/, /ɚ/ or /r̩/, /ɝ/ or /r̩/.
3. The retention of the schwa in the schwa + liquid is not included under VOC.
4. Common full vowels that result from the application of VOC include o, ʊ, ɛ, and ɔ.

Deletion of Final Consonant	DFC	Consonant Harmony	CH	Backing to Velars	BK
Prevocalic Voicing	PVV	Postvocalic Devoicing	PVD	Epenthesis	EPEN
Syllable Reduction	SR	Vocalization	VOC	Metathesis	METATH
Velar Fronting	VF	Palatal Fronting	PF	Coalescence	COAL
Stopping of Fricatives and Affricates	ST	Gliding of Liquids	GL	Palatalization	PAL
Cluster Reduction	CR	Deaffrication	DEAFF	Denasalization	DENAS
Stridency Deletion	STR	Deletion of Initial Consonant	DIC	Idiosyncratic Processes	
		Glottal Replacement	GR		

SECTION 11. PALATAL FRONTING

PALATAL FRONTING (PF) is a process that, when applied, results in the forward production of palatal consonants: /ʃ/, /ʒ/, /tʃ/, /dʒ/. These are generally fronted to alveolars: /s/, /z/, /ts/, /dz/. One example of PF would be SHOE /ʃu/ → [su], where the palatal /ʃ/ has become the _____ [s].

CHAIR /tʃɛr/ → [tsɛr] is another example of _____.

The abbreviation for PALATAL FRONTING is _____.

Another example of PF would be JAM /dʒæm/ → [dzæm], where /dʒ/ → [____], an alveolar affricate.

The use of PF may not cause the listener much difficulty. As in VELAR FRONTING (VF), the listener picks up the phonological pattern quite readily, and interpretation becomes automatic. Thus, we recognize [si] as the word _____ in "[si] has a book."

PF is most commonly applied to palatal fricatives and affricates. If PF alone is applied to these palatal consonants, then /ʃ/ → [s], /ʒ/ → [____], /tʃ/ → [ts], and /dʒ/ → [____].

Even though PF may not affect intelligibility as much as some other processes do, there are homonyms that result from its application. When a single word production

---

alveolar

PALATAL
FRONTING,
or PF

PF

[dz]

SHE

[z], [dz]

/p/ PIG	/n/ NO	/ʃ/ SHE	/w/ WAGON	/ɛ/ BED	/ʌ/ GUN
/b/ BED	/ŋ/ STING	/ʒ/ ROUGE	/ʍ/ WHEEL	/æ/ CAT	/ə/ ABOUT
/t/ TOY	/f/ FOX	/h/ HAVE	/ɚ/ FINGER	/a/ GOT	/aɪ/ KITE
/d/ DUCK	/θ/ THINK	/tʃ/ CHICKEN	/ɝ/ CHURCH	/ɔ/ TALK	/ɔɪ/ TOY
/k/ KEEP	/ð/ THIS	/dʒ/ JUMPING	/i/ SEE	/o/ GOAT	/aʊ/ OUT
/g/ GOAT	/s/ SEE	/l/ LAKE	/ɪ/ PIG	/ʊ/ BOOK	
/m/ ME	/z/ ZOO	/j/ YOU	/eɪ, e/ MAKE	/u/ GLUE	

homonyms	represents several underlying forms, we call these underlying forms _____.
homonyms	For example, [si] may represent SHE, SEE, SEA, SKI, SEAL, and so on. These words are, therefore, _____, because the child uses one production for all of them.
homonym	Although the listener may interpret at the automatic level, there is opportunity for confusion when PALATAL FRONTING results in a _____.

List the productions that would result from the application of PF to the following attempted words:

		Adult Form	Child's Form
[tsik]	CHEEK	/tʃik/	→ [_____]
[sædo]	SHADOW	/ʃædo/	→ [_____]
[dzaɪənt]	GIANT	/dʒaɪənt/	→ [_____]
[ɪts]	ITCH	/ɪtʃ/	→ [_____]
[dɪs]	DISH	/dɪʃ/	→ [_____]
[ɔrɪndz]	ORANGE	/ɔrɪndʒ/	→ [_____]
[kɛtsəp]	KETCHUP	/kɛtʃəp/	→ [_____]
[vekesən]	VACATION	/vekeʃən/	→ [_____]
[mædzɪk]	MAGIC	/mædʒɪk/	→ [_____]

Deletion of Final Consonant	DFC	Consonant Harmony	CH	Backing to Velars	BK
Prevocalic Voicing	PVV	Postvocalic Devoicing	PVD	Epenthesis	EPEN
Syllable Reduction	SR	Vocalization	VOC	Metathesis	METATH
Velar Fronting	VF	Palatal Fronting	PF	Coalescence	COAL
Stopping of Fricatives and Affricates	ST	Gliding of Liquids	GL	Palatalization	PAL
		Deaffrication	DEAFF	Denasalization	DENAS
Cluster Reduction	CR	Deletion of Initial Consonant	DIC	Idiosyncratic Processes	
Stridency Deletion	STR	Glottal Replacement	GR		

When PF alone is applied, the following sound changes will occur:

/ʃ/   →   [___]   [s]

/ʒ/   →   [___]   [z]

/tʃ/   →   [___]   [ts]

/dʒ/   →   [___]   [dz]

As with many sound changes, additional processes may be applied. When /ʃ/ → [t], other processes have been applied in addition to _____.   **PF**

When PF and ST are applied, then /ʃ/ and /ʒ/ may become [ts] or [dz]. If completely stopped, /ts/ and /dz/ or /ʃ/ and /ʒ/ may become [___] or [___].   **[t], [d]**

Specifically, when SHOE /ʃu/ → [tu], we understand that first /ʃ/ → [s] by the process of _____. And then the /s/ → [t] by the processes of STOPPING and STRIDENCY DELETION.   **PF**

Whenever a palatal fricative or affricate becomes an alveolar consonant, _____ has been applied.   **PF**

The palatal affricate /tʃ/ can become [ts], retaining the affrication. Here, the only process involved is _____.   **PF**

/tʃ/ may also become [t], where the frication portion of the affricate has been deleted. When /tʃ/ → [t], the processes of _____ and _____ have been applied in addition to PF.   **ST, STR**

/p/ *PIG*	/n/ *NO*	/ʃ/ *SHE*	/w/ *WAGON*	/ɛ/ *BED*	/ʌ/ *GUN*
/b/ *BED*	/ŋ/ *STING*	/ʒ/ *ROUGE*	/ʍ/ *WHEEL*	/æ/ *CAT*	/ə/ *ABOUT*
/t/ *TOY*	/f/ *FOX*	/h/ *HAVE*	/ɚ/ *FINGER*	/a/ *GOT*	/aɪ/ *KITE*
/d/ *DUCK*	/θ/ *THINK*	/tʃ/ *CHICKEN*	/ɝ/ *CHURCH*	/ɔ/ *TALK*	/ɔɪ/ *TOY*
/k/ *KEEP*	/ð/ *THIS*	/dʒ/ *JUMPING*	/i/ *SEE*	/o/ *GOAT*	/aʊ/ *OUT*
/g/ *GOAT*	/s/ *SEE*	/l/ *LAKE*	/ɪ/ *PIG*	/ʊ/ *BOOK*	
/m/ *ME*	/z/ *ZOO*	/j/ *YOU*	/eɪ, e/ *MAKE*	/u/ *GLUE*	

PF

strident

ST, STR, PVV

PF

PF

PF

STR

PF

strident

When /tʃ/ → [s], the stop portion of the affricate has been deleted and the fricative aspect has been retained. This is called DEAFFRICATION (see Section 13). In this case also, the palatal /ʃ/ has been fronted to a /s/. Thus, the process of _____ has been applied.

STRIDENCY DELETION has not been applied when /tʃ/ → [s], since the [s] is also _____.

The affricate /tʃ/ also becomes [d] fairly frequently among young childen and phonologically disordered children. In this case, the production has retained the stop portion of the affricate, has lost the continuant-strident portion, and has added voicing. The three processes, therefore, that are applied for /tʃ/ to become [d] are _____, _____, and _____.

Similarly, /dʒ/ can become [dz], [d], or [z] if _____ is applied with or without additional processes.

When /dʒ/ → [dz], only the process of _____ has been applied.

When /dʒ/ → [d], both ST and _____ have been applied.

And, since the strident fricative portion has been deleted, _____ has also been applied.

When /dʒ/ → [z], DEAFFRICATION has been applied in addition to _____.

STR has not been applied, since [z] is also a _____ consonant.

Deletion of Final Consonant	DFC	Consonant Harmony	CH	Backing to Velars	BK
Prevocalic Voicing	PVV	Postvocalic Devoicing	PVD	Epenthesis	EPEN
Syllable Reduction	SR	Vocalization	VOC	Metathesis	METATH
Velar Fronting	VF	Palatal Fronting	PF	Coalescence	COAL
Stopping of Fricatives and Affricates	ST	Gliding of Liquids	GL	Palatalization	PAL
Cluster Reduction	CR	Deaffrication	DEAFF	Denasalization	DENAS
Stridency Deletion	STR	Deletion of Initial Consonant	DIC	Idiosyncratic Processes	
		Glottal Replacement	GR		

/ʃ/ may become [s], [t], [ts], [d], [z], [dz] when _____ is applied with or without additional processes.

PF

When /ʃ/ → [s], only _____ has been applied.

PF

When /ʃ/ → [t], PF and _____ and _____ have been applied.

ST, STR

List the sound changes that would result from the use of PF for the following words:

	Adult Form		Child's Form	Sound Change	
CHIN	/tʃɪn/	→	[tsɪn]	/___/ → [___]	/tʃ/ → [ts]
JUMP	/dʒʌmp/	→	[dzʌmp]	/___/ → [___]	/dʒ/ → [dz]
JOKE	/dʒok/	→	[dzok]	/___/ → [___]	/dʒ/ → [dz]
SHEEP	/ʃip/	→	[sip]	/___/ → [___]	/ʃ/ → [s]
RICH	/rɪtʃ/	→	[rɪts]	/___/ → [___]	/tʃ/ → [ts]
OCEAN	/oʃən/	→	[osən]	/___/ → [___]	/ʃ/ → [s]
PAJAMAS	/pədʒæməz/	→	[pədzæməz]	/___/ → [___]	/dʒ/ → [dz]

_____ is the process that, when applied, results in the fronting of a palatal fricative or affricate to an alveolar.

PF

In the examples just given, the stridency has been retained. That is, when /tʃ/ → [ts], or /ʃ/ → [s], there is _____ retained in both.

stridency

/p/ *PIG*	/n/ *NO*	/ʃ/ *SHE*	/w/ *WAGON*	/ɛ/ *BED*	/ʌ/ *GUN*
/b/ *BED*	/ŋ/ *STING*	/ʒ/ *ROUGE*	/ʍ/ *WHEEL*	/æ/ *CAT*	/ə/ *ABOUT*
/t/ *TOY*	/f/ *FOX*	/h/ *HAVE*	/ɚ/ *FINGER*	/a/ *GOT*	/aɪ/ *KITE*
/d/ *DUCK*	/θ/ *THINK*	/tʃ/ *CHICKEN*	/ɝ/ *CHURCH*	/ɔ/ *TALK*	/ɔɪ/ *TOY*
/k/ *KEEP*	/ð/ *THIS*	/dʒ/ *JUMPING*	/i/ *SEE*	/o/ *GOAT*	/aʊ/ *OUT*
/g/ *GOAT*	/s/ *SEE*	/l/ *LAKE*	/ɪ/ *PIG*	/ʊ/ *BOOK*	
/m/ *ME*	/z/ *ZOO*	/j/ *YOU*	/eɪ, e/ *MAKE*	/u/ *GLUE*	

In contrast, when /tʃ/ → [t], or /ʃ/ → [t], the stridency has been deleted. This is because the process of STOPPING has been applied in addition to PF. Recall that when strident fricatives become stop consonants they lose their _____.

stridency

Consider both PF and ST. Then /tʃ/, /ʃ/, /dʒ/, /ʒ/ could change to any one of these: /s/, /z/, /t/, /d/, /ts/, /dz/. A change to ANY of these alveolars would be the result of the application of the process _____.

PF

For example, when CHAIR /tʃɛr/ → [tsɛr], the process of _____ was applied.

PF

When CHAIR /tʃɛr/ → [tɛr], the processes of _____ and _____ have been applied, and the stridency has also been deleted.

PF, ST

When CHAIR /tʃɛr/ → [dɛr], the processes of _____, _____, and _____ were applied as well as the process of PREVOCALIC VOICING (PVV).

PF, ST, STR

List the processes that were applied to result in each of the following sound changes:

	Sound Change	Process(es)
ST	/ʃ/ → [tʃ]	_____
PF, ST	/ʃ/ → [ts]	_____
PF	/ʃ/ → [s]	_____

Deletion of Final Consonant	DFC	Consonant Harmony	CH	Backing to Velars	BK
		Postvocalic Devoicing	PVD	Epenthesis	EPEN
Prevocalic Voicing	PVV	Vocalization	VOC	Metathesis	METATH
Syllable Reduction	SR	Palatal Fronting	PF	Coalescence	COAL
Velar Fronting	VF	Gliding of Liquids	GL	Palatalization	PAL
Stopping of Fricatives and Affricates	ST	Deaffrication	DEAFF	Denasalization	DENAS
Cluster Reduction	CR	Deletion of Initial Consonant	DIC	Idiosyncratic Processes	
Stridency Deletion	STR	Glottal Replacement	GR		

/ʃ/ → [t]   _____   ST, STR, PF

/ʃ/ → [d]   _____   ST, STR, PVV, PF

Note that when /ʃ/ → [ts], STR has not been applied. /ts/ is an alveolar affricate. It contains characteristics of /s/ and therefore also stridency. However, when /ʃ/ becomes /t/ or /d/, _____ has been applied.   STR

Indicate whether each of the following provides an opportunity for PF to be applied:

	Adult Form	YES/NO	
CITY	/sɪɾɪ/	_____	NO, no palatals
PUSH	/puʃ/	_____	YES, /ʃ/
WATCH	/watʃ/	_____	YES, /tʃ/
SISTER	/sɪstɚ/	_____	NO, no palatals
ROUGE	/ruʒ/	_____	YES, /ʒ/
SHOUT	/ʃaʊt/	_____	YES, /ʃ/
PAJAMAS	/pədʒæməz/	_____	YES, /dʒ/

For each of the following responses, enter the sound change(s) and indicate the process(es) that have been applied.

/p/ *PIG*	/n/ *NO*	/ʃ/ *SHE*	/w/ *WAGON*	/ɛ/ *BED*	/ʌ/ *GUN*
/b/ *BED*	/ŋ/ *STING*	/ʒ/ *ROUGE*	/ʍ/ *WHEEL*	/æ/ *CAT*	/ə/ *ABOUT*
/t/ *TOY*	/f/ *FOX*	/h/ *HAVE*	/ɚ/ *FINGER*	/a/ *GOT*	/aɪ/ *KITE*
/d/ *DUCK*	/θ/ *THINK*	/tʃ/ *CHICKEN*	/ɝ/ *CHURCH*	/ɔ/ *TALK*	/ɔɪ/ *TOY*
/k/ *KEEP*	/ð/ *THIS*	/dʒ/ *JUMPING*	/i/ *SEE*	/o/ *GOAT*	/aʊ/ *OUT*
/g/ *GOAT*	/s/ *SEE*	/l/ *LAKE*	/ɪ/ *PIG*	/ʊ/ *BOOK*	
/m/ *ME*	/z/ *ZOO*	/j/ *YOU*	/eɪ, e/ *MAKE*	/u/ *GLUE*	

		Adult Form		Child's Form	Sound Change	Process (es)
/tʃ/ → [ts], PF	LUNCH	/lʌntʃ/	→	[lʌnts]	/__/ → [__]	____
/tʃ/ → [d], PF, ST, STR, PVV	CHEESE	/tʃiz/	→	[diz]	/__/ → [__]	____
/tʃ/ → [t], PF, ST, STR	CHEW	/tʃu/	→	[tu]	/__/ → [__]	____
/tʃ/ → [s], PF, (DEAFF)	KITCHEN	/kɪtʃɪn/	→	[kɪsɪn]	/__/ → [__]	____
/ʃ/ → [s], PF	CRASH	/kræʃ/	→	[kræs]	/__/ → [__]	____
/ʃ/ → [d], PF, ST, STR, PVV	SHUT	/ʃʌt/	→	[dʌt]	/__/ → [__]	____
/dʒ/ → [d], PF, ST, STR	GYM	/dʒɪm/	→	[dɪm]	/__/ → [__]	____
/ndʒ/ → [nz], PF, (DEAFF)	ENGINE	/ɛndʒɪn/	→	[ɛnzɪn]	/__/ → [__]	____
/ʒ/ → [z], PF	TELEVISION	/tɛləvɪʒən/	→	[tɛləvɪzən]	/__/ → [__]	____

SUMMARY
Palatal Fronting

1. PF is a process that, when applied, results in the alveolar production of the palatal consonants /ʃ/, /ʒ/, /tʃ/, and /dʒ/.
2. The application of PF may be accompanied by ST, STR, or DEAFF.

Deletion of Final Consonant	DFC	Consonant Harmony	CH	Backing to Velars	BK
Prevocalic Voicing	PVV	Postvocalic Devoicing	PVD	Epenthesis	EPEN
Syllable Reduction	SR	Vocalization	VOC	Metathesis	METATH
Velar Fronting	VF	Palatal Fronting	PF	Coalescence	COAL
Stopping of Fricatives and Affricates	ST	Gliding of Liquids	GL	Palatalization	PAL
		Deaffrication	DEAFF	Denasalization	DENAS
Cluster Reduction	CR	Deletion of Initial Consonant	DIC	Idiosyncratic Processes	
Stridency Deletion	STR	Glottal Replacement	GR		

SECTION 12. GLIDING OF LIQUIDS

GLIDING OF LIQUIDS (GL) refers to the production of a glide (/w/, /j/) for a liquid (/r/, /l/). The change from LAMP /læmp/ to [wæmp] is an example of _____.

GLIDING OF
LIQUIDS

The abbreviation for GLIDING OF LIQUIDS is _____.

GL

Another example of GL would be RIGHT /raɪt/ → [jaɪt], where the /r/ → [____].

[j]

The application of this process is limited to the target consonants /r/ and /l/. However, this process may occur frequently because many English words contain the consonants /____/ and /____/.

/r/, /l/

The two glides in Standard American English are /____/ and /____/.

/w/, /j/

We recognize GL as a phonological process that is common among young children and is one of the _____ processes to be suppressed.

last

List the productions that would result from applying GL to the following target words:

	Adult Form		Child's Form		
LEAF	/lif/	→	[_____] or	[_____]	[wif], [jif]
LADY	/ledɪ/	→	[_____] or	[_____]	[wedɪ], [jedɪ]

/p/ *PIG*	/n/ *NO*	/ʃ/ *SHE*	/w/ *WAGON*	/ɛ/ *BED*	/ʌ/ *GUN*
/b/ *BED*	/ŋ/ *STING*	/ʒ/ *ROUGE*	/ʍ/ *WHEEL*	/æ/ *CAT*	/ə/ *ABOUT*
/t/ *TOY*	/f/ *FOX*	/h/ *HAVE*	/ɚ/ *FINGER*	/a/ *GOT*	/aɪ/ *KITE*
/d/ *DUCK*	/θ/ *THINK*	/tʃ/ *CHICKEN*	/ɝ/ *CHURCH*	/ɔ/ *TALK*	/ɔɪ/ *TOY*
/k/ *KEEP*	/ð/ *THIS*	/dʒ/ *JUMPING*	/i/ *SEE*	/o/ *GOAT*	/aʊ/ *OUT*
/g/ *GOAT*	/s/ *SEE*	/l/ *LAKE*	/ɪ/ *PIG*	/ʊ/ *BOOK*	
/m/ *ME*	/z/ *ZOO*	/j/ *YOU*	/eɪ, e/ *MAKE*	/u/ *GLUE*	

[wʌn], [jʌn] | RUN /rʌn/ → [_____] or [_____]

[wid], [jid] | READ /rid/ → [_____] or [_____]

[w], [j] | The application of GL results in the liquids /r/ and /l/ becoming one of the glides [____] or [____].

Examine each of the following target words and the child's responses. Give the sound change for each:

		Adult Form	Child's Form	Sound Change
/l/ → [w]	LEMON	/lɛmən/ → [wɛmən]		/____/ → [____]
/l/ → [w]	LOOK	/lʊk/ → [wʊk]		/____/ → [____]
/r/ → [j]	ROCK	/rak/ → [jak]		/____/ → [____]
/r/ → [w]	RING	/rɪŋ/ → [wɪŋ]		/____/ → [____]

Some contexts promote GLIDING more than others. When /r/ is followed by a rounded vowel, it is more likely be become [w]. For example, /r/ may become [w] in ROOF /ruf/ → [wuf] because of the influence of the rounded [____], but it may be retained as /r/ in READ /rid/ → [rid].

[u] OR vowel

Similarly, /r/ may become [w] in ROAD /rod/ → [wod] because of the influence of the ____.

[o] OR rounded vowel

/r/ may be produced less [w]-like in the context of non-rounded vowels. For example, READ /rid/ may be produced [rid], while ROAD /rod/ is produced [wod].

Deletion of Final Consonant	DFC	Consonant Harmony	CH	Backing to Velars	BK
Prevocalic Voicing	PVV	Postvocalic Devoicing	PVD	Epenthesis	EPEN
Syllable Reduction	SR	Vocalization	VOC	Metathesis	METATH
Velar Fronting	VF	Palatal Fronting	PF	Coalescence	COAL
Stopping of Fricatives and Affricates	ST	Gliding of Liquids	GL	Palatalization	PAL
		Deaffrication	DEAFF	Denasalization	DENAS
Cluster Reduction	CR.	Deletion of Initial Consonant	DIC	Idiosyncratic Processes	
Stridency Deletion	STR	Glottal Replacement	GR		

The /r/ is likely to become [＿＿] in the context of a
＿＿＿＿＿＿ vowel.

    [w], rounded

    Similarly, when /l/ is glided in the context of a
rounded vowel, it is likely to be glided to [＿＿] as in
BLUE /blu/ → [bwu].

    [w]

    For the following productions, give the probable
sound change relative to the vowel context. That is,
indicate whether /r/ and /l/ are likely to be glided to a [j]
or [w] on the basis of the adjacent vowel characteristics.

	Adult Form	*Probable Sound Change*	
ROAD	/rod/	/＿＿/ → [＿＿]	/r/ → [w]
ROPE	/rop/	/＿＿/ → [＿＿]	/r/ → [w]
LOAN	/lon/	/＿＿/ → [＿＿]	/l/ → [w]
LOAD	/lod/	/＿＿/ → [＿＿]	/l/ → [w]
ROW	/ro/	/＿＿/ → [＿＿]	/r/ → [w]
ROOF	/ruf/	/＿＿/ → [＿＿]	/r/ → [w]

    In each case, the adjacent vowel involves lip
rounding; the /r/ or /l/ is likely to become a [w] when
this occurs. The coarticulatory influence of anticipated lip
rounding on the vowel may affect the preceding
＿＿＿＿＿＿.

    consonant (/r/, /l/)

    Many word-initial clusters contain a ＿＿＿＿＿＿.

    liquid (/r/ or /l/)

/p/ *PIG*	/n/ *NO*	/ʃ/ *SHE*	/w/ *WAGON*	/ɛ/ *BED*	/ʌ/ *GUN*
/b/ *BED*	/ŋ/ *STING*	/ʒ/ *ROUGE*	/ʍ/ *WHEEL*	/æ/ *CAT*	/ə/ *ABOUT*
/t/ *TOY*	/f/ *FOX*	/h/ *HAVE*	/ɚ/ *FINGER*	/a/ *GOT*	/aɪ/ *KITE*
/d/ *DUCK*	/θ/ *THINK*	/tʃ/ *CHICKEN*	/ɝ/ *CHURCH*	/ɔ/ *TALK*	/ɔɪ/ *TOY*
/k/ *KEEP*	/ð/ *THIS*	/dʒ/ *JUMPING*	/i/ *SEE*	/o/ *GOAT*	/aʊ/ *OUT*
/g/ *GOAT*	/s/ *SEE*	/l/ *LAKE*	/ɪ/ *PIG*	/ʊ/ *BOOK*	
/m/ *ME*	/z/ *ZOO*	/j/ *YOU*	/eɪ, e/ *MAKE*	/u/ *GLUE*	

GL	For example, CLAP /klæp/ might be produced [kwæp], where _____ has been applied to the /l/ in /kl/.
[gwæs], OR [gjæs]	Similarly, GLASS /glæs/ might be produced [_____] with the application of GL.

Indicate whether each of the following words provides an opportunity for GL to be applied:

		Adult Form	YES/NO
YES, /l/	SLIDE	/slaɪd/	_____
NO, no liquids	SWING	/swɪŋ/	_____
YES, /r/	RABBIT	/ræbɪt/	_____
YES, /r/	FRIEND	/frɛnd/	_____
YES, /r/ and/or /l/	PROBLEM	/prabləm/	_____
YES, /r/	GRANDMA	/græma/	_____
YES, /r/	CEREAL	/sɪrɪəl/	_____
YES, /r/ and/or /l/	GORILLA	/gərɪlə/	_____
NO, no consonantal /r/ or /l/	PUZZLE	/pʌzl̩/	_____
NO, no liquids	WINDOW	/wɪndo/	_____

Deletion of Final Consonant	DFC	Consonant Harmony	CH	Backing to Velars	BK
Prevocalic Voicing	PVV	Postvocalic Devoicing	PVD	Epenthesis	EPEN
Syllable Reduction	SR	Vocalization	VOC	Metathesis	METATH
Velar Fronting	VF	Palatal Fronting	PF	Coalescence	COAL
Stopping of Fricatives and Affricates	ST	Gliding of Liquids	GL	Palatalization	PAL
Cluster Reduction	CR	Deaffrication	DEAFF	Denasalization	DENAS
Stridency Deletion	STR	Deletion of Initial Consonant	DIC	Idiosyncratic Processes	
		Glottal Replacement	GR		

Recall that /ɚ/ and /əl/ are generally not glided. The most common process applied to simplify these two syllabics is _____.

VOC

Recall that the vowel context may influence whether the liquid becomes a [w] or a [j]. Specifically, a _____ vowel will tend to result in the production of [w].

rounded

Similarly, the consonants within a cluster may determine whether a [____] or [____] is produced for the liquid.

[w], [j]

When BRING /brɪŋ/ is glided, the bilabial /b/ may influence the /r/ to become a [____] rather than a [____]. The sound change would be noted as /br/ → [bw].

[w], [j]

Similarly, when FLAG /flæg/ is glided, the /fl/ tends to become [____], rather than [____] because of the influence of the labiodental, /f/.

[fw], [fj]

Evaluate the following clusters and determine whether a [w] is likely to be produced, and, if so, which consonant would be influential.

	Adult Form	YES/NO	Influential Consonant
FLOAT	/flot/	_____	_____
BRUSH	/brʌʃ/	_____	_____
FRUIT	/frut/	_____	_____

YES, /f/

YES, /b/

YES, /f/

/p/ *PIG*	/n/ *NO*	/ʃ/ *SHE*	/w/ *WAGON*	/ɛ/ *BED*	/ʌ/ *GUN*
/b/ *BED*	/ŋ/ *STING*	/ʒ/ *ROUGE*	/ʍ/ *WHEEL*	/æ/ *CAT*	/ə/ *ABOUT*
/t/ *TOY*	/f/ *FOX*	/h/ *HAVE*	/ɚ/ *FINGER*	/a/ *GOT*	/aɪ/ *KITE*
/d/ *DUCK*	/θ/ *THINK*	/tʃ/ *CHICKEN*	/ɝ/ *CHURCH*	/ɔ/ *TALK*	/ɔɪ/ *TOY*
/k/ *KEEP*	/ð/ *THIS*	/dʒ/ *JUMPING*	/i/ *SEE*	/o/ *GOAT*	/aʊ/ *OUT*
/g/ *GOAT*	/s/ *SEE*	/l/ *LAKE*	/ɪ/ *PIG*	/ʊ/ *BOOK*	
/m/ *ME*	/z/ *ZOO*	/j/ *YOU*	/eɪ, e/ *MAKE*	/u/ *GLUE*	

YES, /mb/

NO, no labials

UMBRELLA   /əmbrɛlə/ _____ _____

CLEAN   /klin/ _____ _____

GLIDING may be applied selectively. For example, it may apply to clusters only. Examine the following productions and describe the optional rule this child is using:

	Adult Form		Child's Form
CLOWN	/klaʊn/	→	[klaʊn]
LIKE	/laɪk/	→	[laɪk]
RADIO	/redɪo/	→	[wedɪo]
CARROT	/kɛrət/	→	[kɛwət]
HELLO	/hɛlo/	→	[hɛlo]
GREEN	/grin/	→	[gwin]
BRUSH	/brʌʃ/	→	[bwʌʃ]
BLUE	/blu/	→	[blu]

/r/ is glided;
/l/ is not.

Optional Rule:

GL may be applied optionally within /l/ contexts or within /r/ contexts. Examine the following /r/ contexts and describe the optional rule that applies:

Deletion of Final Consonant	DFC	Consonant Harmony	CH	Backing to Velars	BK
Prevocalic Voicing	PVV	Postvocalic Devoicing	PVD	Epenthesis	EPEN
Syllable Reduction	SR	Vocalization	VOC	Metathesis	METATH
Velar Fronting	VF	Palatal Fronting	PF	Coalescence	COAL
Stopping of Fricatives and Affricates	ST	Gliding of Liquids	GL	Palatalization	PAL
		Deaffrication	DEAFF	Denasalization	DENAS
Cluster Reduction	CR	Deletion of Initial Consonant	DIC	Idiosyncratic Processes	
Stridency Deletion	STR	Glottal Replacement	GR		

	Adult Form		*Child's Form*
GREEN	/grin/	→	[grin]
BREEZE	/briz/	→	[bwiz]
DRESS	/drɛs/	→	[dwɛs]
RABBIT	/ræbɪt/	→	[wæbɪt]
SORRY	/sɔri/	→	[sɔwi]
CROWN	/kraʊn/	→	[kraʊn]
GRASS	/græs/	→	[græs]

Optional Rule:

/r/ is not glided in velar clusters; it is glided in the other contexts given.

GLIDING may be applied in conjunction with other processes. For example, even if a liquid cluster is reduced to one member (the liquid), that may be glided. For example, when GREEN /grin/ → [win], the processes _____ and _____ have been applied.

CR, GL

As with previous sound changes, more than one process may be applied to a specific sound change. Another example would be CRACK /kræk/ → [gwæk], where the sound change /kr/ → [gw] has resulted from the application of _____ and _____.

PVV, GL

/p/ PIG	/n/ NO	/ʃ/ SHE	/w/ WAGON	/ɛ/ BED	/ʌ/ GUN
/b/ BED	/ŋ/ STING	/ʒ/ ROUGE	/ʍ/ WHEEL	/æ/ CAT	/ə/ ABOUT
/t/ TOY	/f/ FOX	/h/ HAVE	/ɚ/ FINGER	/a/ GOT	/aɪ/ KITE
/d/ DUCK	/θ/ THINK	/tʃ/ CHICKEN	/ɝ/ CHURCH	/ɔ/ TALK	/ɔɪ/ TOY
/k/ KEEP	/ð/ THIS	/dʒ/ JUMPING	/i/ SEE	/o/ GOAT	/aʊ/ OUT
/g/ GOAT	/s/ SEE	/l/ LAKE	/ɪ/ PIG	/ʊ/ BOOK	
/m/ ME	/z/ ZOO	/j/ YOU	/eɪ, e/ MAKE	/u/ GLUE	

List all processes that have been applied to each of the following:

	Adult Form		Child's Form	Process(es)
GL	TELEPHONE	/tɛləfon/	→ [tɛwəfon]	_____
SR (GL is blocked)	TELEPHONE	/tɛləfon/	→ [tefon]	_____
GL, VF (or CH)	ROCKET	/rakɪt/	→ [watɪt]	_____
ST, STR, GL	SLIDE	/slaɪd/	→ [twaɪd]	_____
GL	CLOWN	/klaʊn/	→ [kwaʊn]	_____
CR	VACUUM	/vækjuəm/	→ [vækuəm]	_____
PVV, GL	TREE	/tri/	→ [dwi]	_____
ST, STR, PVV, GL	SLIPPERY	/slɪpərɪ/	→ [dwɪpərɪ]	_____
CR (GL is blocked)	BROKEN	/brokən/	→ [bokən]	_____
CR, PVV (GL is blocked)	TRUCK	/trʌk/	→ [dʌk]	_____

three   GL was blocked _____ times.

Since GL was applied six times and was blocked four times, the number of potential contexts was actually _____. However, until the child suppresses CR and SR, we will not know whether the blocked liquids would

nine   have been glided.

Deletion of Final Consonant	DFC	Consonant Harmony	CH	Backing to Velars	BK	
Prevocalic Voicing	PVV	Postvocalic Devoicing	PVD	Epenthesis	EPEN	
Syllable Reduction	SR	Vocalization	VOC	Metathesis	METATH	
Velar Fronting	VF	Palatal Fronting	PF	Coalescence	COAL	
Stopping of Fricatives and Affricates	ST	Gliding of Liquids	GL	Palatalization	PAL	
Cluster Reduction	CR	Deaffrication	DEAFF	Denasalization	DENAS	
Stridency Deletion	STR	Deletion of Initial Consonant	DIC	Idiosyncratic Processes		
		Glottal Replacement	GR			

SUMMARY
Gliding of Liquids

1. GL refers to the production of a glide (/w/, /j/) for a liquid (/l/, /r/).
2. Although limited to /l/ and /r/, this process occurs frequently because many English words contain liquids.
3. Gliding to a /w/ often occurs when the liquid is adjacent to a rounded vowel.
4. When the liquid in a cluster becomes /w/ or /j/, the process of GL has been applied.
5. The process of GL may be blocked by CR when the liquid is deleted from a cluster.
6. GL may be applied selectively to either /l/ or /r/ contexts.

/p/ *PIG*	/n/ *NO*	/ʃ/ *SHE*	/w/ *WAGON*	/ɛ/ *BED*	/ʌ/ *GUN*
/b/ *BED*	/ŋ/ *STING*	/ʒ/ *ROUGE*	/ʍ/ *WHEEL*	/æ/ *CAT*	/ə/ *ABOUT*
/t/ *TOY*	/f/ *FOX*	/h/ *HAVE*	/ɚ/ *FINGER*	/a/ *GOT*	/aɪ/ *KITE*
/d/ *DUCK*	/θ/ *THINK*	/tʃ/ *CHICKEN*	/ɝ/ *CHURCH*	/ɔ/ *TALK*	/ɔɪ/ *TOY*
/k/ *KEEP*	/ð/ *THIS*	/dʒ/ *JUMPING*	/i/ *SEE*	/o/ *GOAT*	/aʊ/ *OUT*
/g/ *GOAT*	/s/ *SEE*	/l/ *LAKE*	/ɪ/ *PIG*	/ʊ/ *BOOK*	
/m/ *ME*	/z/ *ZOO*	/j/ *YOU*	/eɪ, e/ *MAKE*	/u/ *GLUE*	

SECTION 13. DEAFFRICATION

DEAFFRICATION (DEAFF) is a process that affects affricates. The change from CHAIR /tʃɛr/ → [ʃɛr] is an example of _____.

DEAFFRICATION, or DEAFF

Another example of DEAFFRICATION would be CHAT /tʃæt/ → [_____], where /tʃ/ → /ʃ/, a fricative.

[ʃæt]

DEAFFRICATION, or DEAFF

Similarly, JUMP /dʒʌmp/ → [ʒʌmp] with the application of _____.

The abbreviation for DEAFFRICATION is _____.

DEAFF

/tʃ/, /dʒ/

There are two English affricates, /____/ and /____/.

fricative

Each affricate is composed of two segments: a stop segment and a _____ segment.

/ʃ/

The stop segment of /tʃ/ is /t/; the fricative segment of /tʃ/ is /____/.

/d/, /ʒ/

The stop segment of /dʒ/ is /____/; the fricative segment of /dʒ/ is /____/.

DEAFF

The application of _____ results in retention of the fricative segment only.

[ʃ], [ʒ]

Thus, the two affricates, /tʃ/ and /dʒ/, become [____] and [____] with the application of DEAFF.

Deletion of Final Consonant	DFC	Consonant Harmony	CH	Backing to Velars	BK
Prevocalic Voicing	PVV	Postvocalic Devoicing	PVD	Epenthesis	EPEN
Syllable Reduction	SR	Vocalization	VOC	Metathesis	METATH
Velar Fronting	VF	Palatal Fronting	PF	Coalescence	COAL
Stopping of Fricatives and Affricates	ST	Gliding of Liquids	GL	Palatalization	PAL
Cluster Reduction	CR	Deaffrication	DEAFF	Denasalization	DENAS
Stridency Deletion	STR	Deletion of Initial Consonant	DIC	Idiosyncratic Processes	
		Glottal Replacement	GR		

Indicate whether each of the following adult forms provides an opportunity for DEAFF to be applied:

	Adult Form	YES/NO	
COUCH	/kaʊtʃ/	_____	YES, /tʃ/
CHIMNEY	/tʃɪmni/	_____	YES, /tʃ/
GIANT	/dʒaɪənt/	_____	YES, /dʒ/
GIFT	/gɪft/	_____	NO, no affricate.
CHRISTMAS	/krɪsməs/	_____	NO, no affricate.
BRIDGE	/brɪdʒ/	_____	YES, /dʒ/

Of the six words listed, _____ provide at least one opportunity for DEAFF to be applied. That is, they contain affricates.

four

If the process of DEAFF is applied to one of the affricates in CHURCH /tʃɝtʃ/, it might become [tʃɝʃ] or [ʃɝtʃ]. If DEAFF is applied to both affricates in this word, it will become [_____].

[ʃɝʃ]

Apply the process of DEAFF to the following attempted words.

	Adult Form	Child's Form	
CHIP	/tʃɪp/	→ [_____]	[ʃɪp]
JAM	/dʒæm/	→ [_____]	[ʒæm]

/p/ PIG	/n/ NO	/ʃ/ SHE	/w/ WAGON	/ɛ/ BED	/ʌ/ GUN
/b/ BED	/ŋ/ STING	/ʒ/ ROUGE	/ʍ/ WHEEL	/æ/ CAT	/ə/ ABOUT
/t/ TOY	/f/ FOX	/h/ HAVE	/ɚ/ FINGER	/a/ GOT	/aɪ/ KITE
/d/ DUCK	/θ/ THINK	/tʃ/ CHICKEN	/ɝ/ CHURCH	/ɔ/ TALK	/ɔɪ/ TOY
/k/ KEEP	/ð/ THIS	/dʒ/ JUMPING	/i/ SEE	/o/ GOAT	/aʊ/ OUT
/g/ GOAT	/s/ SEE	/l/ LAKE	/ɪ/ PIG	/ʊ/ BOOK	
/m/ ME	/z/ ZOO	/j/ YOU	/eɪ, e/ MAKE	/u/ GLUE	

[waʃ] | WATCH /watʃ/ → [_____]

[brɪʒ] | BRIDGE /brɪdʒ/ → [_____]

[pəʒæməz] | PAJAMAS /pədʒæməz/ → [_____]

[kɪʃɪn] | KITCHEN /kɪtʃɪn/ → [_____]

fricative

In each case, the affricate becomes a fricative. When the process of DEAFF is applied to an affricate, it becomes a _____.

DEAFF

In addition to resulting in a homorganic fricative, the application of _____ may result in the production of a non-homorganic fricative.

homorganic

Recall that _____ means "produced at the same place of articulation."

/tʃ/ → [ʃ]

It is possible for the processes of DEAFF and PF to be applied concurrently. For example, CHAIR /tʃɛr/ becomes [ʃɛr] with the application of DEAFF. The sound change is represented by /___/ → [___].

[s]

When PF is then applied, the sound change becomes /ʃ/ → [___].

[ts]

The processes of DEAFF and PF may be applied in the reverse order with the same result. If PF is applied first, then /tʃ/ → [___].

[s]

If DEAFF is then applied, the affricate /ts/ becomes the fricative [___].

Deletion of Final Consonant	DFC	Consonant Harmony	CH	Backing to Velars	BK
Prevocalic Voicing	PVV	Postvocalic Devoicing	PVD	Epenthesis	EPEN
Syllable Reduction	SR	Vocalization	VOC	Metathesis	METATH
Velar Fronting	VF	Palatal Fronting	PF	Coalescence	COAL
Stopping of Fricatives and Affricates	ST	Gliding of Liquids	GL	Palatalization	PAL
Cluster Reduction	CR	Deaffrication	DEAFF	Denasalization	DENAS
Stridency Deletion	STR	Deletion of Initial Consonant	DIC	Idiosyncratic Processes	
		Glottal Replacement	GR		

In both cases, CHAIR /tʃɛr/ → [sɛr] with the application of both _____ and _____.

DEAFF, PF

Apply the processes of PF and DEAFF to the following words. Give the productions that would result from applying first PF and then DEAFF.

	Adult Form		Apply PF		Apply DEAFF	
CHAIR	/tʃɛr/	→	[_____]	→	[_____]	[tsɛr], [sɛr]
JAM	/dʒæm/	→	[_____]	→	[_____]	[dzæm], [zæm]
WATCH	/watʃ/	→	[_____]	→	[_____]	[wats], [was]
BRIDGE	/brɪdʒ/	→	[_____]	→	[_____]	[brɪdz], [brɪz]
PAJAMAS	/pədʒæməz/	→	[_____]	→	[_____]	[pədzæməz], [pəzæməz]
KITCHEN	/kɪtʃɪn/	→	[_____]	→	[_____]	[kɪtsɪn], [kɪsɪn]

When an affricate becomes an allophone of /s/, /z/, /ʃ/, or /ʒ/, the process of _____ has still been applied.

DEAFF

For example, when /tʃ/ → [s̪], where the /s/ has been dentalized, the process of _____ has been applied, resulting in the production of the fricative segment of the affricate.

DEAFF

The most common sound changes involving affricates result in the production of /s/, /z/, /ʃ/, and /ʒ/. However, it is also possible for one of the other fricatives to be produced as the result of the application of _____.

DEAFF

/p/ *PIG*	/n/ *NO*	/ʃ/ *SHE*	/w/ *WAGON*	/ɛ/ *BED*	/ʌ/ *GUN*
/b/ *BED*	/ŋ/ *STING*	/ʒ/ *ROUGE*	/ʍ/ *WHEEL*	/æ/ *CAT*	/ə/ *ABOUT*
/t/ *TOY*	/f/ *FOX*	/h/ *HAVE*	/ɚ/ *FINGER*	/a/ *GOT*	/aɪ/ *KITE*
/d/ *DUCK*	/θ/ *THINK*	/tʃ/ *CHICKEN*	/ɝ/ *CHURCH*	/ɔ/ *TALK*	/ɔɪ/ *TOY*
/k/ *KEEP*	/ð/ *THIS*	/dʒ/ *JUMPING*	/i/ *SEE*	/o/ *GOAT*	/aʊ/ *OUT*
/g/ *GOAT*	/s/ *SEE*	/l/ *LAKE*	/ɪ/ *PIG*	/ʊ/ *BOOK*	
/m/ *ME*	/z/ *ZOO*	/j/ *YOU*	/eɪ, e/ *MAKE*	/u/ *GLUE*	

DEAFF, PF, STR		For example, JEEP /dʒip/ may become [ðip] with the application of DEAFF and PF, where the fronted /ʒ/ has been dentalized and produced without stridency. Therefore, there are three processes that have been applied: _____, _____, and _____.		

/z/ — In addition, the /ʒ/ has been dentalized. This is not considered to be a phonological process, but rather an allophonic form of the phoneme /___/.

Determine which processes were applied to the following target words to result in the given productions. Recall that dentalization is not a phonological process.

			Adult Form		*Child's Form*	*Process(es) Applied*
PF	BENCH	/bɛntʃ/	→	[bɛnts]	_____
PF, DEAFF	BENCH	/bɛntʃ/	→	[bɛns]	_____
PF, DEAFF	BENCH	/bɛntʃ/	→	[bɛns̪]	_____
PF, DEAFF, STR	BENCH	/bɛntʃ/	→	[bɛnθ]	_____
DEAFF	BENCH	/bɛntʃ/	→	[bɛnʃ]	_____
PF	BRIDGE	/brɪdʒ/	→	[brɪdz]	_____
PF, DEAFF	BRIDGE	/brɪdʒ/	→	[brɪz]	_____
PF, DEAFF	BRIDGE	/brɪdʒ/	→	[brɪz̪]	_____
DEAFF	BRIDGE	/brɪdʒ/	→	[brɪʒ]	_____
PF, DEAFF, STR	BRIDGE	/brɪdʒ/	→	[brɪð]	_____

Deletion of Final Consonant	DFC	Consonant Harmony	CH	Backing to Velars	BK
Prevocalic Voicing	PVV	Postvocalic Devoicing	PVD	Epenthesis	EPEN
Syllable Reduction	SR	Vocalization	VOC	Metathesis	METATH
Velar Fronting	VF	Palatal Fronting	PF	Coalescence	COAL
Stopping of Fricatives and Affricates	ST	Gliding of Liquids	GL	Palatalization	PAL
Cluster Reduction	CR	Deaffrication	DEAFF	Denasalization	DENAS
Stridency Deletion	STR	Deletion of Initial Consonant	DIC	Idiosyncratic Processes	
		Glottal Replacement	GR		

Word	Phonemic		Surface		Process(es)
CHEW	/tʃu/	→	[tsu]	_____	PF
CHEW	/tʃu/	→	[su]	_____	PF, DEAFF
CHEW	/tʃu/	→	[θu]	_____	PF, DEAFF, STR
CHEW	/tʃu/	→	[s̪u]	_____	PF, DEAFF
CHEW	/tʃu/	→	[ʃu]	_____	DEAFF
JOB	/dʒab/	→	[ʒab]	_____	DEAFF
JOB	/dʒab/	→	[zab]	_____	DEAFF, PF
JOB	/dʒab/	→	[dzab]	_____	PF
JOB	/dʒab/	→	[z̪ab]	_____	DEAFF, PF
JOB	/dʒab/	→	[ðab]	_____	DEAFF, PF, STR

The application of DEAFF can result in the production of homonyms. For example, when the process of DEAFF is applied to CHEW /tʃu/, it becomes [ʃu]. Thus, the words CHEW and SHOE become _____ because they are represented by the same surface form in the child's production.   homonyms

Give the processes that were applied to result in the following homonyms:

Homonyms	Surface Form	Process(es) Applied	
CHEW-SHOE	/ʃu/	_____	DEAFF
CHEW-SHOE-SUE	/su/	_____	DEAFF, PF

/p/ *PIG*	/n/ *NO*	/ʃ/ *SHE*	/w/ *WAGON*	/ɛ/ *BED*	/ʌ/ *GUN*		
/b/ *BED*	/ŋ/ *STING*	/ʒ/ *ROUGE*	/ʍ/ *WHEEL*	/æ/ *CAT*	/ə/ *ABOUT*		
/t/ *TOY*	/f/ *FOX*	/h/ *HAVE*	/ɚ/ *FINGER*	/ɑ/ *GOT*	/aɪ/ *KITE*		
/d/ *DUCK*	/θ/ *THINK*	/tʃ/ *CHICKEN*	/ɝ/ *CHURCH*	/ɔ/ *TALK*	/ɔɪ/ *TOY*		
/k/ *KEEP*	/ð/ *THIS*	/dʒ/ *JUMPING*	/i/ *SEE*	/o/ *GOAT*	/aʊ/ *OUT*		
/g/ *GOAT*	/s/ *SEE*	/l/ *LAKE*	/ɪ/ *PIG*	/ʊ/ *BOOK*			
/m/ *ME*	/z/ *ZOO*	/j/ *YOU*	/eɪ, e/ *MAKE*	/u/ *GLUE*			

DEAFF, PF, ST, STR	CHEW-SHOE-SUE-TWO	/tu/	_____
PVV	JEEP-CHEEP	/dʒip/	_____
PVV, DEAFF	JEEP-CHEEP-SHEEP	/ʒip/	_____
PVV, DEAFF, CR, PF	JEEP-CHEAP-SHEEP-SLEEP	/zip/	_____
DEAFF	MATCH-MASH	/mæʃ/	_____
DEAFF, PF	MATCH-MASH-MASS	/mæs/	_____
DEAFF, PF, ST, STR	MATCH-MASH-MASS-MAT	/mæt/	_____
PVD	BADGE-BATCH	/bætʃ/	_____
PVD, DEAFF	BADGE-BATCH-BASH	/bæʃ/	_____
PVD, DEAFF, PF	BADGE-BATCH-BASH-BASS	/bæs/	_____

intelligible

The more homonyms the child uses, the less _____ the speech.

The process of DEAFF can be applied selectively. Describe the optional process that the following child is using:

	Adult Form	*Child's Form*
CHAIR	/tʃɛr/	→ [tʃɛr]

Deletion of Final Consonant	DFC	Consonant Harmony	CH	Backing to Velars	BK
Prevocalic Voicing	PVV	Postvocalic Devoicing	PVD	Epenthesis	EPEN
Syllable Reduction	SR	Vocalization	VOC	Metathesis	METATH
Velar Fronting	VF	Palatal Fronting	PF	Coalescence	COAL
Stopping of Fricatives and Affricates	ST	Gliding of Liquids	GL	Palatalization	PAL
Cluster Reduction	CR	Deaffrication	DEAFF	Denasalization	DENAS
Stridency Deletion	STR	Deletion of Initial Consonant	DIC	Idiosyncratic Processes	
		Glottal Replacement	GR		

JAM   /dʒæm/ → [dʒæm]

WATCH   /watʃ/ → [waʃ]

BUDGE   /bʌdʒ/ → [bʌʒ]

KITCHEN   /kɪtʃɪn/ → [kɪtʃɪn]

BADGER   /bædʒɚ/ → [bædʒɚ]

Optional Process:

Describe the optional process that the following child used on the same six words:

	Adult Form		Child's Form
CHAIR	/tʃɛr/	→	[ʃɛr]
JAM	/dʒæm/	→	[dʒæm]
WATCH	/watʃ/	→	[waʃ]
BUDGE	/bʌdʒ/	→	[bʌdʒ]
KITCHEN	/kɪtʃɪn/	→	[kɪʃɪn]
BADGER	/bædʒɚ/	→	[bædʒɚ]

Optional Process:

> DEAFF applies to word-final affricates only.

> DEAFF applies to voiceless affricates only.

/p/ *PIG*	/n/ *NO*	/ʃ/ *SHE*	/w/ *WAGON*	/ɛ/ *BED*	/ʌ/ *GUN*
/b/ *BED*	/ŋ/ *STING*	/ʒ/ *ROUGE*	/ʍ/ *WHEEL*	/æ/ *CAT*	/ə/ *ABOUT*
/t/ *TOY*	/f/ *FOX*	/h/ *HAVE*	/ɚ/ *FINGER*	/a/ *GOT*	/aɪ/ *KITE*
/d/ *DUCK*	/θ/ *THINK*	/tʃ/ *CHICKEN*	/ɝ/ *CHURCH*	/ɔ/ *TALK*	/ɔɪ/ *TOY*
/k/ *KEEP*	/ð/ *THIS*	/dʒ/ *JUMPING*	/i/ *SEE*	/o/ *GOAT*	/aʊ/ *OUT*
/g/ *GOAT*	/s/ *SEE*	/l/ *LAKE*	/ɪ/ *PIG*	/ʊ/ *BOOK*	
/m/ *ME*	/z/ *ZOO*	/j/ *YOU*	/eɪ, e/ *MAKE*	/u/ *GLUE*	

Determine which processes were applied to the following words. Examine the sound changes carefully.

	Adult Form		Child's Form	Sound Changes	Process(es)
[k], CR, STR	ASK	/æsk/	→ [æk]	/sk/ → [___]	___
[ts], ST	BUS	/bʌs/	→ [bʌts]	/s/ → [___]	___
[s], DEAFF, PF	CATCH	/kætʃ/	→ [kæs]	/tʃ/ → [___]	___
[t], ST, STR, PF	CHIMNEY	/tʃɪmnɪ/	→ [tɪmnɪ]	/tʃ/ → [___]	___
[kl], ST, STR, CH	FLAG	/flæg/	→ [klæg]	/fl/ → [___]	___
[dz], PF	JACKET	/dʒækɪt/	→ [dzækɪt]	/dʒ/ → [___]	___
[ʒ], DEAFF	JUNK	/dʒʌŋk/	→ [ʒʌnk]	/dʒ/ → [___]	___
[s], PF, DEAFF	MATCH	/mætʃ/	→ [mæs]	/tʃ/ → [___]	___
[ʃ], DEAFF	OUCH	/autʃ/	→ [auʃ]	/tʃ/ → [___]	___
[s], DEAFF, PF	TEACHER	/titʃɚ/	→ [tisɚ]	/tʃ/ → [___]	___

SUMMARY
Deaffrication
1. DEAFF is a process that results in the retention of the fricative portion of the affricate.
2. Each affricate is composed of two segments: a stop and a fricative.
3. DEAFF and PF may be applied concurrently.

Deletion of Final Consonant	DFC	Consonant Harmony	CH	Backing to Velars	BK
Prevocalic Voicing	PVV	Postvocalic Devoicing	PVD	Epenthesis	EPEN
Syllable Reduction	SR	Vocalization	VOC	Metathesis	METATH
Velar Fronting	VF	Palatal Fronting	PF	Coalescence	COAL
Stopping of Fricatives and Affricates	ST	Gliding of Liquids	GL	Palatalization	PAL
Cluster Reduction	CR	Deaffrication	DEAFF	Denasalization	DENAS
Stridency Deletion	STR	Deletion of Initial Consonant	DIC	Idiosyncratic Processes	
		Glottal Replacement	GR		

Processes Uncharacteristic
of Normal Speech Development

SECTION 14. DELETION OF INITIAL CONSONANT

DELETION OF INITIAL CONSONANT (DIC) is the name for the process that is applied when the child's production does not include a word-initial consonant where one is expected. BOY /bɔɪ/ → [ɔɪ] is an example of _____.

DELETION OF
INITIAL
CONSONANT

We will use the abbreviation _____ to represent DELETION OF INITIAL CONSONANT.

DIC

Another example of DIC would be SEE /si/ → [i], where the /s/ has become _____.

deleted, (ø)

Since the deletion occurs word-initially, we recognize the process as _____.

DIC

_____ is a process which is used by the very young child who is using primarily CV and VC words.

DIC

For example, during the acquisition of the first 50 words, a child may change WALK /wɔk/ → [ɔk] and HOUSE /haʊs/ → [aʊs]. Similarly, WASH may change from /waʃ/ → [____] with the application of DIC.

[aʃ]

List the productions which would result from the application of DIC to the following attempted words:

	Adult Form	Child's Form
[aʊs]	HOUSE /haʊs/	→ [_____]
[ɔg]	DOG /dɔg/	→ [_____]

Deletion of Final Consonant	DFC	Consonant Harmony	CH	Backing to Velars	BK
Prevocalic Voicing	PVV	Postvocalic Devoicing	PVD	Epenthesis	EPEN
Syllable Reduction	SR	Vocalization	VOC	Metathesis	METATH
Velar Fronting	VF	Palatal Fronting	PF	Coalescence	COAL
Stopping of Fricatives and Affricates	ST	Gliding of Liquids	GL	Palatalization	PAL
Cluster Reduction	CR	Deaffrication	DEAFF	Denasalization	DENAS
Stridency Deletion	STR	Deletion of Initial Consonant	DIC	Idiosyncratic Processes	
		Glottal Replacement	GR		

CUP /kʌp/ → [_____] [ʌp]

SOAP /sop/ → [_____] [op]

MOON /mun/ → [_____] [un]

DIC is also applied to words with word-initial clusters. Thus, CLEAN /klin/ → [in] when DIC is applied. The result is a production that lacks a _____ consonant.

prevocalic, OR word-initial

That is, the production begins with a vowel when there should be one or more _____ word-initially.

consonants

Apply the process of DIC to the following attempted words containing clusters. Indicate the altered production which will result:

	Adult Form	Child's Form	
SNAKE	/snek/	→ [_____]	[ek]
BLOCK	/blak/	→ [_____]	[ak]
BRUSH	/brʌʃ/	→ [_____]	[ʌʃ]
TRUCK	/trʌk/	→ [_____]	[ʌk]
SLEEP	/slip/	→ [_____]	[ip]

Whether an attempted word begins with a cluster or a singleton, if the child's production lacks a word-initial consonant, then the process of _____ has been applied.

DIC

/p/ *PIG*	/n/ *NO*	/ʃ/ *SHE*	/w/ *WAGON*	/ɛ/ *BED*	/ʌ/ *GUN*
/b/ *BED*	/ŋ/ *STING*	/ʒ/ *ROUGE*	/ʍ/ *WHEEL*	/æ/ *CAT*	/ə/ *ABOUT*
/t/ *TOY*	/f/ *FOX*	/h/ *HAVE*	/ɚ/ *FINGER*	/a/ *GOT*	/aɪ/ *KITE*
/d/ *DUCK*	/θ/ *THINK*	/tʃ/ *CHICKEN*	/ɝ/ *CHURCH*	/ɔ/ *TALK*	/ɔɪ/ *TOY*
/k/ *KEEP*	/ð/ *THIS*	/dʒ/ *JUMPING*	/i/ *SEE*	/o/ *GOAT*	/aʊ/ *OUT*
/g/ *GOAT*	/s/ *SEE*	/l/ *LAKE*	/ɪ/ *PIG*	/ʊ/ *BOOK*	
/m/ *ME*	/z/ *ZOO*	/j/ *YOU*	/eɪ, e/ *MAKE*	/u/ *GLUE*	

Identify the individual sound changes and the resulting productions of the following attempted words with the application of DELETION OF INITIAL CONSONANT (DIC):

		Adult Form		Child's Form	Sound Change
[up] /s/ → [ø]	SOUP	/sup/	→ [____]	/____/ → [____]
[aɪt] /k/ → [ø]	KITE	/kaɪt/	→ [____]	/____/ → [____]
[æp] /kl/ → [ø]	CLAP	/klæp/	→ [____]	/____/ → [____]
[ɪŋk] /dr/ → [ø]	DRINK	/drɪŋk/	→ [____]	/____/ → [____]
[ɔg] /fr/ → /[ø]	FROG	/frɔg/	→ [____]	/____/ → [____]

When the attempted word contains no word-initial consonant (as in UP or IN) then there is no opportunity for the process of _____ to be applied.

DIC

Indicate whether each of the following words provides an opportunity for DIC to be applied. The first one has been completed:

		Adult Form	Y/N	Phoneme(s) Affected
YES, /l/	LAMP	/læmp/	Yes	/l/

Deletion of Final Consonant	DFC	Consonant Harmony	CH	Backing to Velars	BK
Prevocalic Voicing	PVV	Postvocalic Devoicing	PVD	Epenthesis	EPEN
Syllable Reduction	SR	Vocalization	VOC	Metathesis	METATH
Velar Fronting	VF	Palatal Fronting	PF	Coalescence	COAL
Stopping of Fricatives and Affricates	ST	Gliding of Liquids	GL	Palatalization	PAL
Cluster Reduction	CR	Deaffrication	DEAFF	Denasalization	DENAS
Stridency Deletion	STR	Deletion of Initial Consonant	DIC	Idiosyncratic Processes	
		Glottal Replacement	GR		

BLUE	/blu/	_____	/___/	YES, /bl/
ORANGE	/ɔrɪndʒ/	_____	/___/	NO
WINDOW	/wɪndo/	_____	/___/	YES, /w/
YELLOW	/jɛlo/	_____	/___/	YES, /j/
APPLE	/æpḷ/	_____	/___/	NO
HOUSE	/haʊs/	_____	/___/	YES, /h/

Of the seven attempted words, a total of
_____ words provide an opportunity for DIC to be
applied.

five

Once you have identified the contexts in which DIC
was applied, then go back and look for similarities within
these contexts. Determine whether the process of DIC has
been applied uniformly or only in certain contexts. For
example, all prevocalic nasal consonants may be deleted
while all other prevocalic _____ are retained.

consonants

It is important to look for these specific patterns
within a process category. For example, DIC may be
optionally applied to prevocalic voiceless consonants only.

/p/ *PIG*	/n/ *NO*	/ʃ/ *SHE*	/w/ *WAGON*	/ɛ/ *BED*	/ʌ/ *GUN*
/b/ *BED*	/ŋ/ *STING*	/ʒ/ *ROUGE*	/ʍ/ *WHEEL*	/æ/ *CAT*	/ə/ *ABOUT*
/t/ *TOY*	/f/ *FOX*	/h/ *HAVE*	/ɚ/ *FINGER*	/a/ *GOT*	/aɪ/ *KITE*
/d/ *DUCK*	/θ/ *THINK*	/tʃ/ *CHICKEN*	/ɝ/ *CHURCH*	/ɔ/ *TALK*	/ɔɪ/ *TOY*
/k/ *KEEP*	/ð/ *THIS*	/dʒ/ *JUMPING*	/i/ *SEE*	/o/ *GOAT*	/aʊ/ *OUT*
/g/ *GOAT*	/s/ *SEE*	/l/ *LAKE*	/ɪ/ *PIG*	/ʊ/ *BOOK*	
/m/ *ME*	/z/ *ZOO*	/j/ *YOU*	/eɪ, e/ *MAKE*	/u/ *GLUE*	

List the productions for each of the following attempted words, using this *optional* rule:

	Adult Form	Child's Form
CAT	/kæt/	→ [_____]
DOG	/dɔg/	→ [_____]
SUN	/sʌn/	→ [_____]
ZOO	/zu/	→ [_____]

[æt], voiceless /k/ has been deleted.

[dɔg], /d/ is voiced.

[ʌn], voiceless /s/ has been deleted.

[zu], /z/ is voiced.

In the examples just given, the process of DIC is applied only when the word-initial consonant is voiceless (CAT and SUN). When there are specific conditions for the application of a process, it is called an _____ process.

optional

Recall that whether a singleton or a cluster has been deleted word-initially, _____ has been applied.

DIC

The result is a production that lacks a _____ consonant.

prevocalic, OR word-initial

Although other phonological processes may also apply, if the sound change represents a deletion that results in the deletion of all word-initial consonants, the process applied is _____.

DIC

Deletion of Final Consonant	DFC	Consonant Harmony	CH	Backing to Velars	BK
Prevocalic Voicing	PVV	Postvocalic Devoicing	PVD	Epenthesis	EPEN
Syllable Reduction	SR	Vocalization	VOC	Metathesis	METATH
Velar Fronting	VF	Palatal Fronting	PF	Coalescence	COAL
Stopping of Fricatives and Affricates	ST	Gliding of Liquids	GL	Palatalization	PAL
Cluster Reduction	CR	Deaffrication	DEAFF	Denasalization	DENAS
Stridency Deletion	STR	Deletion of Initial Consonant	DIC	Idiosyncratic Processes	
		Glottal Replacement	GR		

SUMMARY
Deletion of Initial Consonant

1. DIC is a process that results in the deletion of a singleton or cluster from word-initial position.
2. Any process may be applied uniformly (consistently) or selectively (optionally).
3. Once a process such as DIC has been identified, the consistency of its application should be ascertained.

/p/ *P*IG	/n/ *N*O	/ʃ/ *SH*E	/w/ *W*AGON	/ɛ/ B*E*D	/ʌ/ G*U*N
/b/ *B*ED	/ŋ/ STI*NG*	/ʒ/ ROU*GE*	/ʍ/ *WH*EEL	/æ/ C*A*T	/ə/ *A*BOUT
/t/ *T*OY	/f/ *F*OX	/h/ *H*AVE	/ɝ/ FING*ER*	/a/ G*O*T	/aɪ/ K*I*TE
/d/ *D*UCK	/θ/ *TH*INK	/tʃ/ *CH*ICKEN	/ɝ/ *CH*UR*CH*	/ɔ/ T*A*LK	/ɔɪ/ T*OY*
/k/ *K*EEP	/ð/ *TH*IS	/dʒ/ *J*UMPING	/i/ S*EE*	/o/ G*OA*T	/aʊ/ *OU*T
/g/ *G*OAT	/s/ *S*EE	/l/ *L*AKE	/ɪ/ P*I*G	/ʊ/ B*OO*K	
/m/ *M*E	/z/ *Z*OO	/j/ *Y*OU	/eɪ, e/ M*A*KE	/u/ GL*UE*	

SECTION 15. GLOTTAL REPLACEMENT

GLOTTAL REPLACEMENT

GLOTTAL REPLACEMENT (GR) is a process that, when applied, results in the use of a glottal stop /ʔ/ for a consonant. FEET /fit/ → [fiʔ] is an example of _____.

[ʔ]

Another example of GLOTTAL REPLACEMENT would be BACK /bæk/ → [bæʔ], where the /k/ → [___].

GR

The abbreviation for GLOTTAL REPLACEMENT is _____.

GR

GR is not limited to a specific within-word position as are DFC, DIC, and others. BACK /bæk/ → [ʔæk] is also an example of _____.

glottal stop

A glottal stop is produced by bringing the vocal folds together rapidly. This articulation at the level of the larynx results in the production of a _____.

vocal tract

Although a glottal stop is not considered to be an English consonant, it does represent activity within the vocal tract in contrast to a deletion, where there is no activity within the _____.

To illustrate this, examine the following productions for Child A and Child B:

	Adult Form	*Child A*	*Child B*
CAT	/kæt/	[kæ]	[kæʔ]

Deletion of Final Consonant	DFC	Consonant Harmony	CH	Backing to Velars	BK
Prevocalic Voicing	PVV	Postvocalic Devoicing	PVD	Epenthesis	EPEN
Syllable Reduction	SR	Vocalization	VOC	Metathesis	METATH
Velar Fronting	VF	Palatal Fronting	PF	Coalescence	COAL
Stopping of Fricatives and Affricates	ST	Gliding of Liquids	GL	Palatalization	PAL
Cluster Reduction	CR	Deaffrication	DEAFF	Denasalization	DENAS
Stridency Deletion	STR	Deletion of Initial Consonant	DIC	Idiosyncratic Processes	
		Glottal Replacement	GR		

BAG	/bæg/	[bæ]	[bæʔ]
REST	/rɛst/	[rɛ]	[rɛʔ]
TALK	/tɔk/	[tɔ]	[tɔʔ]
MESS	/mɛs/	[mɛ]	[mɛʔ]

Child B has represented word-final consonants by using a _____.

glottal stop

Thus, Child B has applied the process of _____ to all five words.

GR

Child A has applied the process of _____ to all five words.

DFC

Thus, Child A has no representation of _____ consonants in any of the words examined.

word-final

List the sound changes involving glottal stops for the following productions:

	Adult Form		Child's Form	Sound Change	
BOOK	/bʊk/	→	[bʊʔ]	/___/ → [___]	/k/ → [ʔ]
KITE	/kæt/	→	[kæʔ]	/___/ → [___]	/t/ → [ʔ]
GLASS	/glæs/	→	[glæʔ]	/___/ → [___]	/s/ → [ʔ]
CHURCH	/tʃɝtʃ/	→	[tʃɝʔ]	/___/ → [___]	/tʃ/ → [ʔ]
PAGE	/pedʒ/	→	[peʔ]	/___/ → [___]	/dʒ/ → [ʔ]
STOVE	/stov/	→	[stoʔ]	/___/ → [___]	/v/ → [ʔ]

/p/ PIG	/n/ NO	/ʃ/ SHE	/w/ WAGON	/ɛ/ BED	/ʌ/ GUN	
/b/ BED	/ŋ/ STING	/ʒ/ ROUGE	/ʍ/ WHEEL	/æ/ CAT	/ə/ ABOUT	
/t/ TOY	/f/ FOX	/h/ HAVE	/ɚ/ FINGER	/a/ GOT	/aɪ/ KITE	
/d/ DUCK	/θ/ THINK	/tʃ/ CHICKEN	/ɝ/ CHURCH	/ɔ/ TALK	/ɔɪ/ TOY	
/k/ KEEP	/ð/ THIS	/dʒ/ JUMPING	/i/ SEE	/o/ GOAT	/aʊ/ OUT	
/g/ GOAT	/s/ SEE	/l/ LAKE	/ɪ/ PIG	/ʊ/ BOOK		
/m/ ME	/z/ ZOO	/j/ YOU	/eɪ, e/ MAKE	/u/ GLUE		

/ʃ/ → [ʔ]   WASH   /waʃ/   → [waʔ]   /___/ → [___]

Notice that GR may be applied to clusters as well as singletons. Apply GR to each of the word-final clusters in the following words. Assume that the entire cluster is replaced by the glottal stop.

		Adult Form	*Child's Form*
[nɛʔ]	NEST	/nɛst/	→ [_____]
[baʔ]	BOX	/baks/	→ [_____]
[dʒaɪəʔ]	GIANT	/dʒaɪənt/	→ [_____]
[mɪʔ]	MILK	/mɪlk/	→ [_____]
[pɪʔ]	PINCH	/pɪntʃ/	→ [_____]
[ræʔ]	RANK	/ræŋk/	→ [_____]
[lɛʔ]	LEFT	/lɛft/	→ [_____]

GR

When an entire cluster becomes a glottal stop, the process of CLUSTER REDUCTION has been applied in addition to _____.

STR

If a cluster containing a strident consonant (/ʃ/, /ʒ/, /s/, /z/, /tʃ/, /dʒ/, /f/, /v/) is replaced by a glottal stop, the process of _____ has also been applied.

CR, STR, GR

For example, if STORE /stor/ → [ʔor], the sound change is /st/ → [ʔ], and the processes involved are _____, _____, and _____.

Deletion of Final Consonant	DFC	Consonant Harmony	CH	Backing to Velars	BK
Prevocalic Voicing	PVV	Postvocalic Devoicing	PVD	Epenthesis	EPEN
Syllable Reduction	SR	Vocalization	VOC	Metathesis	METATH
Velar Fronting	VF	Palatal Fronting	PF	Coalescence	COAL
Stopping of Fricatives and Affricates	ST	Gliding of Liquids	GL	Palatalization	PAL
		Deaffrication	DEAFF	Denasalization	DENAS
Cluster Reduction	CR	Deletion of Initial Consonant	DIC	Idiosyncratic Processes	
Stridency Deletion	STR	Glottal Replacement	GR		

Recall that GR is not limited to specific within-word positions. Apply GR to the intervocalic singletons and clusters in the following words:

	Adult Form		Child's Form	
BASKET	/bæskɪt/	→	[_____]	[bæʔɪt]
BLANKET	/blæŋkɪt/	→	[_____]	[blæʔɪt]
BRACELET	/breslɪt/	→	[_____]	[breʔɪt]
BATHTUB	/bæθtʌb/	→	[_____]	[bæʔʌb]
CHICKEN	/tʃɪkɪn/	→	[_____]	[tʃɪʔɪn]
MATCHES	/mætʃɪz/	→	[_____]	[mæʔɪz]
PENCIL	/pɛnsl̩/	→	[_____]	[pɛʔl̩]

(Notice that some productions containing glottal stops are regionally characteristic. For example, BOTTLE [baʔl̩] and BUTTON [bʌʔn̩] are adult forms in certain areas of the northeastern United States. The clinician is encouraged to be aware of differences such as these and to interpret the results of any phonological analysis according to local patterns of production.)

GLOTTAL REPLACEMENT may be applied to one member of a cluster as well as to the entire cluster. For example, when PART /part/ → [parʔ], the cluster /rt/ → [__]. [rʔ]

/p/ PIG	/n/ NO	/ʃ/ SHE	/w/ WAGON	/ɛ/ BED	/ʌ/ GUN
/b/ BED	/ŋ/ STING	/ʒ/ ROUGE	/ʍ/ WHEEL	/æ/ CAT	/ə/ ABOUT
/t/ TOY	/f/ FOX	/h/ HAVE	/ɚ/ FINGER	/a/ GOT	/aɪ/ KITE
/d/ DUCK	/θ/ THINK	/tʃ/ CHICKEN	/ɝ/ CHURCH	/ɔ/ TALK	/ɔɪ/ TOY
/k/ KEEP	/ð/ THIS	/dʒ/ JUMPING	/i/ SEE	/o/ GOAT	/aʊ/ OUT
/g/ GOAT	/s/ SEE	/l/ LAKE	/ɪ/ PIG	/ʊ/ BOOK	
/m/ ME	/z/ ZOO	/j/ YOU	/eɪ, e/ MAKE	/u/ GLUE	

/rt/	Here the glottal stop has replaced only the /t/ in the cluster ____.
[mɪlʔ]	Similarly, MILK /mɪlk/ might become ____.

List the sound changes for the following productions in which one member of each cluster has been affected by GR:

		Adult Form		Child's Form	Sound Change
/lp/ → [lʔ]	HELP	/hɛlp/	→	[hɛlʔ]	/____/ → [____]
/rt/ → [rʔ]	HEART	/hart/	→	[harʔ]	/____/ → [____]
/lt/ → [lʔ]	MELT	/mɛlt/	→	[mɛlʔ]	/____/ → [____]
/rt/ → [rʔ]	SHORT	/ʃort/	→	[ʃorʔ]	/____/ → [____]
/rk/ → [rʔ]	SHARK	/ʃark/	→	[ʃarʔ]	/____/ → [____]
/rd/ → [rʔ]	YARD	/jard/	→	[jarʔ]	/____/ → [____]
/rt/ → [rʔ]	START	/start/	→	[starʔ]	/____/ → [____]

The replacement of only one member of a cluster by a glottal stop is not common. Notice that all of the clusters in the examples above are word-final and contain one of the liquids /____/ or /____/.

/r/, /l/

GR can be applied to word-initial singletons and clusters. However, glottal stops are difficult to perceive in this context. For example, there is essentially no difference to the listener between [ʔænd] and [ænd], even though one has had the process of _____ applied.

GR

Deletion of Final Consonant	DFC	Consonant Harmony	CH	Backing to Velars	BK
Prevocalic Voicing	PVV	Postvocalic Devoicing	PVD	Epenthesis	EPEN
Syllable Reduction	SR	Vocalization	VOC	Metathesis	METATH
Velar Fronting	VF	Palatal Fronting	PF	Coalescence	COAL
Stopping of Fricatives and Affricates	ST	Gliding of Liquids	GL	Palatalization	PAL
Cluster Reduction	CR	Deaffrication	DEAFF	Denasalization	DENAS
Stridency Deletion	STR	Deletion of Initial Consonant	DIC	Idiosyncratic Processes	
		Glottal Replacement	GR		

Give the productions that would result from applying GR to the word-initial consonants of the following targets:

	Adult Form		*Child's Form*	
TENT	/tɛnt/	→	[_____]	[ʔɛnt]
BUS	/bʌs/	→	[_____]	[ʔʌs]
DRAGON	/drægən/	→	[_____]	[ʔægən], OR [ʔrægən]
JUICE	/dʒus/	→	[_____]	[ʔus]
CLOWN	/klaʊn/	→	[_____]	[ʔaʊn], OR [ʔlaʊn]
KISS	/kɪs/	→	[_____]	[ʔɪs]
WAGON	/wægən/	→	[_____]	[ʔægən]

Glottal stops are difficult to perceive word-initially because the vocal folds come together rapidly to initiate the vowel just as they would to produce the _____.

glottal stop

Glottal stops are perceived more easily within word-final and intervocalic contexts. For example, when MONKEY /mʌŋkɪ/ → [mʌʔɪ], the _____ is perceptible.

glottal stop

Although young children may use glottal stops to replace consonants, the process of _____ is generally not productive in normal young children.

GR

/p/ *PIG*	/n/ *NO*	/ʃ/ *SHE*	/w/ *WAGON*	/ɛ/ *BED*	/ʌ/ *GUN*
/b/ *BED*	/ŋ/ *STING*	/ʒ/ *ROUGE*	/ʍ/ *WHEEL*	/æ/ *CAT*	/ə/ *ABOUT*
/t/ *TOY*	/f/ *FOX*	/h/ *HAVE*	/ɚ/ *FINGER*	/a/ *GOT*	/aɪ/ *KITE*
/d/ *DUCK*	/θ/ *THINK*	/tʃ/ *CHICKEN*	/ɝ/ *CHURCH*	/ɔ/ *TALK*	/ɔɪ/ *TOY*
/k/ *KEEP*	/ð/ *THIS*	/dʒ/ *JUMPING*	/i/ *SEE*	/o/ *GOAT*	/aʊ/ *OUT*
/g/ *GOAT*	/s/ *SEE*	/l/ *LAKE*	/ɪ/ *PIG*	/ʊ/ *BOOK*	
/m/ *ME*	/z/ *ZOO*	/j/ *YOU*	/eɪ, e/ *MAKE*	/u/ *GLUE*	

process	That is, an occasional glottal stop may be used, but the _____ itself is applied to relatively few potential contexts.
high	Since a glottal stop could be used for any consonant anywhere, the number of opportunities to apply the process of GR is quite _____.
productive	GR is not a *productive* process in young children. That is, it occurs a very small percentage of the time. For a process to be _____, the ratio of applications to number of opportunities would need to be greater than 0.30 (30%).
glottal stop	The important thing to note about GR is that its application results in a more articulatory complex form than would the application of one of the deletion processes. The use of a _____ approaches the adult form of a word more closely than a deletion.
DFC	For example, when BACK /bæk/ → [bæʔ], the glottal stop marks the location of a consonant. However, when _____ is applied, the production becomes [bæ], and no consonant is represented in word-final position.
consonants	When children who are in therapy begin to apply GR instead of DFC or DIC, it may be a sign of progress toward including prevocalic and postvocalic _____ and thus suppressing the deletion processes.
	Determine which processes were applied to the following words and their sound changes:

Deletion of Final Consonant	DFC	Consonant Harmony	CH	Backing to Velars	BK
		Postvocalic Devoicing	PVD	Epenthesis	EPEN
Prevocalic Voicing	PVV	Vocalization	VOC	Metathesis	METATH
Syllable Reduction	SR	Palatal Fronting	PF	Coalescence	COAL
Velar Fronting	VF	Gliding of Liquids	GL	Palatalization	PAL
Stopping of Fricatives and Affricates	ST	Deaffrication	DEAFF	Denasalization	DENAS
		Deletion of Initial Consonant	DIC	Idiosyncratic Processes	
Cluster Reduction	CR				
Stridency Deletion	STR	Glottal Replacement	GR		

	Adult Form		Child's Form	Sound Change			Process
AFRAID	/əfred/	→	[pwed]	/ə/	→	[ø] _____	SR
				/fr/	→	[pw] _____	ST, STR, GL
BREAKFAST	/brɛkfəst/	→	[brɛkəs]	/kf/	→	[k] _____	CR, STR
				/st/	→	[s] _____	CR
CRAZY	/krezɪ/	→	[edɪ]	/kr/	→	[ø] _____	CR, DIC
				/z/	→	[d] _____	ST, STR
CATCH	/kætʃ/	→	[tætʃ]	/k/	→	[t] _____	VF or CH
CHIMNEY	/tʃɪmnɪ/	→	[dɪmnɪ]	/tʃ/	→	[d] _____	ST, STR, PVV, PF
CRASH	/kræʃ/	→	[twæʃ]	/kr/	→	[tw] _____	VF or CH, GL
FAST	/fæst/	→	[bæs]	/f/	→	[b] _____	ST, STR, PVV
				/st/	→	[s] _____	CR
FLAG	/flæg/	→	[fæ]	/fl/	→	[f] _____	CR
				/g/	→	[ø] _____	DFC
FRIEND	/frɛnd/	→	[fwɛnt]	/fr/	→	[fw] _____	GL
				/nd/	→	[nt] _____	PVD
JACKET	/dʒækɪt/	→	[dækɪ]	/dʒ/	→	[d] _____	ST, STR, PF
				/t/	→	[ø] _____	DFC
JUNGLE	/dʒʌŋgl̩/	→	[dʌndo]	/dʒ/	→	[d] _____	ST, STR, PF
				/ŋg/	→	[nd] _____	VF or CH
				/l/	→	[o] _____	VOC

/p/ PIG	/n/ NO	/ʃ/ SHE	/w/ WAGON	/ɛ/ BED	/ʌ/ GUN
/b/ BED	/ŋ/ STING	/ʒ/ ROUGE	/ʍ/ WHEEL	/æ/ CAT	/ə/ ABOUT
/ɩ/ TOY	/f/ FOX	/h/ HAVE	/ɚ/ FINGER	/a/ GOT	/aɪ/ KITE
/d/ DUCK	/θ/ THINK	/tʃ/ CHICKEN	/ɝ/ CHURCH	/ɔ/ TALK	/ɔɪ/ TOY
/k/ KEEP	/ð/ THIS	/dʒ/ JUMPING	/i/ SEE	/o/ GOAT	/aʊ/ OUT
/g/ GOAT	/s/ SEE	/l/ LAKE	/ɪ/ PIG	/ʊ/ BOOK	
/m/ ME	/z/ ZOO	/j/ YOU	/eɪ, e/ MAKE	/u/ GLUE	

ST, STR, PF	JUNK	/dʒʌŋk/	→ [dʌŋk]	/dʒ/ →	[d] _____
GR, ST, STR	LAUGH	/læf/	→ [læʔ]	/f/ →	[ʔ] _____
ST, STR, PF	OUCH	/aʊtʃ/	→ [aʊt]	/tʃ/ →	[t] _____
CR, STR	PANTS	/pænts/	→ [pæn]	/nts/ →	[n] _____
ST, STR VOC	PUZZLE	/pʌzl̩/	→ [pʌdo]	/z/ → /l̩/ →	[d] _____ [o] _____
GL ST, STR	ROOF	/ruf/	→ [wup]	/r/ → /f/ →	[w] _____ [p] _____
CR, STR, PVV VOC	SPILL	/spɪl/	→ [bɪo]	/sp/ → /l/ →	[b] _____ [o] _____
ST, STR CR	ZEBRA	/zibrə/	→ [dibə]	/z/ → /br/ →	[d] _____ [b] _____

Deletion of Final		Consonant Harmony	CH	Backing to Velars	BK
Consonant	DFC	Postvocalic Devoicing	PVD	Epenthesis	EPEN
Prevocalic Voicing	PVV	Vocalization	VOC	Metathesis	METATH
Syllable Reduction	SR	Palatal Fronting	PF	Coalescence	COAL
Velar Fronting	VF	Gliding of Liquids	GL	Palatalization	PAL
Stopping of Fricatives		Deaffrication	DEAFF	Denasalization	DENAS
and Affricates	ST	Deletion of Initial		Idiosyncratic	
Cluster Reduction	CR	Consonant	DIC	Processes	
Stridency Deletion	STR	Glottal Replacement	GR		

SUMMARY
Glottal Replacement

1. GR is a process that, when applied, results in the use of a glottal stop /ʔ/ for a consonant.

2. Although a glottal stop is not considered to be an English consonant, it does represent activity within the vocal tract.

3. When an entire cluster becomes a glottal stop, the process of CR has also been applied.

4. The use of intervocalic glottal stops is characteristic of acceptable adult production in certain regions throughout the United States.

5. It is difficult to differentiate word-initial glottal stops from vowel initiation.

/p/ *PIG*	/n/ *NO*	/ʃ/ *SHE*	/w/ *WAGON*	/ɛ/ *BED*	/ʌ/ *GUN*
/b/ *BED*	/ŋ/ *STING*	/ʒ/ *ROUGE*	/ʍ/ *WHEEL*	/æ/ *CAT*	/ə/ *ABOUT*
/t/ *TOY*	/f/ *FOX*	/h/ *HAVE*	/ɚ/ *FINGER*	/a/ *GOT*	/aɪ/ *KITE*
/d/ *DUCK*	/θ/ *THINK*	/tʃ/ *CHICKEN*	/ɝ/ *CHURCH*	/ɔ/ *TALK*	/ɔɪ/ *TOY*
/k/ *KEEP*	/ð/ *THIS*	/dʒ/ *JUMPING*	/i/ *SEE*	/o/ *GOAT*	/aʊ/ *OUT*
/g/ *GOAT*	/s/ *SEE*	/l/ *LAKE*	/ɪ/ *PIG*	/ʊ/ *BOOK*	
/m/ *ME*	/z/ *ZOO*	/j/ *YOU*	/eɪ, e/ *MAKE*	/u/ *GLUE*	

SECTION 16. BACKING

BACKING (BK) is a process that is applied to non-velar consonants. Its application results in the production of a velar consonant or an /h/. NUT /nʌt/ → [nʌk] is an example of _____.

BACKING, or BK

MOUSE /maʊs/ → [maʊk] is also an example of _____.

BACKING, or BK

The abbreviation for BACKING is _____.

BK

The velar consonants are /___/, /___/, and /___/.

/k/, /g/, /ŋ/

Consonants are backed to velars or /h/ when the process of _____ is applied.

BK, or BACKING

Thus, /d/ → [g], /p/ → [k], /n/ → [ŋ] when the same manner of production is used. When any sound change to a velar occurs, the process of _____ is considered.

BK

Another example of BK would be TIME /taɪm/ → [kaɪm], where /t/ → [___], a velar consonant.

[k]

Recall that VF is the process that results in fronting velars to the alveolar ridge. BK affects non-velar consonants, which then become _____ or /___/.

velar(s), /h/

While BK may be applied to alveolar consonants, VF is applied to _____ consonants.

velar

For example, when BK is applied to TEA /ti/, it becomes [ki]. However, when VF is applied to KEY /ki/, it becomes [___].

[ti]

Deletion of Final Consonant	DFC	Consonant Harmony	CH	Backing to Velars	BK
Prevocalic Voicing	PVV	Postvocalic Devoicing	PVD	Epenthesis	EPEN
Syllable Reduction	SR	Vocalization	VOC	Metathesis	METATH
Velar Fronting	VF	Palatal Fronting	PF	Coalescence	COAL
Stopping of Fricatives and Affricates	ST	Gliding of Liquids	GL	Palatalization	PAL
Cluster Reduction	CR	Deaffrication	DEAFF	Denasalization	DENAS
Stridency Deletion	STR	Deletion of Initial Consonant	DIC	Idiosyncratic Processes	
		Glottal Replacement	GR		

BK, like GR, is not common among young normal children. It is unusual for a child to use _____ productively.

BK

By productively, we mean that it is applied to greater than _____% of available opportunities.

30

List the sound changes that have resulted from the application of BK to the following adult forms:

	Adult Form	*Child's Form*	*Sound Change*	
TAR	/tar/	→ [kar]	/___/ → [___]	/t/ → [k]
DONE	/dʌn/	→ [gʌn]	/___/ → [___]	/d/ → [g]
PIT	/pɪt/	→ [pɪk]	/___/ → [___]	/t/ → [k]
MR.	/mɪstɚ/	→ [mɪskɚ]	/___/ → [___]	/st/ → [sk]
SAD	/sæd/	→ [sæg]	/___/ → [___]	/d/ → [g]
TEETH	/tiθ/	→ [hiθ]	/___/ → [___]	/t/ → [h]
ZIPPER	/zɪpɚ/	→ [zɪkɚ]	/___/ → [___]	/p/ → [k]

Additional processes may be applied. This results in a production that is further from the target. For example, when /p/ → [k], as in SOAP /sop/ → [sok], the process of _____ accounts for the entire sound change.

BK

However, when /v/ → [k], as in GLOVE /glʌv/ → [glʌk], additional processes are involved. Since /v/ is voiced and [k] is not, the process of _____ was applied in addition to the process of BK.

PVD

/p/ *PIG*	/n/ *NO*	/ʃ/ *SHE*	/w/ *WAGON*	/ɛ/ *BED*	/ʌ/ *GUN*
/b/ *BED*	/ŋ/ *STING*	/ʒ/ *ROUGE*	/ʍ/ *WHEEL*	/æ/ *CAT*	/ə/ *ABOUT*
/t/ *TOY*	/f/ *FOX*	/h/ *HAVE*	/ɚ/ *FINGER*	/a/ *GOT*	/aɪ/ *KITE*
/d/ *DUCK*	/θ/ *THINK*	/tʃ/ *CHICKEN*	/ɝ/ *CHURCH*	/ɔ/ *TALK*	/ɔɪ/ *TOY*
/k/ *KEEP*	/ð/ *THIS*	/dʒ/ *JUMPING*	/i/ *SEE*	/o/ *GOAT*	/aʊ/ *OUT*
/g/ *GOAT*	/s/ *SEE*	/l/ *LAKE*	/ɪ/ *PIG*	/ʊ/ *BOOK*	
/m/ *ME*	/z/ *ZOO*	/j/ *YOU*	/eɪ, e/ *MAKE*	/u/ *GLUE*	

STR		Also, /v/ is a strident consonant and [k] is not. Therefore, the process of _____ was also applied.
ST		And, since /v/ is continuant and [k] is a stop consonant, the process of _____ was applied.

Give the sound changes for the following productions. Each consonant that has been backed has had additional processes applied to it. Give the processes that were responsible for each sound change.

		Adult Form	Child's Form	Sound Change	Pro-cesses
/tʃ/ → [k], ST, STR, BK	CHAIR	/tʃɛr/	→ [kɛr]	/___/ → [___]	___
/s/ → [k], ST, STR, BK	HOUSE	/haʊs/	→ [haʊk]	/___/ → [___]	___
/dʒ/ → [g], ST, STR, BK	JAM	/dʒæm/	→ [gæm]	/___/ → [___]	___
/tʃ/ → [k], ST, STR, BK	WATCH	/watʃ/	→ [wak]	/___/ → [___]	___
/s/ → [g], ST, STR, PVV, BK	SUN	/sʌn/	→ [gʌn]	/___/ → [___]	___
/θ/ → [k], ST, BK or CH	THING	/θɪŋ/	→ [kɪŋ]	/___/ → [___]	___
/dʒ/ → [k], ST, STR, PVD, BK	BRIDGE	/brɪdʒ/	→ [brɪk]	/___/ → [___]	___

Deletion of Final Consonant	DFC	Consonant Harmony	CH	Backing to Velars	BK
Prevocalic Voicing	PVV	Postvocalic Devoicing	PVD	Epenthesis	EPEN
Syllable Reduction	SR	Vocalization	VOC	Metathesis	METATH
Velar Fronting	VF	Palatal Fronting	PF	Coalescence	COAL
Stopping of Fricatives and Affricates	ST	Gliding of Liquids	GL	Palatalization	PAL
Cluster Reduction	CR	Deaffrication	DEAFF	Denasalization	DENAS
Stridency Deletion	STR	Deletion of Initial Consonant	DIC	Idiosyncratic Processes	
		Glottal Replacement	GR		

CHIP	/tʃɪp/	→ [gɪp]	/___/ → [___] ___	/tʃ/ → [g], ST, STR, PVV, BK
GIRAFFE	/dʒəræf/	→ [gəræf]	/___/ → [___] ___	/dʒ/ → [g], ST, STR, BK
SHOP	/ʃap/	→ [gap]	/___/ → [___] ___	/ʃ/ → [g], ST, STR, PVV, BK
TREASURE	/trɛʒɚ/	→ [trɛgɚ]	/___/ → [___] ___	/ʒ/ → [g], ST, STR, BK
TALK	/tɔk/	→ [kɔk]	/___/ → [___] ___	/t/ → [k], BK or CH

Any consonant other than a velar or an /h/ may be backed to a velar or an [h] by applying the process of _____.

BK

_____ is not limited to a specific position within a word.

BK

For each of the following words, give the number of consonants available for BACKING:

	Adult Form	Number of Consonants	
TO	/tu/	_____	one
BYE	/baɪ/	_____	one
TELEPHONE	/tɛləfon/	_____	four
BOAT	/bot/	_____	two

/p/ PIG   /n/ NO   /ʃ/ SHE   /w/ WAGON   /ɛ/ BED   /ʌ/ GUN
/b/ BED   /ŋ/ STING   /ʒ/ ROUGE   /ʍ/ WHEEL   /æ/ CAT   /ə/ ABOUT
/t/ TOY   /f/ FOX   /h/ HAVE   /ɚ/ FINGER   /a/ GOT   /aɪ/ KITE
/d/ DUCK   /θ/ THINK   /tʃ/ CHICKEN   /ɝ/ CHURCH   /ɔ/ TALK   /ɔɪ/ TOY
/k/ KEEP   /ð/ THIS   /dʒ/ JUMPING   /i/ SEE   /o/ GOAT   /aʊ/ OUT
/g/ GOAT   /s/ SEE   /l/ LAKE   /ɪ/ PIG   /ʊ/ BOOK
/m/ ME   /z/ ZOO   /j/ YOU   /eɪ, e/ MAKE   /u/ GLUE

two	BABY	/bebɪ/	_____
three	BANANA	/bənænə/	_____
two	SOAP	/sop/	_____

reduced

BK can be applied to clusters. The entire cluster may be *retained*, as in TREE /tri/ → [kri] or _____ as in /tri/ → [ki].

CR, BK

When a complete non-velar cluster becomes a velar singleton, then the processes of _____ and _____ are probable.

For the following words containing clusters, apply BK to the stop consonant of each cluster and reduce the cluster to retain the velar. The first one has been done for you.

		Adult Form		*Child's Form*
	TRY	/traɪ/	→	[kaɪ]
[gu] (/bl/ → [gl] → [g])	BLUE	/blu/	→	[_____]
[kov] (/st/ → [sk] → [k])	STOVE	/stov/	→	[_____]
[bækəb] (/θt/ → [θk] → [k])	BATHTUB	/bæθtəb/	→	[_____]
[nɛk] (/st/ → [sk] → [k])	NEST	/nɛst/	→	[_____]

Deletion of Final Consonant	DFC	Consonant Harmony	CH	Backing to Velars	BK
Prevocalic Voicing	PVV	Postvocalic Devoicing	PVD	Epenthesis	EPEN
Syllable Reduction	SR	Vocalization	VOC	Metathesis	METATH
Velar Fronting	VF	Palatal Fronting	PF	Coalescence	COAL
Stopping of Fricatives and Affricates	ST	Gliding of Liquids	GL	Palatalization	PAL
		Deaffrication	DEAFF	Denasalization	DENAS
Cluster Reduction	CR	Deletion of Initial Consonant	DIC	Idiosyncratic Processes	
Stridency Deletion	STR	Glottal Replacement	GR		

TRAP   /træp/ →   [_____]   [kæp]
                                                        (/tr/ → [kr] → [k])

HELP   /hɛlp/ →   [_____]   [hɛk]
                                                        (/lp/ → [lk] → [k])

The process of BK has been applied to those seven
words along with the process of _____.   CR

Children may apply the process of BK selectively. For
example, a child may apply BK to only intervocalic
clusters and singletons. Thus, TABLE /tebl̩/ → [tegl̩] (/b/
→ [g]), but BOY /bɔɪ/ → [_____] (/b/ → [b]).   [bɔɪ]

Describe the optional process used by this child on
the following 15 words:

	Adult Form	Child's Form
BANANA	/bənænə/ →	[bənænə]
CHIN	/tʃɪn/ →	[hɪn]
GIRAFFE	/dʒəræf/ →	[dʒəræk]
FIVE	/faɪv/ →	[haɪv]
FAT	/fæt/ →	[hæk]
LAMP	/læmp/ →	[læmp]
MUD	/mʌd/ →	[mʌd]
KNIFE	/naɪf/ →	[naɪk]
PEACH	/pitʃ/ →	[hik]
READ	/rid/ →	[rid]
SOAP	/sop/ →	[hok]

/p/ PIG	/n/ NO	/ʃ/ SHE	/w/ WAGON	/ɛ/ BED	/ʌ/ GUN
/b/ BED	/ŋ/ STING	/ʒ/ ROUGE	/ʍ/ WHEEL	/æ/ CAT	/ə/ ABOUT
/t/ TOY	/f/ FOX	/h/ HAVE	/ɚ/ FINGER	/a/ GOT	/aɪ/ KITE
/d/ DUCK	/θ/ THINK	/tʃ/ CHICKEN	/ɝ/ CHURCH	/ɔ/ TALK	/ɔɪ/ TOY
/k/ KEEP	/ð/ THIS	/dʒ/ JUMPING	/i/ SEE	/o/ GOAT	/aʊ/ OUT
/g/ GOAT	/s/ SEE	/l/ LAKE	/ɪ/ PIG	/ʊ/ BOOK	
/m/ ME	/z/ ZOO	/j/ YOU	/eɪ, e/ MAKE	/u/ GLUE	

SPINACH	/spɪnɪtʃ/	→	[hɪnɪk]
TRAIN	/tren/	→	[hren]
WINDOW	/wɪndo/	→	[wɪndo]
ZIP	/zɪp/	→	[zɪk]

BK is applied to voiceless consonants only; they become [h] in initial position and [k] elsewhere.

Optional Process:

optional

Since not all consonants are backed, the application of BK is _____.

selectively

As an optional process, it is applied _____ rather than uniformly.

assimilation, OR CH

BK often occurs in words that already contain velar consonants. For example, DUCK /dʌk/ → [gʌk]. By the definition of BK, the non-velar consonant has been backed to a velar. However, there is already a velar, /k/, in the word DUCK, which may have influenced the place of articulation. There is then the possibility that some type of _____ occurred.

Indicate for each of the following words whether CH is or is not a possible process:

	Adult Form		Child's Form		CH is a Possibility
DUCK	/dʌk/	→	[gʌk]		YES
YES CUP	/kʌp/	→	[kʌk]		_____

Deletion of Final Consonant	DFC	Consonant Harmony	CH	Backing to Velars	BK
Prevocalic Voicing	PVV	Postvocalic Devoicing	PVD	Epenthesis	EPEN
Syllable Reduction	SR	Vocalization	VOC	Metathesis	METATH
Velar Fronting	VF	Palatal Fronting	PF	Coalescence	COAL
Stopping of Fricatives and Affricates	ST	Gliding of Liquids	GL	Palatalization	PAL
Cluster Reduction	CR	Deaffrication	DEAFF	Denasalization	DENAS
Stridency Deletion	STR	Deletion of Initial Consonant	DIC	Idiosyncratic Processes	
		Glottal Replacement	GR		

BAD	/bæd/	→ [bæg]	_____	NO
CHIMNEY	/tʃɪmnɪ/	→ [tʃɪŋgɪ]	_____	NO
DIVE	/daɪv/	→ [gaɪv]	_____	NO
ELEPHANT	/ɛləfənt/	→ [ɛləfənk]	_____	NO
FLAG	/flæg/	→ [gwæg]	_____	YES

Of these seven words, BACKING to velar consonants could have been the result of CH in _____ of them.

three

BK was the only possibility in _____ of them because these words contained no velars that could have influenced the place of production.

four

The following child has used the process of BK selectively. Describe the rule this child is using:

	Adult Form	*Child's Form*
BAD	/bæd/	→ [bæk]
BUS	/bʌs/	→ [bʌk]
CATCH	/kætʃ/	→ [kæk]
FRIEND	/frɛnd/	→ [frɛŋk]
MATCH	/mætʃ/	→ [mæk]
ROOF	/ruf/	→ [ruk]
NUT	/nʌt/	→ [nʌk]
PIT	/pɪt/	→ [pɪk]

/p/ *PIG*	/n/ *NO*	/ʃ/ *SHE*	/w/ *WAGON*	/ɛ/ *BED*	/ʌ/ *GUN*
/b/ *BED*	/ŋ/ *STING*	/ʒ/ *ROUGE*	/ʍ/ *WHEEL*	/æ/ *CAT*	/ə/ *ABOUT*
/t/ *TOY*	/f/ *FOX*	/h/ *HAVE*	/ɚ/ *FINGER*	/a/ *GOT*	/aɪ/ *KITE*
/d/ *DUCK*	/θ/ *THINK*	/tʃ/ *CHICKEN*	/ɝ/ *CHURCH*	/ɔ/ *TALK*	/ɔɪ/ *TOY*
/k/ *KEEP*	/ð/ *THIS*	/dʒ/ *JUMPING*	/i/ *SEE*	/o/ *GOAT*	/aʊ/ *OUT*
/g/ *GOAT*	/s/ *SEE*	/l/ *LAKE*	/ɪ/ *PIG*	/ʊ/ *BOOK*	
/m/ *ME*	/z/ *ZOO*	/j/ *YOU*	/eɪ, e/ *MAKE*	/u/ *GLUE*	

SOAP   /sop/   → [sok]

Optional Rule:

All word-final consonants are backed to [k].

SUMMARY
Backing

1. BK is a process that is applied to non-velar consonants, resulting in the production of a velar or an /h/.
2. BK is an unusual process and is not used productively by young normal speakers.
3. BK may occur in words that already contain velar consonants or /h/; CH must then be considered.

Deletion of Final Consonant	DFC	Consonant Harmony	CH	Backing to Velars	BK
Prevocalic Voicing	PVV	Postvocalic Devoicing	PVD	Epenthesis	EPEN
Syllable Reduction	SR	Vocalization	VOC	Metathesis	METATH
Velar Fronting	VF	Palatal Fronting	PF	Coalescence	COAL
Stopping of Fricatives and Affricates	ST	Gliding of Liquids	GL	Palatalization	PAL
Cluster Reduction	CR	Deaffrication	DEAFF	Denasalization	DENAS
Stridency Deletion	STR	Deletion of Initial Consonant	DIC	Idiosyncratic Processes	
		Glottal Replacement	GR		

SECTION 17. EPENTHESIS

EPENTHESIS (EPEN) is a process that results in the insertion of a schwa (/ə/) between two consonants. BLUE /blu/ → [bəlu] is an example of _____.

EPENTHESIS

Similarly, GREEN /grin/ → [_____] with the application of EPENTHESIS.

[gərin]

The abbreviation for EPENTHESIS is _____.

EPEN

When a schwa is inserted between two consonants, as in the word BLUE, the syllable shape is altered from CCV to CVCV. Producing this _____ form is more natural for the child.

CVCV

Insert a schwa between the appropriate consonants for each of the following words. Give their sound changes.

	Adult Form	Child's Form	Sound Changes	
GRASS	/græs/	→ [_____]	/___/ → [___]	[gəræs] /gr/ → [gər]
BRUSH	/brʌʃ/	→ [_____]	/___/ → [___]	[bərʌʃ] /br/ → [bər]
PLANE	/plen/	→ [_____]	/___/ → [___]	[pəlen] /pl/ → [pəl]
AFRAID	/əfred/	→ [_____]	/___/ → [___]	[əfəred] /fr/ → [fər]
CLASS	/klæs/	→ [_____]	/___/ → [___]	[kəlæs] /kl/ → [kəl]
DRINK	/drɪŋk/	→ [_____]	/___/ → [___]	[dərɪŋk] /dr/ → [dər]

/p/ *PIG*	/n/ *NO*	/ʃ/ *SHE*	/w/ *WAGON*	/ɛ/ *BED*	/ʌ/ *GUN*
/b/ *BED*	/ŋ/ *STING*	/ʒ/ *ROUGE*	/ʍ/ *WHEEL*	/æ/ *CAT*	/ə/ *ABOUT*
/t/ *TOY*	/f/ *FOX*	/h/ *HAVE*	/ɚ/ *FINGER*	/a/ *GOT*	/aɪ/ *KITE*
/d/ *DUCK*	/θ/ *THINK*	/tʃ/ *CHICKEN*	/ɝ/ *CHURCH*	/ɔ/ *TALK*	/ɔɪ/ *TOY*
/k/ *KEEP*	/ð/ *THIS*	/dʒ/ *JUMPING*	/i/ *SEE*	/o/ *GOAT*	/aʊ/ *OUT*
/g/ *GOAT*	/s/ *SEE*	/l/ *LAKE*	/ɪ/ *PIG*	/ʊ/ *BOOK*	
/m/ *ME*	/z/ *ZOO*	/j/ *YOU*	/eɪ, e/ *MAKE*	/u/ *GLUE*	

[ɛləfənət]

/nt/ → [nət]

ELEPHANT   /ɛləfənt/ → [_____] /___/ → [____]

schwa

EPEN is a type of cluster simplification when it is used in this way. The insertion of a _____ breaks up the cluster (CC) into a CVCV form.

cluster

Since it does not specifically *reduce* the cluster, it is not considered under CLUSTER REDUCTION. Its application does, however, simplify the production of a _____.

EPEN

The addition of a consonant is sometimes included under EPEN. For example, when FORK /fork/ → [fwɔɚk], the addition of the /w/ results from the application of _____ (Hodson and Paden, 1983, p. 17).

PVD

Another example that has been reported is the addition of a weak consonant, as in WING /wɪŋ/ → [wɪŋk]. Since this effectively devoices the word-final /ŋ/, it has been included in this text under _____.

The most common usage of EPEN is the schwa insertion between consonants within a *cluster*; even this is not common. It does appear, however, that some children include EPEN as a stage toward the development of adult-like _____.

clusters

As with other processes, EPEN may be one of several processes applied to a word. Determine which processes were used *in addition to* EPEN for the following child's productions:

Deletion of Final		Consonant Harmony	CH	Backing to Velars	BK
Consonant	DFC	Postvocalic Devoicing	PVD	Epenthesis	EPEN
Prevocalic Voicing	PVV	Vocalization	VOC	Metathesis	METATH
Syllable Reduction	SR	Palatal Fronting	PF	Coalescence	COAL
Velar Fronting	VF	Gliding of Liquids	GL	Palatalization	PAL
Stopping of Fricatives		Deaffrication	DEAFF	Denasalization	DENAS
and Affricates	ST	Deletion of Initial		Idiosyncratic	
Cluster Reduction	CR	Consonant	DIC	Processes	
Stridency Deletion	STR	Glottal Replacement	GR		

	Adult Form	Child's Form	Processes	
BRUSH	/brʌʃ/	→ [bəwʌ]	_____	GL, DFC, STR
PLANE	/plen/	→ [pen]	_____	CR, EPEN is blocked
THROW	/θro/	→ [dəwo]	_____	ST, PVV, GL
TRUCK	/trʌk/	→ [dəwʌt]	_____	PVV, GL, VF (CH)
FRIEND	/frɛnd/	→ [bəwɛnd]	_____	ST, STR, PVV, GL
AFRAID	/əfred/	→ [əfəwed]	_____	GL
CLASS	/klæs/	→· [kəlæs]	_____	None besides EPEN

SUMMARY
Epenthesis

1. EPEN is a process that results in the insertion of a schwa (/ə/) between two consonants.
2. The syllable shape is altered from CCV to CVCV by the application of EPEN.
3. EPEN is a type of cluster simplification when a schwa is inserted between two consonants within a cluster.

/p/ *PIG*	/n/ *NO*	/ʃ/ *SHE*	/w/ *WAGON*	/ɛ/ *BED*	/ʌ/ *GUN*
/b/ *BED*	/ŋ/ *STING*	/ʒ/ *ROUGE*	/ʍ/ *WHEEL*	/æ/ *CAT*	/ə/ *ABOUT*
/t/ *TOY*	/f/ *FOX*	/h/ *HAVE*	/ɚ/ *FINGER*	/a/ *GOT*	/aɪ/ *KITE*
/d/ *DUCK*	/θ/ *THINK*	/tʃ/ *CHICKEN*	/ɝ/ *CHURCH*	/ɔ/ *TALK*	/ɔɪ/ *TOY*
/k/ *KEEP*	/ð/ *THIS*	/dʒ/ *JUMPING*	/i/ *SEE*	/o/ *GOAT*	/aʊ/ *OUT*
/g/ *GOAT*	/s/ *SEE*	/l/ *LAKE*	/ɪ/ *PIG*	/ʊ/ *BOOK*	
/m/ *ME*	/z/ *ZOO*	/j/ *YOU*	/eɪ, e/ *MAKE*	/u/ *GLUE*	

SECTION 18. METATHESIS

METATHESIS

METATHESIS (METATH) is a transposition or sequence alteration of consonants. CUP /kʌp/ → [pʌk] is an example of _____.

METATHESIS

The /k/ and /p/ have exchanged locations within the word. The *sequence* has been altered through the application of _____.

METATH

The abbreviation for METATHESIS is _____.

altered, OR reversed

Another example of METATH is BASKET /bæskɪt/ → [bæksɪt]. The sequence of the /s/ and /k/ has been _____.

METATH

SPAGHETTI /spagɛɾɪ/ → [bəsgɛɾɪ] results from the application of _____.

PVV

The /s/ has been transposed from word-initial position to follow the first vowel. In addition, the /p/ → [b], which is an example of _____.

Determine whether METATH has been applied to each of the following words:

	Adult Form	*Child's Form*	*YES/NO*
YES, /k/ and /s/ were reversed. ACCIDENT	/æksədɛnt/ →	[æskədɛnt]	_____
YES, /k/ and /s/ were exchanged. BICYCLE	/baɪsɪkl̩/ →	[baɪkɪsl̩]	_____

Deletion of Final Consonant	DFC	Consonant Harmony	CH	Backing to Velars	BK
Prevocalic Voicing	PVV	Postvocalic Devoicing	PVD	Epenthesis	EPEN
Syllable Reduction	SR	Vocalization	VOĊ	Metathesis	METATH
Velar Fronting	VF	Palatal Fronting	PF	Coalescence	COAL
Stopping of Fricatives and Affricates	ST	Gliding of Liquids	GL	Palatalization	PAL
Cluster Reduction	CR	Deaffrication	DEAFF	Denasalization	DENAS
Stridency Deletion	STR	Deletion of Initial Consonant	DIC	Idiosyncratic Processes	
		Glottal Replacement	GR		

BROKEN	/brokən/	→ [bronək]	_____	YES, /k/ and /n/ were exchanged.
CARROT	/kɛrət/	→ [tɛrək]	_____	YES, /t/ and /k/ were exchanged.
ELEPHANT	/ɛləfənt/	→ [ɛfələnt]	_____	YES, /f/ and /l/ were exchanged.
STOP	/stap/	→ [taps]	_____	YES, /s/ has been transposed.
CATS	/kæts/	→ [skæt]	_____	YES, /s/ has been transposed.
TEACHER	/titʃɚ/	→ [tʃitɚ]	_____	YES, /t/ and /tʃ/ were exchanged.
SPOON	/spun/	→ [puns]	_____	YES, /s/ has been transposed.
PAJAMAS	/pədʒæməz/	→ [dʒəbæməz]	_____	YES, /p/ (as /b/) and /dʒ/ have been exchanged.

All of the words just given provided contexts for the application of _____.

METATH

One phoneme may be moved to another location within the word. This type of METATH is called _____.

transposition

Or, two consonants may have their sequence altered by the application of _____.

METATH

/p/ *PIG*	/n/ *NO*	/ʃ/ *SHE*	/w/ *WAGON*	/ɛ/ *BED*	/ʌ/ *GUN*
/b/ *BED*	/ŋ/ *STING*	/ʒ/ *ROUGE*	/ʍ/ *WHEEL*	/æ/ *CAT*	/ə/ *ABOUT*
/t/ *TOY*	/f/ *FOX*	/h/ *HAVE*	/ɚ/ *FINGER*	/a/ *GOT*	/aɪ/ *KITE*
/d/ *DUCK*	/θ/ *THINK*	/tʃ/ *CHICKEN*	/ɝ/ *CHURCH*	/ɔ/ *TALK*	/ɔɪ/ *TOY*
/k/ *KEEP*	/ð/ *THIS*	/dʒ/ *JUMPING*	/i/ *SEE*	/o/ *GOAT*	/aʊ/ *OUT*
/g/ *GOAT*	/s/ *SEE*	/l/ *LAKE*	/ɪ/ *PIG*	/ʊ/ *BOOK*	
/m/ *ME*	/z/ *ZOO*	/j/ *YOU*	/eɪ, e/ *MAKE*	/u/ *GLUE*	

METATH	Productions such as [bæksɪt] and [bəsɡɛɪɪ] are fairly common. The more complex the word form, the more likely it is that _____ will be applied.
unintelligible	If METATH is used productively (>30%), the child is likely to be one who has unintelligible speech. That is, METATH is often found in the speech of _____ children.
common	The occasional use of METATH to produce a word like [bæksɪt] is common. The application of METATH to >30% of available contexts is not _____.

Determine which of the following words provides an opportunity for METATH to be applied:

		Adult Form	*YES/NO*
YES	PLAY	/pleɪ/	_____
YES	FISH	/fɪʃ/	_____
YES	SCHOOL	/skul/	_____
YES	OUCH	/aʊtʃ/	_____
YES	CHEESE	/tʃiz/	_____
YES	JUNGLE	/dʒʌngl̩/	_____
YES	KITE	/kaɪt/	_____

METATH	Because transposition is one type of METATH, any word containing one or more consonants provides an opportunity for _____ to be applied.

Deletion of Final Consonant	DFC	Consonant Harmony	CH	Backing to Velars	BK
Prevocalic Voicing	PVV	Postvocalic Devoicing	PVD	Epenthesis	EPEN
Syllable Reduction	SR	Vocalization	VOC	Metathesis	METATH
Velar Fronting	VF	Palatal Fronting	PF	Coalescence	COAL
Stopping of Fricatives and Affricates	ST	Gliding of Liquids	GL	Palatalization	PAL
Cluster Reduction	CR	Deaffrication	DEAFF	Denasalization	DENAS
Stridency Deletion	STR	Deletion of Initial Consonant	DIC	Idiosyncratic Processes	
		Glottal Replacement	GR		

For example, in the word BOY /bɔɪ/, the /b/ may be transposed to word-final position. The child's production would then be _____.

[ɔɪb]

For the following words, give the production that would result from the sequence reversal of the consonants. The first one has been done for you:

	Adult Form		Child's Form
AFTER	/æftɚ/	→	[ætfɚ]
BOAT	/bot/	→	[_____]
CAP	/kæp/	→	[_____]
JACKET	/dʒækɪt/	→	[_____]
PENCIL	/pɛnsl̩/	→	[_____]
SHAPE	/ʃep/	→	[_____]
YELLOW	/jɛlo/	→	[_____]

[tob]

[pæk]

[dʒætɪk] or [kædʒɪt] or [tædʒɪk] or [kætɪdʒ]

[pɛsn̩l̩], [nɛpsl̩], or [sɛnpl̩]

[peʃ]

[lɛjo]

As with other processes, it is possible for several processes to be applied to a single sound change. For example, when CARD /kard/ → [dak] the process of CR has been applied in addition to _____.

METATH

Similarly, when MESS /mɛs/ → [tɛm], the /s/ has exchanged places with the /m/, but it has become [t]. When /s/ → [t], the processes applied are _____.

ST, STR

/p/ PIG	/n/ NO	/ʃ/ SHE	/w/ WAGON	/ɛ/ BED	/ʌ/ GUN
/b/ BED	/ŋ/ STING	/ʒ/ ROUGE	/ʍ/ WHEEL	/æ/ CAT	/ə/ ABOUT
/t/ TOY	/f/ FOX	/h/ HAVE	/ɚ/ FINGER	/a/ GOT	/aɪ/ KITE
/d/ DUCK	/θ/ THINK	/tʃ/ CHICKEN	/ɝ/ CHURCH	/ɔ/ TALK	/ɔɪ/ TOY
/k/ KEEP	/ð/ THIS	/dʒ/ JUMPING	/i/ SEE	/o/ GOAT	/aʊ/ OUT
/g/ GOAT	/s/ SEE	/l/ LAKE	/ɪ/ PIG	/ʊ/ BOOK	
/m/ ME	/z/ ZOO	/j/ YOU	/eɪ, e/ MAKE	/u/ GLUE	

METATH

It is easiest to identify and analyze the sound changes after applying METATH. That is, /s/ → [t] would be analyzed after _____ was applied.

For example, when SHAPE /ʃep/ → [bes], we note METATH and then we note the following sound changes and processes:

/ʃ/	→	[s]	PF
/p/	→	[b]	PVV

Similarly, when FIGHT /faɪt/ → [daɪp], we note METATH and then we note the sound changes and processes:

/f/	→	[p]	ST, STR
/t/	→	[___]	_____

[d], PVV

If the sound changes were analyzed prior to assigning METATH, then the /t/ would be voiced in word-final position, which is harder to account for than in word-initial position. If the exchange is made first, then /t/ → [d] occurs word-initially and is assigned the process of _____.

PVV

Analyze the following productions for all processes applied. The first one has been done for you.

	Adult Form	Child's Form	Processes
SICK	/sɪk/	→ [gɪs]	METATH
		/k/ → [g]	PVV

Deletion of Final Consonant	DFC	Consonant Harmony	CH	Backing to Velars	BK
Prevocalic Voicing	PVV	Postvocalic Devoicing	PVD	Epenthesis	EPEN
Syllable Reduction	SR	Vocalization	VOC	Metathesis	METATH
Velar Fronting	VF	Palatal Fronting	PF	Coalescence	COAL
Stopping of Fricatives and Affricates	ST	Gliding of Liquids	GL	Palatalization	PAL
		Deaffrication	DEAFF	Denasalization	DENAS
Cluster Reduction	CR	Deletion of Initial Consonant	DIC	Idiosyncratic Processes	
Stridency Deletion	STR	Glottal Replacement	GR		

BATH	/bæθ/	→ [dæp]	_____	METATH
	/b/ → [___]	_____	[p], PVD
	/θ/ → [___]	_____	[d], ST, PVV

| CHIMNEY | /tʃɪmnɪ/ | → [tʃɪnmɪ] | _____ | METATH; no other processes |

| BULLDOZER | /bʊldozɚ/ | → [bʊdwozɚ] | _____ | METATH |
| | /l/ → [___] | _____ | [w], GL |

BICYCLE	/baɪsɪkl̩/	→ [baɪpɪfl̩]	_____	METATH
	/k/ → [p]	_____	CH (with /b/)
	/s/ → [f]	_____	CH (with /b/)

KETCHUP	/ˈkɛtʃəp/	→ [dʒɛpəp]	_____	METATH
	/k/ → [___]	_____	[p], CH
	/tʃ/ → [___]	_____	[dʒ], PVV

| RADISH | /rædɪʃ/ | → [dæwɪʃ] | _____ | METATH |
| | /r/ → [___] | _____ | [w], GL |

STRAWBERRY	/strɔberɪ/	→ [bwɔsterɪ]	_____	METATH
	/r/ → [___]	_____	[w], GL
(Note that the /r/ in the /str/ cluster remained prevocalic.)			

| ICE CREAM | /aɪskrim/ | → [aɪtsrim] | _____ | METATH |
| | /k/ → [___] | _____ | [t], VF or CH |

| FEATHER | /fɛðɚ/ | → [fɛvɚ] | _____ | CH; no other changes |

/p/ PIG	/n/ NO	/ʃ/ SHE	/w/ WAGON	/ɛ/ BED	/ʌ/ GUN
/b/ BED	/ŋ/ STING	/ʒ/ ROUGE	/ʍ/ WHEEL	/æ/ CAT	/ə/ ABOUT
/t/ TOY	/f/ FOX	/h/ HAVE	/ɚ/ FINGER	/a/ GOT	/aɪ/ KITE
/d/ DUCK	/θ/ THINK	/tʃ/ CHICKEN	/ɝ/ CHURCH	/ɔ/ TALK	/ɔɪ/ TOY
/k/ KEEP	/ð/ THIS	/dʒ/ JUMPING	/i/ SEE	/o/ GOAT	/aʊ/ OUT
/g/ GOAT	/s/ SEE	/l/ LAKE	/ɪ/ PIG	/ʊ/ BOOK	
/m/ ME	/z/ ZOO	/j/ YOU	/eɪ, e/ MAKE	/u/ GLUE	

SUMMARY
Metathesis
1. METATH refers to both the transposition and the sequence alteration of consonants within a word.
2. METATH has the potential for producing a high degree of listener confusion.

Deletion of Final Consonant	DFC	Consonant Harmony	CH	Backing to Velars	BK
		Postvocalic Devoicing	PVD	Epenthesis	EPEN
Prevocalic Voicing	PVV	Vocalization	VOC	Metathesis	METATH
Syllable Reduction	SR	Palatal Fronting	PF	Coalescence	COAL
Velar Fronting	VF	Gliding of Liquids	GL	Palatalization	PAL
Stopping of Fricatives and Affricates	ST	Deaffrication	DEAFF	Denasalization	DENAS
		Deletion of Initial Consonant	DIC	Idiosyncratic Processes	
Cluster Reduction	CR				
Stridency Deletion	STR	Glottal Replacement	GR		

SECTION 19. COALESCENCE

COALESCENCE (COAL) is a process that compresses two adjacent consonants or syllables into one unit. For example, SHOVEL /ʃʌvəl/ → [ʃʌl], where the word has been collapsed from two syllables into one by combining the first part of the word, /ʃʌ/, with the last part of the word, /l/. When adjacent syllables are compressed or collapsed, the process that has been applied. may be _____.

COALESCENCE

Similarly, when BROKEN /brokən/ → [bron], the /bro/ from the first syllable and the /n/ from the second syllable have been _____ to produce a monosyllabic word, [bron].

compressed OR
collapsed

The abbreviation for COALESCENCE is _____.

COAL

The two examples just given show how collapsing may take place across syllables. COAL has also been used to account for collapsing across phonemes. For example, when SPOON /spun/ → [fun], both the /s/ (a voiceless strident fricative) and the /p/ (a bilabial) have been compressed into [f], a labial, voiceless, strident fricative. The [f] is composed of characteristics of both /____/ and /____/.

/s/, /p/

Similarly, when SLEEP /slip/ → [ɬip], the voiceless /s/ and the lateral /l/ collapse to form a voiceless lateral [ɬ]. The process applied was _____.

COAL

It is sometimes difficult to recognize coalescence. For example, when CH and CR are applied to SPOON

/p/ *PIG*	/n/ *NO*	/ʃ/ *SHE*	/w/ *WAGON*	/ɛ/ *BED*	/ʌ/ *GUN*
/b/ *BED*	/ŋ/ *STING*	/ʒ/ *ROUGE*	/ʍ/ *WHEEL*	/æ/ *CAT*	/ə/ *ABOUT*
/t/ *TOY*	/f/ *FOX*	/h/ *HAVE*	/ɚ/ *FINGER*	/a/ *GOT*	/aɪ/ *KITE*
/d/ *DUCK*	/θ/ *THINK*	/tʃ/ *CHICKEN*	/ɝ/ *CHURCH*	/ɔ/ *TALK*	/ɔɪ/ *TOY*
/k/ *KEEP*	/ð/ *THIS*	/dʒ/ *JUMPING*	/i/ *SEE*	/o/ *GOAT*	/aʊ/ *OUT*
/g/ *GOAT*	/s/ *SEE*	/l/ *LAKE*	/ɪ/ *PIG*	/ʊ/ *BOOK*	
/m/ *ME*	/z/ *ZOO*	/j/ *YOU*	/eɪ, e/ *MAKE*	/u/ *GLUE*	

COAL

/spun/, it becomes [fpun] and then [fun]. This is also the production obtained from the application of

_____.

COAL

It may be appropriate to consider /sp/ → [f] as the result of CH ([fp]) followed by CR ([f]). If this order is assumed, then the primary treatment goal would be CR followed by CH. If _____ is assumed, there are no direct implications for treatment.

COAL

However, when a production collapses a word across syllables (as in BROKEN /brokən/ → [bron]), the process of _____ has been applied.

In the word STRAWBERRY /strɔbɛrɪ/, if the /r/ is glided to a [w], producing [stw], and CH is applied (with the [w] as the influential consonant), and the cluster is reduced, the production will be one of the following:

[fwɔbɛrɪ]

[pwɔbɛrɪ]

COAL

Although some have described this collapsing across phonemes as _____, we will consider it to be CH followed by CR (see Schane, 1973, p. 68).

The significance of COAL may be observed when a word is collapsed across syllables. Indicate whether or not a word has been collapsed for the following examples:

	Adult Form		Child's Form	YES/NO

YES   SUPPER   /sʌpɚ/   → [sɝ]   _____

YES   TELEPHONE /tɛləfon/ → [tɛon]   _____

Deletion of Final Consonant	DFC	Consonant Harmony	CH	Backing to Velars	BK
Prevocalic Voicing	PVV	Postvocalic Devoicing	PVD	Epenthesis	EPEN
Syllable Reduction	SR	Vocalization	VOC	Metathesis	METATH
Velar Fronting	VF	Palatal Fronting	PF	Coalescence	COAL
Stopping of Fricatives and Affricates	ST	Gliding of Liquids	GL	Palatalization	PAL
Cluster Reduction	CR	Deaffrication	DEAFF	Denasalization	DENAS
Stridency Deletion	STR	Deletion of Initial Consonant	DIC	Idiosyncratic Processes	
		Glottal Replacement	GR		

TRAFFIC	/træfɪk/	→ [trɪk]	_____	YES
VANILLA	/vənɪlə/	→ [nɪlə]	_____	NO, SR
WELCOME	/wɛlkəm/	→ [wɛm]	_____	YES
WINDOW	/wɪndo/	→ [wo]	_____	YES
KITCHEN	/kɪtʃɪn/	→ [kɪnɪtʃ]	_____	NO, METATH
JELLY	/dʒɛlɪ/	→ [dʒɪ]	_____	YES
GIRAFFE	/dʒɜræf/	→ [dʒæf]	_____	YES
ELEPHANT	/ɛləfənt/	→ [ɛfən]	_____	NO, SR and CR

Although COAL may be used to account for collapsing across both consonants and syllables, collapsing across consonants can be alternatively, and perhaps more appropriately, accounted for by applying _____ and _____.

CH, CR

SUMMARY
Coalescence

1. COAL is a process that compresses two adjacent consonants or syllables into one unit.
2. Elements of both units are retained.
3. COAL may be explained by the co-occurrence of CH and CR in clusters that are reduced to one member that shares characteristics of both.

/p/ *PIG*	/n/ *NO*	/ʃ/ *SHE*	/w/ *WAGON*	/ɛ/ *BED*	/ʌ/ *GUN*
/b/ *BED*	/ŋ/ *STING*	/ʒ/ *ROUGE*	/ʍ/ *WHEEL*	/æ/ *CAT*	/ə/ *ABOUT*
/t/ *TOY*	/f/ *FOX*	/h/ *HAVE*	/ɚ/ *FINGER*	/a/ *GOT*	/aɪ/ *KITE*
/d/ *DUCK*	/θ/ *THINK*	/tʃ/ *CHICKEN*	/ɝ/ *CHURCH*	/ɔ/ *TALK*	/ɔɪ/ *TOY*
/k/ *KEEP*	/ð/ *THIS*	/dʒ/ *JUMPING*	/i/ *SEE*	/o/ *GOAT*	/aʊ/ *OUT*
/g/ *GOAT*	/s/ *SEE*	/l/ *LAKE*	/ɪ/ *PIG*	/ʊ/ *BOOK*	
/m/ *ME*	/z/ *ZOO*	/j/ *YOU*	/eɪ, e/ *MAKE*	/u/ *GLUE*	

SECTION 20. PALATALIZATION

PALATALIZATION | PALATALIZATION (PAL) is a process which alters the place of articulation from a non-palatal location to the palate. SAND /sænd/ → [ʃænd] is an example of _____.

PALATALIZATION | Similarly, when BOYS /bɔɪz/ → [bɔɪʒ], the process of _____ has been applied.

PAL | The abbreviation for PALATALIZATION is _____.

/s/, /z/ | The consonants affected by PAL are primarily the alveolar fricatives, which are /___/ and /___/.

Apply the process of PAL to the following words containing alveolar fricatives. Give the production that would result.

		Adult Form		*Child's Form*
[baɪʃɪkl̩]	BICYCLE	/baɪsɪkl̩/	→	[_____]
[bʌʒd]	BUZZED	/bʌzd/	→	[_____]
[ʃɪrɪəl]	CEREAL	/sɪrɪəl/	→	[_____]
[iʒɪ]	EASY	/izɪ/	→	[_____]
[fɝʃt]	FIRST	/fɝst/	→	[_____]
[gæʃ]	GAS	/gæs/	→	[_____]

Deletion of Final Consonant	DFC	Consonant Harmony	CH	Backing to Velars	BK
Prevocalic Voicing	PVV	Postvocalic Devoicing	PVD	Epenthesis	EPEN
Syllable Reduction	SR	Vocalization	VOC	Metathesis	METATH
Velar Fronting	VF	Palatal Fronting	PF	Coalescence	COAL
Stopping of Fricatives and Affricates	ST	Gliding of Liquids	GL	Palatalization	PAL
Cluster Reduction	CR	Deaffrication	DEAFF	Denasalization	DENAS
Stridency Deletion	STR	Deletion of Initial Consonant	DIC	Idiosyncratic Processes	
		Glottal Replacement	GR		

LASSO   /læso/   → [_____]   [læʃo]

If both PAL and ST are applied to an alveolar fricative, the result may be a palatal affricate. For example, initially when PLEASE /pliz/ → [pliʒ], the process of _____ has been applied.   PAL

When ST is then applied to the /ʒ/ in /pliʒ/, it becomes [_____].   [plidʒ]

Apply both PAL and ST to the following words. The first one has been done for you.

	Adult Form	Apply PAL	Apply ST
BICYCLE	/baɪsɪkl̩/	→ [baɪʃɪkl̩]	→ [baɪtʃɪkl̩]
BUZZED	/bʌzd/	→ [_____]	→ [_____]
CEREAL	/sɪrɪəl/	→ [_____]	→ [_____]
EASY	/izɪ/	→ [_____]	→ [_____]
FIRST	/fɝst/	→ [_____]	→ [_____]
GAS	/gæs/	→ [_____]	→ [_____]
LASSO	/læso/	→ [_____]	→ [_____]

[bʌʒd], [bʌdʒd]

[ʃɪrɪəl], [tʃɪrɪəl]

[iʒɪ], [idʒɪ]

[fɝʃt], [fɝtʃt]

[gæʃ], [gætʃ]

[læʃo], [lætʃo]

It is possible for other non-palatal consonants to be palatalized, especially during casual or fast speech. For example, the /t/ is palatalized when MEET YOU /mit ju/ → [mitʃu] because of the influence of the palatal /j/. This is characteristic of normal conversational speech styles. The alteration of an alveolar fricative to a palatal

/p/ *PIG*	/n/ *NO*	/ʃ/ *SHE*	/w/ *WAGON*	/ɛ/ *BED*	/ʌ/ *GUN*
/b/ *BED*	/ŋ/ *STING*	/ʒ/ *ROUGE*	/ʍ/ *WHEEL*	/æ/ *CAT*	/ə/ *ABOUT*
/t/ *TOY*	/f/ *FOX*	/h/ *HAVE*	/ɚ/ *FINGER*	/a/ *GOT*	/aɪ/ *KITE*
/d/ *DUCK*	/θ/ *THINK*	/tʃ/ *CHICKEN*	/ɝ/ *CHURCH*	/ɔ/ *TALK*	/ɔɪ/ *TOY*
/k/ *KEEP*	/ð/ *THIS*	/dʒ/ *JUMPING*	/i/ *SEE*	/o/ *GOAT*	/aʊ/ *OUT*
/g/ *GOAT*	/s/ *SEE*	/l/ *LAKE*	/ɪ/ *PIG*	/ʊ/ *BOOK*	
/m/ *ME*	/z/ *ZOO*	/j/ *YOU*	/eɪ, e/ *MAKE*	/u/ *GLUE*	

fricative, affricate | _____ or _____ is the most common result of the application of PAL.

SUMMARY
Palatalization

1. PAL is a process that alters the place of articulation from non-palatal to palatal.
2. The consonants affected by PAL are primarily the alveolar fricatives, /s/ and /z/.
3. PAL occurs frequently in casual adult speech.

Deletion of Final Consonant	DFC	Consonant Harmony	CH	Backing to Velars	BK	
Prevocalic Voicing	PVV	Postvocalic Devoicing	PVD	Epenthesis	EPEN	
Syllable Reduction	SR	Vocalization	VOC	Metathesis	METATH	
Velar Fronting	VF	Palatal Fronting	PF	Coalescence	COAL	
Stopping of Fricatives and Affricates	ST	Gliding of Liquids	GL	Palatalization	PAL	
		Deaffrication	DEAFF	Denasalization	DENAS	
Cluster Reduction	CR	Deletion of Initial Consonant	DIC	Idiosyncratic Processes		
Stridency Deletion	STR	Glottal Replacement	GR			

SECTION 21. DENASALIZATION

DENASALIZATION (DEN) is a process that results in a nasal consonant becoming non-nasal. When MUD /mʌd/ → [bʌd] the process of _____ has been applied.

Similarly, HAMMER /hæmɚ/ → [_____] with the application of DENASALIZATION.

The abbreviation for DENASALIZATION is _____.

It is likely that the application of DEN to a nasal consonant will result in the production of a homorganic non-nasal consonant. Recall that when one consonant is produced at the same place of articulation as another, it is called a _____ consonant.

The homorganic non-nasal cognates for the nasal consonants are as follows:

Nasals	Non-Nasal Homorganic
/m/	/____/
/n/	/____/
/ŋ/	/____/

When a child has a cold with a stuffy nose, nasal consonants may become _____ temporarily.

DENASALIZATION

[hæbɚ]

DEN

homorganic

/b/

/d/

/g/

non-nasal

/p/ *PIG*	/n/ *NO*	/ʃ/ *SHE*	/w/ *WAGON*	/ɛ/ *BED*	/ʌ/ *GUN*
/b/ *BED*	/ŋ/ *STING*	/ʒ/ *ROUGE*	/ʍ/ *WHEEL*	/æ/ *CAT*	/ə/ *ABOUT*
/t/ *TOY*	/f/ *FOX*	/h/ *HAVE*	/ɚ/ *FINGER*	/a/ *GOT*	/aɪ/ *KITE*
/d/ *DUCK*	/θ/ *THINK*	/tʃ/ *CHICKEN*	/ɝ/ *CHURCH*	/ɔ/ *TALK*	/ɔɪ/ *TOY*
/k/ *KEEP*	/ð/ *THIS*	/dʒ/ *JUMPING*	/i/ *SEE*	/o/ *GOAT*	/aʊ/ *OUT*
/g/ *GOAT*	/s/ *SEE*	/l/ *LAKE*	/ɪ/ *PIG*	/ʊ/ *BOOK*	
/m/ *ME*	/z/ *ZOO*	/j/ *YOU*	/eɪ, e/ *MAKE*	/u/ *GLUE*	

Apply the process of DEN to the following words containing nasals. Assume that homorganic consonants are produced.

		Adult Form		Child's Form
[fɪdɪʃ]	FINISH	/fɪnɪʃ/	→ [	]
[farb]	FARM	/farm/	→ [	]
[grid]	GREEN	/grin/	→ [	]
[gʌb]	GUM	/gʌm/	→ [	]
[hʌbd]	HUMMED	/hʌmd/	→ [	]
[kɪg]	KING	/kɪŋ/	→ [	]
[lɔgɚ], but this is actually CR	LONGER	/lɔŋgɚ/	→ [	]

DEN can be applied as one of several processes resulting in a single sound change. For example, PLANE /plen/ → [plet] results from the application of DEN (/pled/) and _____.   PVD

Determine which processes were applied to the following words containing nasals.

		Adult Form	Child's Form	Process(es)
CR	LUNCH	/lʌntʃ/	→ [lʌtʃ]	_____
CR	LONGER	/lɔŋgɚ/	→ [lɔgɚ]	_____

Deletion of Final		Consonant Harmony	CH	Backing to Velars	BK
Consonant	DFC	Postvocalic Devoicing	PVD	Epenthesis	EPEN
Prevocalic Voicing	PVV	Vocalization	VOC	Metathesis	METATH
Syllable Reduction	SR	Palatal Fronting	PF	Coalescence	COAL
Velar Fronting	VF	Gliding of Liquids	GL	Palatalization	PAL
Stopping of Fricatives		Deaffrication	DEAFF	Denasalization	DENAS
and Affricates	ST	Deletion of Initial		Idiosyncratic	
Cluster Reduction	CR	Consonant	DIC	Processes	
Stridency Deletion	STR	Glottal Replacement	GR		

LOAN	/lon/	→ [lot]	_____	DEN, PVD
MAN	/mæn/	→ [mæt]	_____	DEN, PVD
MAN	/mæn/	→ [næd]	_____	DEN, CH
TON	/tʌn/	→ [gʌk]	_____	/t/ → [g]: PVV, BK /n/ → [k]: BK, DEN, PVD
TRAIN	/tren/	→ [tred]	_____	DEN
WIN	/wɪn/	→ [wɪt]	_____	DEN, PVD
YARN	/jarn/	→ [jard]	_____	DEN
BURN	/bɝn/	→ [bɝd]	_____	DEN

SUMMARY
Denasalization
1. DEN is a process that results in a nasal consonant becoming non-nasal.
2. When a speaker has a cold accompanied by a stuffy nose, nasal consonants may become non-nasal.

/p/ PIG /n/ NO /ʃ/ SHE /w/ WAGON /ɛ/ BED /ʌ/ GUN
/b/ BED /ŋ/ STING /ʒ/ ROUGE /ʍ/ WHEEL /æ/ CAT /ə/ ABOUT
/t/ TOY /f/ FOX /h/ HAVE /ɚ/ FINGER /a/ GOT /aɪ/ KITE
/d/ DUCK /θ/ THINK /tʃ/ CHICKEN /ɝ/ CHURCH /ɔ/ TALK /ɔɪ/ TOY
/k/ KEEP /ð/ THIS /dʒ/ JUMPING /i/ SEE /o/ GOAT /aʊ/ OUT
/g/ GOAT /s/ SEE /l/ LAKE /ɪ/ PIG /ʊ/ BOOK
/m/ ME /z/ ZOO /j/ YOU /eɪ, e/ MAKE /u/ GLUE

SECTION 22. IDIOSYNCRATIC PROCESSES

idiosyncratic	IDIOSYNCRATIC PROCESSES are those which are unique to an individual child or uncommon in normal development. For example, while STOPPING OF FRICATIVES (ST) is a common process, stops rarely *become* fricatives. When a child uses a unique or uncommon pattern productively, we refer to it as an _____ process.
idiosyncratic, OR idiosyncratic processes	If a child produces an uncommon form for a target adult word, it does not necessarily mean that an idiosyncratic process has been applied. There should be a sufficient number of occurrences of the uncommon pattern for it to qualify as a *process*. That is, a unique or uncommon process should be used productively before it is included under the category of _____.
idiosyncratic	Another example of an idiosyncratic process would be one that affects glides. While GLIDING OF LIQUIDS (GL) is a common phonological process, glides rarely become liquids. LIGHT /laɪt/ → [waɪt], but WHITE /waɪt/ rarely becomes [laɪt]. If a child alters glides to liquids productively, then the child uses an _____ process.
productively	There are examples of idiosyncratic processes in the literature. Waterson (1971) reported the overuse of /ŋ/ even in word-initial position. For example, FINGER /fɪŋgɚ/ → [ɲeːŋe] and RANDALL /rændļ/ → [ɲaŋo]. If there is a predictable pattern to these errors, and if that pattern is used _____, then the child demonstrates an idiosyncratic process.

Deletion of Final Consonant	DFC	Consonant Harmony	CH	Backing to Velars	BK
		Postvocalic Devoicing	PVD	Epenthesis	EPEN
Prevocalic Voicing	PVV	Vocalization	VOC	Metathesis	METATH
Syllable Reduction	SR	Palatal Fronting	PF	Coalescence	COAL
Velar Fronting	VF	Gliding of Liquids	GL	Palatalization	PAL
Stopping of Fricatives and Affricates	ST	Deaffrication	DEAFF	Denasalization	DENAS
Cluster Reduction	CR	Deletion of Initial Consonant	DIC	Idiosyncratic Processes	
Stridency Deletion	STR	Glottal Replacement	GR		

In Waterson's examples, the predictable pattern might be that when words contain nasals, all consonants become [ŋ], including the nasals themselves. Thus, we would predict that a word like MAYBE /mebɪ/ would become [ŋeŋɪ], where all consonants within the word have become [ŋ]. If this same pattern occurs often enough to be productive (>30% of possible occurrences), then it must be considered as a probable _____.

idiosyncratic process

However, if FINGER and RANDALL were the only two lexical forms for which the child overused [ŋ], then these errors would hardly qualify as an idiosyncratic *process* because there would not be sufficient evidence that the pattern was used _____.

productively

Young children may make one or two novel misproductions without demonstrating a *pattern* of errors. It is important to determine whether there is a pattern and whether it is applied fairly regularly (productively). If so, then it may qualify as an _____.

idiosyncratic process

The use of idiosyncratic processes contributes to overall unintelligibility. When a productive process is characteristic of normal development, the listener is better able to comprehend the child's altered forms than when an unusual process is used productively by the child. Thus, when the child uses the process of GL (changing liquids into glides) the listener is better able to comprehend the child's words than when the child changes glides into _____.

liquids

Ingram (1976, p. 116) used the term "unusual" process to include both unique processes and _____ processes. He suggested that more data on

uncommon

/p/ PIG	/n/ NO	/ʃ/ SHE	/w/ WAGON	/ɛ/ BED	/ʌ/ GUN
/b/ BED	/ŋ/ STING	/ʒ/ ROUGE	/ʍ/ WHEEL	/æ/ CAT	/ə/ ABOUT
/t/ TOY	/f/ FOX	/h/ HAVE	/ɚ/ FINGER	/a/ GOT	/aɪ/ KITE
/d/ DUCK	/θ/ THINK	/tʃ/ CHICKEN	/ɝ/ CHURCH	/ɔ/ TALK	/ɔɪ/ TOY
/k/ KEEP	/ð/ THIS	/dʒ/ JUMPING	/i/ SEE	/o/ GOAT	/aʊ/ OUT
/g/ GOAT	/s/ SEE	/l/ LAKE	/ɪ/ PIG	/ʊ/ BOOK	
/m/ ME	/z/ ZOO	/j/ YOU	/eɪ, e/ MAKE	/u/ GLUE	

normal development were needed prior to distinguishing between the two.

Hodson and Paden (1983, p. 16) describe an idiosyncratic rule as a "deficient pattern which does not fit into any of the [major process] classifications." They acknowledge that any individual child may use a unique pattern that may interfere significantly with overall

intelligibility

_____.

Hodson and Paden (1983) report the use of a /w/ to initiate *final* syllables in multisyllabic words. The example given is BASKET /bæskɪt/ → [bæwə]. Note that [wə] replaces the final syllable here. Similarly, PENCIL /pɛnsl̩/ might become [pɛnwə]. If a child used this particular idiosyncratic process, how would the following target words be produced? The first example has been done for you.

		Adult Form	*Child's Form*
	BOTTLE	/baɾl̩/	→ [bawə]
[bewə]	BABY	/bebɪ/	→ [_____]
[tɛwə]	TEDDY	/tɛdɪ/	→ [_____]
[tɛləwə]	TELEPHONE	/tɛləfon/	→ [_____]
[blæwə]	BLANKET	/blæŋkɪt/	→ [_____]
[tiwə]	T.V.	/tivi/	→ [_____]

Deletion of Final Consonant	DFC	Consonant Harmony	CH	Backing to Velars	BK
Prevocalic Voicing	PVV	Postvocalic Devoicing	PVD	Epenthesis	EPEN
Syllable Reduction	SR	Vocalization	VOC	Metathesis	METATH
Velar Fronting	VF	Palatal Fronting	PF	Coalescence	COAL
Stopping of Fricatives and Affricates	ST	Gliding of Liquids	GL	Palatalization	PAL
		Deaffrication	DEAFF	Denasalization	DENAS
Cluster Reduction	CR	Deletion of Initial Consonant	DIC	Idiosyncratic Processes	
Stridency Deletion	STR	Glottal Replacement	GR		

According to this child's idiosyncratic process, whether a word contains two or three syllables, the final syllable is represented by [_____].

[wə]

Ingram and Terselic (1983) describe the use of a voiceless *ingressive* alveolar fricative (ɬ) to replace word-final /s/, /z/, /ʒ/, and /f/. This is both unusual and uncommon. Thus, to produce a word like DRESS /drɛs/, the child may produce the /drɛ/ portion of the word correctly using an egressive airflow. Then, for the final portion of the word, the child produces a fricative using the opposite airflow direction: an _____ airflow. This change in direction must take place rapidly during coarticulation.

ingressive

The child appears to be making production more difficult. This use of ingressive production has also been cited by Grunwell (1981). Again, the direction of the _____ must change rapidly in order to produce a word containing both ingressive and egressive phonemes.

airflow

Assuming that a child uses the idiosyncratic process described by Ingram and Terselic, determine how the following target words would be produced:

	Adult Form	Child's Form	
BUS	/bʌs/	→ [_____]	[bʌɬ]
BUZZ	/bʌz/	→ [_____]	[bʌɬ]
WITH	/wɪθ/	→ [_____]	[wɪθ]

/p/ *PIG*	/n/ *NO*	/ʃ/ *SHE*	/w/ *WAGON*	/ɛ/ *BED*	/ʌ/ *GUN*
/b/ *BED*	/ŋ/ *STING*	/ʒ/ *ROUGE*	/ʍ/ *WHEEL*	/æ/ *CAT*	/ə/ *ABOUT*
/t/ *TOY*	/f/ *FOX*	/h/ *HAVE*	/ɚ/ *FINGER*	/a/ *GOT*	/aɪ/ *KITE*
/d/ *DUCK*	/θ/ *THINK*	/tʃ/ *CHICKEN*	/ɝ/ *CHURCH*	/ɔ/ *TALK*	/ɔɪ/ *TOY*
/k/ *KEEP*	/ð/ *THIS*	/dʒ/ *JUMPING*	/i/ *SEE*	/o/ *GOAT*	/aʊ/ *OUT*
/g/ *GOAT*	/s/ *SEE*	/l/ *LAKE*	/ɪ/ *PIG*	/ʊ/ *BOOK*	
/m/ *ME*	/z/ *ZOO*	/j/ *YOU*	/eɪ, e/ *MAKE*	/u/ *GLUE*	

[ruɬ]   ROUGE   /ruʒ/   → [_____]

[tʌɬ]   TOUGH   /tʌf/   → [_____]

[faɪv]   FIVE   /faɪv/   → [_____]

[ɬ]

Because the idiosyncratic process affects only certain consonants (those listed by the authors), we must assume that other consonants are not affected. Thus, the word-final /θ/ and /v/ did not become [____].

One other case study described the use of ingressive phoneme production as a possible process. Edwards and Bernhardt (1973) reported the use of a voiceless nasal snort/fricative for several fricatives and affricates. If these unusual patterns are used productively, then they may fit the definition of an _____ process.

idiosyncratic

Pollack (1983) discussed Mike, who preferred the consonants /n/ and /d/ word-initially. Examples were as follows:

BEHIND   /bəhaɪnd/ → [na]

OUTSIDE   /aʊtsaɪd/ → [da]

ENVELOPE   /ɛnvəlop/ → [nɛ]

It appears that when the stressed syllable of the word contained a nasal, then the child's form began with /n/. When the stressed syllable did not contain a nasal, the child's form began with /____/.

/d/

Using this idiosyncratic process, how would this child produce the following target words? Because Pollack does not comment about the form of the vowels when this rule

Deletion of Final Consonant	DFC	Consonant Harmony	CH	Backing to Velars	BK	
Prevocalic Voicing	PVV	Postvocalic Devoicing	PVD	Epenthesis	EPEN	
Syllable Reduction	SR	Vocalization	VOC	Metathesis	METATH	
Velar Fronting	VF	Palatal Fronting	PF	Coalescence	COAL	
Stopping of Fricatives and Affricates	ST	Gliding of Liquids	GL	Palatalization	PAL	
Cluster Reduction	CR	Deaffrication	DEAFF	Denasalization	DENAS	
Stridency Deletion	STR	Deletion of Initial Consonant	DIC	Idiosyncratic Processes		
		Glottal Replacement	GR			

is used, we cannot predict with certainty that they will resemble the primary vowels of the target words.

	Adult Form		*Child's Form*		
BACON	/bekən/	→	[_____]		[de]
NOBODY	/nobadɪ/	→	[_____]		[na]
NOTHING	/nʌθɪŋ/	→	[_____]		[na]
TELEPHONE	/tɛləfon/	→	[_____]		[dɛ]

Grunwell (1983) also reported a child with a /d/ preference. These sound preferences can sometimes be explained by the application of multiple processes to a word. For example, when OUTSIDE /aʊtsaɪd/ → [da], the child may have used the following processes to arrive at [da]:

Adult Form		*Child's Form*	*Process*
/aʊtsaɪd/	→	[saɪd]	SR
/saɪd/	→	[daɪd]	ST, PVV, STR
/daɪd/	→	[daɪ]	DFC
/daɪ/	→	[da]	Vowel Neutralization

While there may appear to be a /d/ preference, the use of /d/ may be explained through the examination of the multiple _____ that may have been applied to the target word. These multiple processes constitute the production's *derivation*.

processes

/p/	*PIG*	/n/	*NO*	/ʃ/	*SHE*	/w/	*WAGON*	/ɛ/	*BED*	/ʌ/	*GUN*
/b/	*BED*	/ŋ/	*STING*	/ʒ/	*ROUGE*	/ʍ/	*WHEEL*	/æ/	*CAT*	/ə/	*ABOUT*
/t/	*TOY*	/f/	*FOX*	/h/	*HAVE*	/ɝ/	*FINGER*	/a/	*GOT*	/aɪ/	*KITE*
/d/	*DUCK*	/θ/	*THINK*	/tʃ/	*CHICKEN*	/ɝ/	*CHURCH*	/ɔ/	*TALK*	/ɔɪ/	*TOY*
/k/	*KEEP*	/ð/	*THIS*	/dʒ/	*JUMPING*	/i/	*SEE*	/o/	*GOAT*	/aʊ/	*OUT*
/g/	*GOAT*	/s/	*SEE*	/l/	*LAKE*	/ɪ/	*PIG*	/ʊ/	*BOOK*		
/m/	*ME*	/z/	*ZOO*	/j/	*YOU*	/eɪ, e/	*MAKE*	/u/	*GLUE*		

Similarly, for BEHIND /bəhaɪnd/ → [na], the child may have used the following processes to arrive at [na]:

Adult Form		Child's Form	Process
/bəhaɪnd/	→	[bənaɪnd]	CH
/bənaɪnd/	→	[naɪnd]	SR
/naɪnd/	→	[naɪ]	CR, DFC
/naɪ/	→	[na]	Vowel Neutralization

idiosyncratic process, OR sound preference

Again, we see that it is sometimes possible to explain what appears to be a _____ by examining the various processes that may have contributed to the production of the preferred sound.

Usually, evidence for these additional processes can be found in the speech sample of the child. That is, if the child uses ST, PVV, and DFC productively within the entire sample, then there is evidence that the child may have done so to change OUTSIDE /aʊtsaɪd/ to [da]. It is entirely possible for the child to demonstrate a sound preference without the alternative explanation that

multiple

_____ processes were applied to the target word.

The advantage of examining the sample for these multiple process examples is the help that it may provide in determining goals for treatment. If the child is described as using an idiosyncratic process that happens to be a sound preference, there are no immediate implications for treatment. However, if there are multiple processes that contribute to the production of the preferred sound, goals for _____ may be more

treatment

obvious.

Deletion of Final Consonant	DFC	Consonant Harmony	CH	Backing to Velars	BK
Prevocalic Voicing	PVV	Postvocalic Devoicing	PVD	Epenthesis	EPEN
Syllable Reduction	SR	Vocalization	VOC	Metathesis	METATH
Velar Fronting	VF	Palatal Fronting	PF	Coalescence	COAL
Stopping of Fricatives and Affricates	ST	Gliding of Liquids	GL	Palatalization	PAL
Cluster Reduction	CR	Deaffrication	DEAFF	Denasalization	DENAS
Stridency Deletion	STR	Deletion of Initial Consonant	DIC	Idiosyncratic Processes	
		Glottal Replacement	GR		

In the example of OUTSIDE just given, the processes of DFC, ST, and PVV (and perhaps also STR and SR) would be worked on individually during treatment, with the end result that the idiosyncratic sound preference would be eliminated. If the sound preference is not considered to be the result of the application of _____, then it must be worked on directly.

multiple processes

To illustrate this principle more directly, if the child needs to work on DFC, ST, and PVV anyway, and if the elimination of these processes also eliminates the use of /d/ (a sound preference), then it is difficult to justify working directly on elimination of the overused /d/. In effect, it will be eliminated as a byproduct of working on _____, _____, and _____.

DFC, ST, PVV

For many clinicians, it is more difficult to develop programs for eliminating an idiosyncratic process than for eliminating one of the developmental processes. In addition, treatment programs may be more efficient if one process is _____ as the result of working on the elimination of another process.

eliminated

Another type of unusual process has been described by Ingram (1976, p. 116ff). This is the tendency for /f/ to become [t], which he terms *tetism*. For example,

	Adult Form	*Child's Form*
FUN	/fʌn/	→ [tʌn]
FOOD	/fud/	→ [tud]
KNIFE	/naɪf/	→ [naɪt]
OFTEN	/ɔfn̩/	→ [ɔtn̩]

/p/ *PIG*	/n/ *NO*	/ʃ/ *SHE*	/w/ *WAGON*	/ɛ/ *BED*	/ʌ/ *GUN*
/b/ *BED*	/ŋ/ *STING*	/ʒ/ *ROUGE*	/ʍ/ *WHEEL*	/æ/ *CAT*	/ə/ *ABOUT*
/t/ *TOY*	/f/ *FOX*	/h/ *HAVE*	/ɚ/ *FINGER*	/a/ *GOT*	/aɪ/ *KITE*
/d/ *DUCK*	/θ/ *THINK*	/tʃ/ *CHICKEN*	/ɝ/ *CHURCH*	/ɔ/ *TALK*	/ɔɪ/ *TOY*
/k/ *KEEP*	/ð/ *THIS*	/dʒ/ *JUMPING*	/i/ *SEE*	/o/ *GOAT*	/aʊ/ *OUT*
/g/ *GOAT*	/s/ *SEE*	/l/ *LAKE*	/ɪ/ *PIG*	/ʊ/ *BOOK*	
/m/ *ME*	/z/ *ZOO*	/j/ *YOU*	/eɪ, e/ *MAKE*	/u/ *GLUE*	

Using this unusual process, how would a child produce the following target words?

		Adult Form		*Child's Form*
[tɪŋgɚ]	FINGER	/fɪŋgɚ/	→	[_____]
[ɔtl̩]	AWFUL	/ɔfl̩/	→	[_____]
[taemlɪ]	FAMILY	/fæmlɪ/	→	[_____]
[dʒəræt]	GIRAFFE	/dʒəræf/	→	[_____]
[tɛðɚ]	FEATHER	/fɛðɚ/	→	[_____]

Within the examples just given, nearly all of the sound changes (/f/ to [t]) can be explained by the application of multiple processes to the /f/ target phoneme. For example, in the word FUN /fʌn/ → [tʌn], the processes of CH and ST (along with STR) may have been applied. The sequence (or *derivation*) would look like this:

$$/fʌn/ → [sʌn] \quad CH$$
$$/sʌn/ → [tʌn] \quad ST, STR$$

The same sort of derivation might apply to KNIFE:

$$/naɪf/ → [naɪs] \quad CH$$
$$/naɪs/ → [naɪt] \quad ST, STR$$

Before a process is labeled as "unusual" or idiosyncratic, it is important to see whether the child's production may be explained by the sequential application

multiple processes

of _____.

Deletion of Final Consonant	DFC	Consonant Harmony	CH	Backing to Velars	BK
Prevocalic Voicing	PVV	Postvocalic Devoicing	PVD	Epenthesis	EPEN
Syllable Reduction	SR	Vocalization	VOC	Metathesis	METATH
Velar Fronting	VF	Palatal Fronting	PF	Coalescence	COAL
Stopping of Fricatives and Affricates	ST	Gliding of Liquids	GL	Palatalization	PAL
Cluster Reduction	CR	Deaffrication	DEAFF	Denasalization	DENAS
Stridency Deletion	STR	Deletion of Initial Consonant	DIC	Idiosyncratic Processes	
		Glottal Replacement	GR		

Whether you as the examiner/clinician choose to treat the pattern, or process, as unusual or as a sequence of processes may be a matter of personal preference. The suggestion has already been made that examining for the _____ may be more helpful for therapy program development.

multiple processes

Ingram also lists as possible unusual processes two allophones of /s/. When /s/ → a dental /s/, which lacks stridency, the child is actually producing a [____].

[θ]

The sound change /s/ → [θ] has been included in this text under the process of STR. This is also referred to as the substitution of /____/ for /____/.

/θ/, /s/

The second /s/-allophone that Ingram includes is the lateral /s/: /ʂ/. He states that this never occurs in normal development. This is similar to the ingressive lateral fricative discussed earlier; the difference is that the airflow is _____ for a lateral /ʂ/.

egressive

Nasal preference has also been described as an unusual process (Ingram, 1976). Consonants become nasals either obligatorily or selectively. The following are examples of a child's productions that illustrate nasal preference:

	Adult Form		*Child's Form*
WASH	/waʃ/	→	[maʃ]
FLOWER	/flaʊɚ/	→	[namɚ]
NIGHT	/naɪt/	→	[naɪn]
CIRCLE	/sɝkl/	→	[nɝnl̩]

/p/ *PIG*	/n/ *NO*	/ʃ/ *SHE*	/w/ *WAGON*	/ɛ/ *BED*	/ʌ/ *GUN*
/b/ *BED*	/ŋ/ *STING*	/ʒ/ *ROUGE*	/ʍ/ *WHEEL*	/æ/ *CAT*	/ə/ *ABOUT*
/t/ *TOY*	/f/ *FOX*	/h/ *HAVE*	/ɚ/ *FINGER*	/a/ *GOT*	/aɪ/ *KITE*
/d/ *DUCK*	/θ/ *THINK*	/tʃ/ *CHICKEN*	/ɝ/ *CHURCH*	/ɔ/ *TALK*	/ɔɪ/ *TOY*
/k/ *KEEP*	/ð/ *THIS*	/dʒ/ *JUMPING*	/i/ *SEE*	/o/ *GOAT*	/aʊ/ *OUT*
/g/ *GOAT*	/s/ *SEE*	/l/ *LAKE*	/ɪ/ *PIG*	/ʊ/ *BOOK*	
/m/ *ME*	/z/ *ZOO*	/j/ *YOU*	/eɪ, e/ *MAKE*	/u/ *GLUE*	

NIGHT

When there is a nasal consonant within the word, the use of additional nasals may be explained by some type of assimilation in manner of production. For example, of the four words just listed, the word _____ might have been the result of nasal consonant assimilation.

reduced

Fricative Preference was described by Ingram as a tendency to retain and/or move fricatives and affricates. For example, STOP /stap/ → [sap] or FREE /fri/ → [fi]. In both examples, the fricative has been retained although the cluster has been _____ from two members to one.

[tap]

Ingram includes specifically /s/ retention in clusters under this category of fricative preference. As stated within the section on CR, the consonant that is deleted from an /s/ + stop cluster tends to be the /s/. Thus, STOP /stap/ is more likely to become [_____] than [sap].

fricative OR /s/

The child who demonstrates a fricative preference often retains the _____ member of the /s/ cluster.

[tʃ]

It appears that Ingram also included the movement (transposition) of fricatives and affricates within words. This has been covered under the section on METATH. An example cited by Ingram is the change from SOCK /sak/ → [ætʃ]. Here the /s/ has been retained and moved to word-final position as the affricate [____].

transposed OR moved

Similarly, STOP /stap/ → [taps] and SOUP /sup/ → [ups]. The /s/ has been retained and _____ to the end of the word in both examples.

Deletion of Final Consonant	DFC	Consonant Harmony	CH	Backing to Velars	BK
Prevocalic Voicing	PVV	Postvocalic Devoicing	PVD	Epenthesis	EPEN
Syllable Reduction	SR	Vocalization	VOC	Metathesis	METATH
Velar Fronting	VF	Palatal Fronting	PF	Coalescence	COAL
Stopping of Fricatives and Affricates	ST	Gliding of Liquids	GL	Palatalization	PAL
Cluster Reduction	CR	Deaffrication	DEAFF	Denasalization	DENAS
Stridency Deletion	STR	Deletion of Initial Consonant	DIC	Idiosyncratic Processes	
		Glottal Replacement	GR		

Each of the idiosyncratic, unusual, uncommon processes introduced here has been reported in the literature. Because children are such unique individuals, there is no limit to the ability to demonstrate a unique pattern or apply a unique process to the spoken word. It is important to recognize that there may be a describable _____ to the errors, no matter how bizarre they may seem.

pattern

Give the idiosyncratic and also developmental processes (or rules) that are used by the following child. Include examples of the pertinent sound changes.

	Adult Form	Child's Form
SAD	/sæd/	→ [tlæd]
FUN	/fʌn/	→ [pʌn]
ZOO	/zu/	→ [du]
THING	/θɪŋ/	→ [tɪŋ]
SICK	/sɪk/	→ [tlɪk]
FISH	/fɪʃ/	→ [pɪʃ]
ZIPPER	/zɪpɚ/	→ [dɪpɚ]
THUMB	/θʌm/	→ [tʌm]

Developmental process(es) with sound changes:

Word-initial fricatives are stopped and, if strident, the stridency is deleted. /f/ → [p], /z/ → [d]

/p/ PIG	/n/ NO	/ʃ/ SHE	/w/ WAGON	/ɛ/ BED	/ʌ/ GUN
/b/ BED	/ŋ/ STING	/ʒ/ ROUGE	/ʍ/ WHEEL	/æ/ CAT	/ə/ ABOUT
/t/ TOY	/f/ FOX	/h/ HAVE	/ɚ/ FINGER	/a/ GOT	/aɪ/ KITE
/d/ DUCK	/θ/ THINK	/tʃ/ CHICKEN	/ɝ/ CHURCH	/ɔ/ TALK	/ɔɪ/ TOY
/k/ KEEP	/ð/ THIS	/dʒ/ JUMPING	/i/ SEE	/o/ GOAT	/aʊ/ OUT
/g/ GOAT	/s/ SEE	/l/ LAKE	/ɪ/ PIG	/ʊ/ BOOK	
/m/ ME	/z/ ZOO	/j/ YOU	/eɪ, e/ MAKE	/u/ GLUE	

		Adult Form	Child's Form
Word-initial /s/ becomes [tl] /s/ → [tl]	Unusual rule(s) with sound changes:		

Using the same rules/processes, determine how the following words would be produced:

		Adult Form	Child's Form
[tlak]	SOCK	/sak/	→ [_____]
[pæt]	FAT	/fæt/	→ [_____]
[dibrə]	ZEBRA	/zibrə/	→ [_____]
[tæŋk] OR [t̪æŋk]	THANK	/θæŋk/	→ [_____]
[tlʌn]	SUN	/sʌn/	→ [_____]
[paɪv]	FIVE	/faɪv/	→ [_____]
[tʌndɚ]	THUNDER	/θʌndɚ/	→ [_____]

<table>
<tr><td>/s/ → [tl]</td><td>Since the rules/processes apply only to word-initial fricatives, the word-final fricative /v/ has not been affected. The unusual sound change is /___/ → [___].</td></tr>
</table>

Give the unusual and also the developmental processes used by the following child. Include pertinent sound changes as examples.

	Adult form	Child's Form
LAUGH	/læf/	→ [læf]

Deletion of Final Consonant	DFC	Consonant Harmony	CH	Backing to Velars	BK
Prevocalic Voicing	PVV	Postvocalic Devoicing	PVD	Epenthesis	EPEN
Syllable Reduction	SR	Vocalization	VOC	Metathesis	METATH
Velar Fronting	VF	Palatal Fronting	PF	Coalescence	COAL
Stopping of Fricatives and Affricates	ST	Gliding of Liquids	GL	Palatalization	PAL
		Deaffrication	DEAFF	Denasalization	DENAS

Cluster Reduction	CR	Deletion of Initial
		   Consonant
			DIC	Idiosyncratic
				   Processes	

Stridency Deletion	STR	Glottal Replacement	GR		

LIKE	/laɪk/	→ [laɪt]
READ	/rid/	→ [rid]
WRONG	/rɔŋ/	→ [rɔn]
WINDOW	/wɪndo/	→ [rɪndo]
WENT	/wɛnt/	→ [rɛnt]
WALK	/wɔk/	→ [rɔt]
YARD	/jard/	→ [lard]
YES	/jɛs/	→ [lɛs]

Developmental process(es) with sound changes:

VF /k/ → [t], /ŋ/ → [n]

Unusual rule(s) with sound changes:

Glides become liquids in word-initial position; /w/ → [r], /j/ → [l]

Using this developmental process and unusual rule, determine how the same child would produce the following target words:

	Adult Form	*Child's Form*	
LOOK	/lʊk/	→ [_____]	[lʊk]
YOU	/ju/	→ [_____]	[lu]
ROCKET	/rakɪt/	→ [_____]	[ratɪt]
WORK	/wɝk/	→ [_____]	[rɝt]

/p/ *PIG*	/n/ *NO*	/ʃ/ *SHE*	/w/ *WAGON*	/ɛ/ *BED*	/ʌ/ *GUN*
/b/ *BED*	/ŋ/ *STING*	/ʒ/ *ROUGE*	/ʍ/ *WHEEL*	/æ/ *CAT*	/ə/ *ABOUT*
/t/ *TOY*	/f/ *FOX*	/h/ *HAVE*	/ɚ/ *FINGER*	/a/ *GOT*	/aɪ/ *KITE*
/d/ *DUCK*	/θ/ *THINK*	/tʃ/ *CHICKEN*	/ɜ/ *CHURCH*	/ɔ/ *TALK*	/ɔɪ/ *TOY*
/k/ *KEEP*	/ð/ *THIS*	/dʒ/ *JUMPING*	/i/ *SEE*	/o/ *GOAT*	/aʊ/ *OUT*
/g/ *GOAT*	/s/ *SEE*	/l/ *LAKE*	/ɪ/ *PIG*	/ʊ/ *BOOK*	
/m/ *ME*	/z/ *ZOO*	/j/ *YOU*	/eɪ, e/ *MAKE*	/u/ *GLUE*	

[rɪn]	WING /wɪŋ/ → [_____]
[trim]	CREAM /krim/ → [_____]

Since there is no evidence that word-initial clusters are included in the application of this unusual rule, nor is there any evidence to the contrary, the use of either a liquid or a glide would be correct in the cluster examples just given. When there are examples of how the child treats the affected consonants in both singleton and cluster contexts, this should be included in the statement of the rule. If this child does apply the rule to glides within clusters, then the unusual rule would be stated as follows: Word-initial glides, both _____ and _____, become liquids.

singleton, cluster

Give the unusual and the developmental processes that are used by the following child. Include examples of pertinent sound changes.

	Adult Form	*Child's Form*
HAND	/hænd/	→ [næn]
NEST	/nɛst/	→ [nɛn]
STONE	/ston/	→ [non]
STATION	/steʃən/	→ [nenən]
CREAM	/krim/	→ [mim]
STAMP	/stæmp/	→ [mæm]
STING	/stɪŋ/	→ [ŋɪŋ]
NOBODY	/nobadɪ/	→ [nonanɪ]

Deletion of Final Consonant	DFC	Consonant Harmony	CH	Backing to Velars	BK
		Postvocalic Devoicing	PVD	Epenthesis	EPEN
Prevocalic Voicing	PVV	Vocalization	VOC	Metathesis	METATH
Syllable Reduction	SR	Palatal Fronting	PF	Coalescence	COAL
Velar Fronting	VF	Gliding of Liquids	GL	Palatalization	PAL
Stopping of Fricatives and Affricates	ST	Deaffrication	DEAFF	Denasalization	DENAS
Cluster Reduction	CR	Deletion of Initial Consonant	DIC	Idiosyncratic Processes	
Stridency Deletion	STR	Glottal Replacement	GR		

		CR
Developmental process(es) with sound changes:		/nd/ → [n]
		/st/ → [ŋ]
		/kr/ → [m]

Unusual rule(s) with sound changes:

When there is a nasal consonant within the word, all other consonants become that nasal.

/h, st, ʃ/ → [n]
/kr, st/ → [m]
/st/ → [ŋ]

Using this developmental process and unusual rule, how would the following words be produced by this child?

	Adult Form		Child's Form	
MISTER	/mɪstɚ/	→ [_____]		[mɪmɚ]
BANANA	/bənænə/	→ [_____]		[nənænə]
COUNT	/kaʊnt/	→ [_____]		[naʊnt]
HUNGRY	/hʌŋgrɪ/	→ [_____]		[ŋʌŋɪ]
ICE CREAM	/aɪskrim/	→ [_____]		[aɪmim]

Remember that idiosyncratic processes should occur a sufficient number of times in potential contexts in order to qualify as an additional process. Any pattern that is unusual or extremely uncommon in normal development may be identified as an _____.

idiosyncratic process

/p/ *PIG*	/n/ *NO*	/ʃ/ *SHE*	/w/ *WAGON*	/ɛ/ *BED*	/ʌ/ *GUN*
/b/ *BED*	/ŋ/ *STING*	/ʒ/ *ROUGE*	/ʍ/ *WHEEL*	/æ/ *CAT*	/ə/ *ABOUT*
/t/ *TOY*	/f/ *FOX*	/h/ *HAVE*	/ɚ/ *FINGER*	/a/ *GOT*	/aɪ/ *KITE*
/d/ *DUCK*	/θ/ *THINK*	/tʃ/ *CHICKEN*	/ɝ/ *CHURCH*	/ɔ/ *TALK*	/ɔɪ/ *TOY*
/k/ *KEEP*	/ð/ *THIS*	/dʒ/ *JUMPING*	/i/ *SEE*	/o/ *GOAT*	/aʊ/ *OUT*
/g/ *GOAT*	/s/ *SEE*	/l/ *LAKE*	/ɪ/ *PIG*	/ʊ/ *BOOK*	
/m/ *ME*	/z/ *ZOO*	/j/ *YOU*	/eɪ, e/ *MAKE*	/u/ *GLUE*	

SUMMARY
Idiosyncratic Processes
1. Idiosyncratic processes are those which are unique to an individual child or uncommon in normal development.
2. This unique or uncommon pattern should occur productively (30% of opportunities) in order to be considered a phonological process.
3. Some "idiosyncratic" processes can be explained by the sequential application of several processes.
4. Idiosyncratic processes probably contribute significantly to overall unintelligibility.

APPENDICES

I

PHONETIC SYMBOLS AND DIACRITICAL MARKS FOR PHONETIC TRANSCRIPTION

ENGLISH VOWELS

Symbol	Example	Phonetic Transcription
i	SEE	[si]
ɪ	PIG	[pɪg]
e, eɪ	MAKE	[mek], [meɪk]
ɛ	BED	[bɛd]
æ	CAT	[kæt]
a	GOT	[gat]
ɔ	TALK	[tɔk]
o	GOAT	[got]
ʊ	BOOK	[bʊk]
u	GLUE	[glu]
ʌ	GUN	[gʌn] (stressed)
ə	ABOUT	[əbaʊt] (unstressed)
aɪ	KITE	[kaɪt]
aʊ	HOUSE	[haʊs]
ɔɪ	TOY	[tɔɪ]
ɝ	CHURCH	[tʃɝtʃ] (stressed)
ɚ	FINGER	[fɪŋgɚ] (unstressed)

---

*All English vowel and consonant phonetic symbols presented in this appendix are those of the International Phonetic Alphabet as they appear in Kenyon and Knott (1953) and Shriberg and Kent (1982). It is generally recognized that /ɪ/ and /ι/ represent the identical phoneme and /ʊ/ and /ɷ/ represent the identical phoneme. These additional phonetic symbols may be found in Ladefoged (1982) and Shriberg and Kent (1982).

ENGLISH CONSONANTS

Symbol	Example	Phonetic Transcription
p	PIG	[pɪg]
b	BED	[bɛd]
t	TOY	[tɔɪ]
d	DUCK	[dʌk]
k	KEEP	[kip]
g	GOAT	[got]
h	HAVE	[hæv]
ʔ	BOTTLE	[baʔl̩]
m	ME	[mi]
n	NO	[no]
ŋ	SING	[sɪŋ]
f	FOX	[faks]
v	VACUUM	[vækjuəm]
θ	THINK	[θɪŋk]
ð	THIS	[ðɪs]
s	SEE	[si]
z	ZOO	[zu]
ʃ	SHE	[ʃi]
ʒ	ROUGE	[ruʒ]
tʃ	CHICKEN	[tʃɪkɪn]
dʒ	JUMPING	[dʒʌmpɪŋ]
l	LAKE	[lek]
r	RABBIT	[ræbɪt]
j	YOU	[ju]
w	WAGON	[wægən]
ʍ	WHEEL	[ʍil] (also pronounced [wil])

ALLOPHONES

Natural Allophones of /r/ that Occur in These Specific Coarticulatory Contexts

ɪɚ	NEAR	[nɪɚ]
ɛɚ	THERE	[ðɛɚ]
aɚ	FAR	[faɚ]
ɔɚ	STORE	[stɔɚ]
ʊɚ	TOUR	[tʊɚ]

ɚ	SISTER	[sɪstɚ]
ɾ	PIERCE	[pɾs]
ʄ	SHORT	[ʃʄt]
ɛˠ	CARED	[kɛˠd]
ʊˠ	TOURED	[tʊˠd]
ɝ	HURT	hɝt]

Allophones Related to Other English Consonants†

Phonetic Symbol	Explanation
ɸ	Voiceless bilabial fricative
β	Voiced bilabial fricative
ɬ̥	Voiceless lateral emission of a fricative ("lateral lisp")
ɬ	Voiced lateral emission of a fricative ("lateral lisp")
x	Voiceless velar fricative
γ̇	Voiced velar fricative
ɾ	Alveolar flap (BUTTER /bʌɾɚ/)

DIACRITICAL MARKS ‡

Phonetic Symbol	Definition	Phonetic Transcription
~	Nasalization	[fɪʃ̃ĩ]
⊓	Dentalization	[haus̪]
^	Lateralization	[s̭kwɝl]
ˇ	Partial Voicing	[k̬ʌp]
°	Partial Devoicing	[gʌn]
:	Lengthened	[bɛ:]
˥	Unreleased	[k˥ɛrət]
ʟ	Released	[kʟ ɛrət]
·	Syllabic	[pɛnsl̩]
h	Aspirated	[tʰɛləfon]
ɯ	Rounded	[s̫orɪ]
m	Unrounded	[s̫i]

---

†From Fisher and Logemann (1971).

‡From Bush et al. (1973) and Shriberg and Kent (1982).

II
COMPARISON CHART FOR PHONOLOGICAL PROCESS TERMINOLOGY

A COMPARISON OF PHONOLOGICAL PROCESS TERMS USED IN EACH OF FIVE ASSESSMENT PROCEDURES

Weiner (1979)	Shriberg and Kwiatkowski (1980)	Hodson (1980)	Ingram (1981)	Khan and Lewis (in press)
SYLLABLE STRUCTURE PROCESSES				
		Prevocalic Singleton Obstruent Omission	Deletion of Initial Consonant	Deletion of Initial Consonant
Final Consonant Deletion	Final Consonant Deletion	Postvocalic Singleton Obstruent Omission	Final Consonant Deletion Nasals Voiced Stops Voiceless Stops Voiceless Frics	Deletion of Final Consonant
Weak Syllable Deletion	Unstressed Syllable Deletion	Syllable Reduction	Unstressed Syllable Deletion Reduction of Disyllable	Syllable Reduction
Cluster Reduction Init. Stop + Liquid Init. Fric + Liquid	Cluster Reduction	Cluster Reduction Obstruent Omission Sonorant Omission	Cluster Reduction Liquid Nasal /s/C	Cluster Simplification

Weiner (1979	Shriberg and Kwiatkowski (1980)	Hodson (1980)	Ingram (1981)	Khan and Lewis (in press)
Init. /s/ + Final /s/ + Stop Final Liquid + Stop Final Nasal + Stop				
Syllable Duplication			Reduplication	

ASSIMILATION PROCESSES

Weiner (1979	Shriberg and Kwiatkowski (1980)	Hodson (1980)	Ingram (1981)	Khan and Lewis (in press)
Labial Alveolar Velar }	Progressive Regressive	{ Labial Alveolar Velar Nasal	Labial Velar }	Consonant Harmony
Devoicing of Final Consonant		Postvocalic Devoicing	Devoicing of Final Consonant	Final Devoicing
Prevocalic Voicing		Prevocalic Voicing	Prevocalic Voicing	Initial Devoicing

SUBSTITUTION PROCESSES

Weiner (1979	Shriberg and Kwiatkowski (1980)	Hodson (1980)	Ingram (1981)	Khan and Lewis (in press)
Stopping of Fricatives	Stopping	Stopping	Stopping Init. Voiceless Fricatives Init. Voiced Fricatives Initial Affricates	Stopping of Fricatives and Affricates
	Palatal Fronting	Depalatalization	Palatal Fronting	Palatal Fronting
Fronting	Velar Fronting	Velar Fronting	Velar Fronting	Velar Fronting
Affrication		Affrication		Stopping of Fricatives
Denasalization			Denasalization	
Vocalization	Liquid Simplification	{ Vowelization Gliding Omission	Vocalization	Liquid Simplification
Gliding of Liquids }			Liquid Gliding }	
Gliding of Affricates				

Weiner (1979)	Shriberg and Kwiatkowski (1980)	Hodson (1980)	Ingram (1981)	Khan and Lewis (in press)
Glottal Replacement		Glottal Replacement Deaffrication Backing Stridency Deletion Nasal Omission Palatalization	Deaffrication	Glottal Replacement Deaffrication Backing Stridency Deletion
			Apicalization Labialization	
		Velar Omissions Coalescence Epenthesis Metathesis Vowel Deviations		

III
PROTOCOL FOR SCORING AND ANALYSIS

Score the following protocol, which utilizes the stimulus words from the *Goldman-Fristoe Test of Articulation*.* List the appropriate sound changes and then assign the phonological processes that were applied. Use only those processes that have been introduced in the text.

Target	Adult Form		Child's Form	Sound Changes	Processes			
HOUSE	/haʊs/	→	[haʊ]	_____	_____		s → ø	DFC, STR
				_____	_____			
				_____	_____			
TELEPHONE	/tɛləfon/	→	[tɛfo]	_____	_____		lə → ø	SR
				_____	_____		n → ø	DFC
				_____	_____			

*From Goldman and Fristoe (1969). Used by permission of American Guidance Service, © 1969.

		Target	Adult Form		Child's Form	Sound Changes	Processes
p → ø	DFC	CUP	/kʌp/	→	[kʌ]	_____	_____
						_____	_____
						_____	_____
n → ø	DFC	GUN	/gʌn/	→	[gʌ]	_____	_____
						_____	_____
						_____	_____
f → ø	DFC, STR	KNIFE	/naɪf/	→	[naɪ]	_____	_____
						_____	_____
						_____	_____
nd → n	CR	WINDOW	/wɪndo/	→	[wɪno]	_____	_____
						_____	_____
						_____	_____
g → d	VF	WAGON	/wægən/	→	[wædə]	_____	_____
n → ø	DFC					_____	_____
						_____	_____
l → o	VOC	WHEEL	/wil/	→	[wio]	_____	_____
						_____	_____
						_____	_____
n → ø	DFC	CHICKEN	/tʃɪkɪn/	→	[tʃɪkɪ]	_____	_____
						_____	_____
						_____	_____
z → dʒ	PAL, ST	ZIPPER	/zɪpɚ/	→	[dʒɪpʊ]	_____	_____
ɚ → ʊ	VOC					_____	_____
						_____	_____

Deletion of Final Consonant	DFC	Consonant Harmony	CH	Backing to Velars	BK
Prevocalic Voicing	PVV	Postvocalic Devoicing	PVD	Epenthesis	EPEN
Syllable Reduction	SR	Vocalization	VOC	Metathesis	METATH
Velar Fronting	VF	Palatal Fronting	PF	Coalescence	COAL
Stopping of Fricatives and Affricates	ST	Gliding of Liquids	GL	Palatalization	PAL
		Deaffrication	DEAFF	Denasalization	DENAS
Cluster Reduction	CR	Deletion of Initial Consonant	DIC	Idiosyncratic Processes	
Stridency Deletion	STR	Glottal Replacement	GR		

Target	Adult Form		Child's Form	Sound Changes	Processes		Sound Changes	Processes
SCISSORS	/sɪzɚz/	→	[sɪzʊz]	_____	_____		ɚ → ʊ	VOC
				_____	_____			
				_____	_____			
DUCK	/dʌk/	→	[dʌ]	_____	_____		k → ø	DFC
				_____	_____			
				_____	_____			
YELLOW	/jɛlo/	→	[jɛlo]	_____	_____		none	
				_____	_____			
				_____	_____			
VACUUM								
	/vaekjuəm/	→	[bækuə]	_____	_____		v → b	ST, STR
				_____	_____		kj → k	CR
				_____	_____		m → ø	DFC
MATCHES	/mætʃɪz/	→	[mæʃɪʃ]	_____	_____		tʃ → ʃ	DEAFF
				_____	_____		z → ʃ	CH, PVD
				_____	_____			
LAMP	/læmp/	→	[wæm]	_____	_____		l → w	GL
				_____	_____		mp → m	CR
				_____	_____			
SHOVEL	/ʃʌvl̩/	→	[sʌbo]	_____	_____		ʃ → s	PF
				_____	_____		v → b	ST, STR
				_____	_____		l̩ → o	VOC

/p/ *PIG*	/n/ *NO*	/ʃ/ *SHE*	/w/ *WAGON*	/ɛ/ *BED*	/ʌ/ *GUN*
/b/ *BED*	/ŋ/ *STING*	/ʒ/ *ROUGE*	/ʍ/ *WHEEL*	/æ/ *CAT*	/ə/ *ABOUT*
/t/ *TOY*	/f/ *FOX*	/h/ *HAVE*	/ɚ/ *FINGER*	/a/ *GOT*	/aɪ/ *KITE*
/d/ *DUCK*	/θ/ *THINK*	/tʃ/ *CHICKEN*	/ɝ/ *CHURCH*	/ɔ/ *TALK*	/ɔɪ/ *TOY*
/k/ *KEEP*	/ð/ *THIS*	/dʒ/ *JUMPING*	/i/ *SEE*	/o/ *GOAT*	/aʊ/ *OUT*
/g/ *GOAT*	/s/ *SEE*	/l/ *LAKE*	/ɪ/ *PIG*	/ʊ/ *BOOK*	
/m/ *ME*	/z/ *ZOO*	/j/ *YOU*	/eɪ, e/ *MAKE*	/u/ *GLUE*	

			Target	Adult Form	Child's Form	Sound Changes	Processes
r → ø		DFC	CAR	/kar/	→ [ka]	_____ _____ _____	_____ _____ _____
t → ø		DFC	RABBIT	/ræbɪt/	→ [ræbɪ]	_____ _____ _____	_____ _____ _____
ŋ → ø		DFC	FISHING	/fɪʃɪŋ/	→ [fɪʃɪ]	_____ _____ _____	_____ _____ _____
none			CHURCH	/tʃɝtʃ/	→ [tʃɝtʃ]	_____ _____ _____	_____ _____ _____
ð → d		ST	FEATHER	/fɛðɚ/	→ [fɛdɔ]	_____ _____ _____	_____ _____ _____
ɚ → ɔ		VOC					
ns → s		CR	PENCILS	/pɛnsl̩z/	→ [pɛsos]	_____ _____ _____	_____ _____ _____
l̩ → o		VOC					
z → s		PVD					
none			THIS	/ðɪs/	→ [ðɪs]	_____ _____ _____	_____ _____ _____
t → ø		DFC	CARROT	/kɛrət/	→ [kɛrə]	_____ _____ _____	_____ _____ _____

Deletion of Final Consonant	DFC	Consonant Harmony	CH	Backing to Velars	BK
Prevocalic Voicing	PVV	Postvocalic Devoicing	PVD	Epenthesis	EPEN
Syllable Reduction	SR	Vocalization	VOC	Metathesis	METATH
Velar Fronting	VF	Palatal Fronting	PF	Coalescence	COAL
Stopping of Fricatives and Affricates	ST	Gliding of Liquids	GL	Palatalization	PAL
		Deaffrication	DEAFF	Denasalization	DENAS
Cluster Reduction	CR	Deletion of Initial Consonant	DIC	Idiosyncratic Processes	
Stridency Deletion	STR	Glottal Replacement	GR		

Target	Adult Form		Child's Form	Sound Changes	Processes			
ORANGE	/ɔrɪndʒ/	→	[ɔwɪʒ]	_____	_____	r → w		GL
				_____	_____	ndʒ → ʒ	CR, DEAFF	
				_____	_____			
BATHTUB	/bæθtəb/	→	[bætə]	_____	_____	θt → t		CR
				_____	_____	b → ø		DFC
				_____	_____			
BATH	/baeθ/	→	[bæf]	_____	_____	θ → f		CH
				_____	_____			
				_____	_____			
THUMB	/θʌm/	→	[t̪ʌm]	_____	_____	θ → t̪		ST
				_____	_____			
				_____	_____			
FINGER	/fɪŋgɚ/	→	[fɪŋgʊ]	_____	_____	ɚ → ʊ		VOC
				_____	_____			
				_____	_____			
RING	/rɪŋ/	→	[rɪŋk]	_____	_____	ŋ → ŋk		PVD
				_____	_____			
				_____	_____			
JUMPING	/dʒʌmpɪŋ/	→	[dʒʌmpɪn]	_____	_____	ŋ → n		VF
				_____	_____			
				_____	_____			
PAJAMAS	/pədʒæməz/	→	[pədʒæmə]	_____	_____	z → ø	DFC, STR	
				_____	_____			
				_____	_____			

/p/ *PIG*	/n/ *NO*	/ʃ/ *SHE*	/w/ *WAGON*	/ɛ/ *BED*	/ʌ/ *GUN*
/b/ *BED*	/ŋ/ *STING*	/ʒ/ *ROUGE*	/ʍ/ *WHEEL*	/æ/ *CAT*	/ə/ *ABOUT*
/t/ *TOY*	/f/ *FOX*	/h/ *HAVE*	/ɚ/ *FINGER*	/a/ *GOT*	/aɪ/ *KITE*
/d/ *DUCK*	/θ/ *THINK*	/tʃ/ *CHICKEN*	/ɝ/ *CHURCH*	/ɔ/ *TALK*	/ɔɪ/ *TOY*
/k/ *KEEP*	/ð/ *THIS*	/dʒ/ *JUMPING*	/i/ *SEE*	/o/ *GOAT*	/aʊ/ *OUT*
/g/ *GOAT*	/s/ *SEE*	/l/ *LAKE*	/ɪ/ *PIG*	/ʊ/ *BOOK*	
/m/ *ME*	/z/ *ZOO*	/j/ *YOU*	/eɪ, e/ *MAKE*	/u/ *GLUE*	

			Target	Adult Form		Child's Form	Sound Changes	Processes
pl → pw		GL	PLANE	/plen/	→	[pwen]	_____ _____ _____	_____ _____ _____
bl → b		CR	BLUE	/blu/	→	[bu]	_____ _____ _____	_____ _____ _____
br → b		CR	BRUSH	/brʌʃ/	→	[bʌs]	_____ _____ _____	_____ _____ _____
ʃ → s		PF						
dr → dw		GL	DRUM	/drʌm/	→	[dwʌ]	_____ _____ _____	_____ _____ _____
m → ø		DFC						
fl → f		CR	FLAG	/flæg/	→	[fæk]	_____ _____ _____	_____ _____ _____
g → k		PVD						

SANTA CLAUS

							Sound Changes	Processes
ntə → ø		SR, CR	/sæntə klɔz/		→	[sækɔz]	_____ _____ _____	_____ _____ _____
kl → k		CR						

CHRISTMAS TREE

						Sound Changes	Processes
kr → k		CR	/krɪsmɪs tri/	→	[kɪsmɪsti]	_____ _____ _____	_____ _____ _____
str → st		CR					

Deletion of Final Consonant	DFC	Consonant Harmony	CH	Backing to Velars	BK
Prevocalic Voicing	PVV	Postvocalic Devoicing	PVD	Epenthesis	EPEN
Syllable Reduction	SR	Vocalization	VOC	Metathesis	METATH
Velar Fronting	VF	Palatal Fronting	PF	Coalescence	COAL
Stopping of Fricatives and Affricates	ST	Gliding of Liquids	GL	Palatalization	PAL
		Deaffrication	DEAFF	Denasalization	DENAS
Cluster Reduction	CR	Deletion of Initial Consonant	DIC	Idiosyncratic Processes	
Stridency Deletion	STR	Glottal Replacement	GR		

Target	Adult Form		Child's Form	Sound Changes	Processes		
SQUIRREL	/skwɝl/	→	[skɝ]	_____ _____	skw → sk	CR
				_____ _____	l → ø	DFC
				_____ _____		
SLEEPING	/slipɪŋ/	→	[swipɪŋ]	_____ _____	sl → sw	GL
				_____ _____		
				_____ _____		
BED	/bɛd/	→	[bɛt]	_____ _____	d → t	PVD
				_____ _____		
				_____ _____		
STOVE	/stov/	→	[sto]	_____ _____	v → ø	DFC, STR
				_____ _____		
				_____ _____		

/p/ *PIG*	/n/ *NO*	/ʃ/ *SHE*	/w/ *WAGON*	/ɛ/ *BED*	/ʌ/ *GUN*
/b/ *BED*	/ŋ/ *STING*	/ʒ/ *ROUGE*	/ʍ/ *WHEEL*	/æ/ *CAT*	/ə/ *ABOUT*
/t/ *TOY*	/f/ *FOX*	/h/ *HAVE*	/ɚ/ *FINGER*	/a/ *GOT*	/aɪ/ *KITE*
/d/ *DUCK*	/θ/ *THINK*	/tʃ/ *CHICKEN*	/ɝ/ *CHURCH*	/ɔ/ *TALK*	/ɔɪ/ *TOY*
/k/ *KEEP*	/ð/ *THIS*	/dʒ/ *JUMPING*	/i/ *SEE*	/o/ *GOAT*	/aʊ/ *OUT*
/g/ *GOAT*	/s/ *SEE*	/l/ *LAKE*	/ɪ/ *PIG*	/ʊ/ *BOOK*	
/m/ *ME*	/z/ *ZOO*	/j/ *YOU*	/eɪ, e/ *MAKE*	/u/ *GLUE*	

EXERCISE PROTOCOL SUMMARY SHEET

	Process	Number of Applications	÷	Number of Opportunities	×100	Per cent
18, 45%	DFC	_____		_____40_____		_____%
0, 0%	PVV	_____		_____22_____		_____%
2, 9%	SR	_____		_____23_____		_____%
2, 12%	VF	_____		_____17_____		_____%
5, 13%	ST	_____		_____38_____		_____%
14, 64%	CR	_____		_____20_____		_____%
4, 11%	STR	_____		_____36_____		_____%
2, 5%	CH	_____		_____42_____		_____%
4, 14%	PVD	_____		_____29_____		_____%
7, 64%	VOC	_____		_____11_____		_____%
2, 20%	PF	_____		_____10_____		_____%
5, 31%	GL	_____		_____16_____		_____%
2, 28%	DEAFF	_____		_____7_____		_____%
0, 0%	DIC	_____		_____43_____		_____%
0, 0%	GR	_____		_____106_____		_____%
0, 0%	BK	_____		_____88_____		_____%
0, 0%	EPEN	_____		_____18_____		_____%
0, 0%	METATH	_____		_____41_____		_____%
0, 0%	COAL	_____		_____26_____		_____%
1, 6%	PAL	_____		_____17_____		_____%
0, 0%	DENAS	_____		_____22_____		_____%

IV.
SYLLABICATION ISSUES

Syllabication refers to the process of dividing a word into syllables. There is relatively better agreement among judgments of the number of syllables within a word than for identifying the actual location of the boundaries between syllables. A word like TELEPHONE /tɛləfon/ contains three discrete vowel nuclei: ɛ, ə, and o. Each vowel nucleus represents one syllable. However, a word like FRIGHTENING /fraɪtənɪŋ/ or /fraɪtnɪŋ/ has three or two vowel nuclei depending upon its pronunciation. Words like HIRE and HOUR may be judged as monosyllabic and bisyllabic while pronounced identically (Ladefoged, 1982, p. 221). Thus, the determination of syllable number may vary from speaker to speaker.

There appears to be less agreement on determination of syllable boundaries (Sloat et al., 1978, p. 57). For example, TELEPHONE may be divided in several ways:

> tɛ lə fon
> tɛ ləf on
> tɛl ə fon
> tɛl əf on

Each division contains three distinct syllables. However, the position of certain consonants (viz. /l/, /f/) varies within and across syllables. The /l/ may be a postvocalic consonant in the syllable /tɛl/ or a prevocalic consonant in the syllable /lə/; /f/ may be a postvocalic consonant in /ləf/ or /əf/ or a prevocalic consonant in /fon/.

Similarly, the syllable boundaries in SANTA CLAUS might be determined by several groupings:

> sæn tə klɔz
> sænt ə klɔz
> sænt ək lɔz
> sæn tək lɔz
> sæ ntə klɔz
> sæ ntək lɔz

The first four are quite possible, while the final two have less acceptable second syllables.

Possible rules for syllable division have been suggested (Pulgram, 1970; Paden, 1971). An example of the application of Pulgram's rules appears in Edwards and Shriberg (1983), p. 31:

1. "A syllable boundary...is inserted after every vowel or diphthong of a word (except the last) so that at least the first syllable is open."

e.g.,
> tɛ lə fon
> wɪ ndo
> væ kjuəm
> pɛ nsəlz
> bæ θtəb
> fɪ ŋgɚ
> dʒʌ mpɪŋ
> sæ ntə klɔz
> krɪ smɪ stri

2. "A consonant can be transferred from the beginning of one syllable to the end of the preceding syllable in order to give a permissible sequence."

Not Affected	*Affected*
tɛ lə fon	wɪn do
væ kjuəm	pɛn səlz
krɪ smɪ stri	bæθ təb
	fɪŋ gɚ
	dʒʌm pɪŋ
	sæn tə klɔz

3. "Additional consonants can be transferred from the beginning of one syllable to the end of the preceding syllable until the second syllable begins with a word-initial permissible sequence." (Not applicable to the words just given.)

In phonological analysis, the choice of one syllable boundary over another will depend upon the individual child's pattern of simplification. The choice may influence the phonological processes which are assigned to each sound change. For example, when /tɛləfon/ → [tɛləbon], the identified sound change is /f/ → [b]. The change in phonological processes would be as follows:

tɛ lə bon	ST,PVV
tɛ ləb on	ST, Postvocalic Voicing

Similarly, if /sæntəklɔz/ → [sænəglɔz], the change in phonological processes for each of two differently divided words would be as follows:

sæn tə klɔz	n → ø	DFC
	kl → gl	PVV
sænt ə klɔz	nt → n	CR
	kl → gl	PVV

The choice of syllabication type particularly influences the assignment of processes to intervocalic clusters. This text considers as clusters all consonant sequences occurring within a word, rather than applying Pulgram's rules. That is, a cluster can be word-initial (BLUE), word-final (LAMP), or word-medial (WINDOW). The assignment of phonological processes reflects this. Clinical experience indicates that in most cases either method of determining syllable boundaries will result in a similar phonological profile for an individual. Although clusters with non-permissible sequences are considered to be clusters in this programmed learning text, the performance of the individual child may justify further examination of syllable boundaries.

REFERENCES

Bush, C.N., Edwards, M.L., Luckau, J.M., Stoel, C.M., Macken, M.A., and Petersen, J.D. (1973). *On specifying a system for transcribing consonants in child language.* Unpublished manuscript, Stanford University, Stanford, CA.

Edwards, M.L. (1984). *Lab workbook for introduction to applied phonetics.* Syracuse University, Syracuse, NY.

Edwards, M.L., and Bernhardt, B. (1973). *Phonological analyses of the speech of four children with language disorders.* Unpublished manuscript, Stanford University, Institute for Childhood Aphasia, Stanford, CA.

Edwards, M.L., and Shriberg, L.D. (1983). *Phonology: Applications in communicative disorders.* San Diego: College-Hill Press.

Compton, A.J., and Hutton, J.S. (1978). *Compton-Hutton phonological assessment.* San Francisco: Carousel House.

Fisher, H.B., and Logemann, J.A. (1971). *Therapists' manual for the Fisher-Logemann test of articulation competence.* Boston: Houghton Mifflin.

Goldman, R., and Fristoe, M. (1969). *Test of articulation.* Circle Pines, MN: American Guidance Service.

Grunwell, P. (1981). *The nature of phonological disability in children.* New York: Academic Press.

Grunwell, P. (1983). Phonological development in phonological disability. *Topics in Language Disorders, 3,* 62–76.

Hodson, B.W. (1980). *The assessment of phonological processes.* Danville, IL: Interstate Printers and Publishers.

Hodson, B.W., and Paden, E.P. (1983). *Targeting intelligible speech: A phonological approach to remediation.* San Diego: College-Hill Press.

Ingram, D. (1976). *Phonological disability in children.* New York: American Elsevier.

Ingram, D. (1981). *Procedures for the phonological analysis of children's language.* Baltimore: University Park Press.

Ingram, D., and Terselic, B. (1983). Final ingression: A case of deviant child phonology. *Topics in Language Disorders, 3,* 45–50.

Kenyon, J.S., and Knott, T.A. (1953). *A pronouncing dictionary of American English*. Springfield, IL: G. and C. Merriam.

Khan, L.M., and Lewis, N.P. *Khan-Lewis Phonological Analysis (for use with the Goldman-Fristoe Test of Articulation)*. Circle Pines, MN: American Guidance Service.

Ladefoged, P. (1982). *A course in phonetics*. New York: Harcourt, Brace, Jovanovich.

McDade, H.L., Khan, L.M., and Seay, L. (1982, November). *The relationship between listener severity ratings and three articulation measures*. Paper presented at the American Speech-Language-Hearing Association Convention, Toronto.

Paden, E.P. (1971). *Exercises in phonetic transcription*. Danville, IL: Interstate Printers and Publishers.

Pollack, K. (1983). Individual preferences: Case study of a phonologically delayed child. *Topics in Language Disorders*, *3*, 10–23.

Pulgram, E. (1970). *Syllable, word, nexus, cursus*. The Hague, Netherlands: Mouton.

Schane, S. A. (1973). *Generative phonology*. Englewood Cliffs, NJ: Prentice-Hall.

Shriberg, L.D., and Kent, R. (1982). *Clinical phonetics*. New York: John Wiley and Sons.

Shriberg, L.D., and Kwiatkowski, J. (1980). *Natural process analysis (NPA): A procedure for phonological analysis of continuous speech samples*. New York: John Wiley and Sons.

Sloat, C., Taylor, S.H., and Hoard, J.E. (1978). *Introduction to phonology*. Englewood Cliffs, NJ: Prentice-Hall.

Stampe, D. (1969). The acquisition of phonetic representation. In R. T. Binnick et al. (Eds.), *Papers from the Fifth Regional Meeting, Chicago Linguistic Society*.

Templin, M.C., and Darley, F.L. (1960). *The Templin-Darley tests of articulation*. Iowa City: Bureau of Educational Research and Service, Extension Division, State University of Iowa.

Waterson, N. (1971). Child phonology: A prosodic view. *Journal of Linguistics*, *7*, 179–211.

Weiner, F.F. (1979). *Phonological process analysis*. Baltimore: University Park Press.

—NOTES—

—NOTES—

—NOTES—

—NOTES—

—NOTES—